DISASTER ME
INTERVENTIONS

Disaster Mental Health Interventions uses DSM-5 diagnostic criteria and the latest research to help build disaster mental health intervention skills that will last a lifetime. Students and emerging professionals across the fields of mental health counseling, social work, school counseling, spiritual care, and emergency management will appreciate the accessible tone, level of detail, and emphasis on practice. Case studies and anecdotes from experienced professionals add an additional level of depth and interest for readers.

James Halpern, PhD, is Professor Emeritus and founding director of the Institute for Disaster Mental Health. He has received many federal, state, and United Nations grants to develop curricula and deliver trainings throughout the United States and abroad.

Karla Vermeulen, PhD, is the Deputy Director of the Institute for Disaster Mental Health and an assistant professor of psychology at the State University of New York at New Paltz, where she oversees an advanced certificate in trauma and disaster mental health and develops trainings for disaster responders.

DISASTER MENTAL HEALTH INTERVENTIONS

CORE PRINCIPLES AND PRACTICES

James Halpern
Karla Vermeulen

Routledge
Taylor & Francis Group

NEW YORK AND LONDON

First published 2017
by Routledge
711 Third Avenue, New York, NY 10017

and by Routledge
2 Park Square, Milton Park, Abingdon, Oxon, OX14 4RN

Routledge is an imprint of the Taylor & Francis Group, an informa business

Library of Congress Cataloging in Publication Data
Names: Halpern, James, author. | Vermeulen, Karla, author.
Title: Disaster mental health interventions: core principles and practices / by James Halpern and Karla Vermeulen.
Description: New York : Routledge, 2017. |
Includes bibliographical references and index.
Identifiers: LCCN 2016041907| ISBN 9781138644557 (hbk) |
ISBN 9781138644588 (pbk) | ISBN 9781315623825 (ebk)
Subjects: LCSH: Crisis intervention (Mental health services)
Classification: LCC RC480.6 .H346 2017 | DDC 362.2/04251–dc23
LC record available at https://lccn.loc.gov/2016041907

ISBN: 978-1-138-64455-7 (hbk)
ISBN: 978-1-138-64458-8 (pbk)
ISBN: 978-1-315-62382-5 (ebk)

Typeset in New Baskerville
by Out of House Publishing

For Gail—always.
—JH

For my wonderful family, for all of their support and inspiration.
And for Michael—for everything, and forever.
—KV

Contents

Acknowledgments   xi

Introduction   1

1 What Is Disaster Mental Health?   3
   A Brief History   4
   The Role of the Helper   7
   "I Don't Need Mental Health"   8
   Who Provides the Mental Health Response?   9
   Settings   11
   The DMH Role over Time   14
   Who Are Your Clients?   15

2 Describing Disasters   18
   Types and Frequencies of Events   20
   Disasters versus Routine Emergencies   21
   Disaster Characteristics   22

3 Disaster's Impact: Typical Reactions   35
   Reactions by Realm   37
   Reactions by Time: Throughout the Disaster Life Cycle   41
   Reactions by Location: Proximity and the Dose–Response
      Relationship   46
   Survivor Guilt, Self-Blame, and Shame   48
   Resilience   49
   Posttraumatic Growth   50

4   Early Interventions: Psychological First Aid   53
The Importance of Early Intervention   54
Evidence-Based Principles of Early Intervention   55
Psychological First Aid   56
Some Cautions when Using PFA   66

5   Early Interventions: Other Actions   68
Assisting with Problem-Solving   69
Correcting Distorted Self-Cognitions   70
Rumor Control   72
Conflict Mitigation   73
Assessment, Triage, and Screening   73
Referrals for Long-Term Care   77
Psychological Debriefing: Criticisms and Cautions   77
An Ounce of Prevention …   79

6   Disaster Loss and Grief   85
Reactions to Loss   87
Characteristics of Disaster-Caused Deaths   88
Private Rituals   91
Public Rituals   94
Supporting the Bereaved   95
Anniversary Reactions   99

7   Disaster's Impact: Extreme Reactions   102
Risk Factors for PTSD and Other Illnesses   104
Trajectories following Traumatic Events   107
Posttraumatic Stress Disorder in Adults   108
Major Depressive Disorder   113
Complicated/Traumatic/Prolonged Grief   114
Other Health and Mental Health Problems   115
Referrals for Long-Term Care   116

8   Children and Families   122
Children's Trauma Reactions   123
Risk Factors   125
Helping Children and Families   127
Talking with Children   132
Making Referrals   133

9   Vulnerable Populations   136
Frail Older Adults   138
People with Physical Disabilities   142

People with Mental Disabilities   145
Other Vulnerable Populations   150

10 Cultural Competence   156
How Culture Shapes Reactions to Disaster   158
Cross-Cultural Issues in Shelters   162
Improving Your Ability to Help Across Cultures   164

11 Maintaining Helper Wellness and Competence   167
Logistics of Deployment   168
Helper Reactions   172
Self-Care   178

12 Conclusions and New Directions   186
Adapting the Response to Chronic Threats   186
Incorporating Technology   193
The Continuing Need for Research   194
A Final Note   195

Index   198

Acknowledgments

We would like to thank current and former colleagues and graduate assistants from the State University of New York (SUNY) at New Paltz who have provided support, advice, and guidance: all of our colleagues on the Psychology Department faculty, Rebecca Rodriguez, Dr. Amy Nitza, Dr. Gerald Benjamin, Dr. Glenn Geher, Dr. Laura Barrett, Dr. Phyllis Freeman, Meredith Johnson, Shelly Wright, Erica Marks, Diane Webb, Jessica Purcell, Rachael Bisceglie, Gillian Hammond, and—most especially—SUNY New Paltz president Don Christian.

We deeply appreciate the opportunities we've had to collaborate with colleagues and friends from other universities and agencies around the world who have added to our understanding of the field. We're grateful for the insights and guidance provided by: Steven Moskowitz, Judith LeComb, Diane Ryan, Valerie Cole, Christie Rogers, Jacki Brownstein, Ali Gheith, Elizabeth Cronin, Kevin Wisely, Gregory Brunelle, Dr. Athena Drewes, Dr. Patricia Findley, Dr. Richard Isralowitz, Dr. Monica Indart, Dr. Mary Tramontin, Dr. Mohammed Afifi, Dr. Majed Alloush, Dr. Bob Raymond, Dr. Lou Cassotta, Dr. Gloria Leon, Dr. Jeffry Levitt, Talia Levanon, Dr. Wayne Daily, and Itay Pruginin.

We also thank the countless mental health professionals we've trained over the years for their dedication and compassion, and for the lessons they've taught us in return. And we applaud the thousands of undergraduate and graduate students we've had the privilege to teach. We often boast about preparing the next generation of disaster responders, and we look forward to seeing our students' energy and drive to improve the world come to fruition.

The case studies and examples used in the book are based on our and colleagues' experiences working with disaster survivors. However, they have been altered to protect the privacy of these individuals. We offer our deepest appreciation to the many helpers and survivors whose resilience and wisdom inspired us and have been our most influential teachers.

Introduction

To every person there comes in their lifetime that special moment when you are figuratively tapped on the shoulder and offered the chance to do a very special thing, unique to you and your talents. What a tragedy if that moment finds you unprepared or unqualified for work which could have been your finest hour.

—Sir Winston Churchill

This book is intended to help you to prepare for that "tap on the shoulder"—for the moment when disaster strikes and you have the opportunity to help people at a time in their lives when they most need it. By understanding how disaster characteristics impact individuals, recognizing disaster stress and reactions, understanding risk and resilience, and learning early intervention best practices, this book will make you better equipped to provide the supportive recovery environment that is so crucial to the healing of those whose lives have been touched by disaster.

Whether you are a student or professional this book is intended to accomplish the following goals and objectives.

- Describe how characteristics of disasters, including their size, cause, levels of expectedness and intentionality, and timing tend to influence survivors' mental health reactions.
- Understand the range of typical reactions that are expectable in survivors following a disaster, including physical, emotional, cognitive, behavioral, and spiritual responses.
- Understand and be able to recognize the extreme reactions experienced by some disaster survivors, including Posttraumatic Stress Disorder (PTSD) and other clinical conditions such as depression, anxiety, and substance abuse.

- Identify risk factors that make certain groups or individuals more vulnerable during and after disasters.
- Review the principles of the recommended early intervention, Psychological First Aid.
- Understand the importance and use of triage to identify those most at risk.
- Review early interventions beyond Psychological First Aid, including rumor control, conflict mediation, and cognitive restructuring.
- Understand the role of screening and referral to identify and assist those demonstrating a need for traditional assessment and longer-term therapy.
- Identify evidence-based best practices for longer-term treatment of PTSD and other reactions.
- Understand why psychological debriefings are no longer recommended for the general public.
- Understand disaster loss and grief and how to assist the bereaved.
- Review how to assist vulnerable populations, including children and those with functional needs.
- Understand how culture shapes reactions to disaster and how to provide culturally competent help.
- Address occupational hazards faced by first responders and other helpers who work at the scene of a disaster, including vicarious traumatization and compassion fatigue.
- Develop a self-care plan to address the impact of this type of work on the counselor.

We begin each chapter with a case study drawn from experiences in the field. Identifying details have been changed to protect survivors' privacy, but we hope these examples demonstrate the vast range of experiences and reactions you may encounter if you decide to get involved in disaster mental health response.

As you'll see throughout the book, the practice of disaster mental health can be intensely challenging, but also intensely rewarding. We hope this text will give you the information and confidence you need to support disaster survivors at a time when their world seems chaotic and out of control, so that your finest hour can help lighten their darkest hour.

Chapter 1

What Is Disaster Mental Health?

Consider the following case study and think about how it differs from your typical counseling or social work training or your current work situation.

> *Tropical Storm Allison dropped as much as 40 inches of rain in Southern Texas and Louisiana in spring 2001. There were 41 fatalities, most by drowning. In rural Louisiana, there was talk of copperhead snakes and alligators roaming the neighborhood as their habitats were disturbed. Fire ants too were considered a danger; as one resident said: "Don't worry about the gators, but if you see a stick on the ground that appears to undulate—do not touch it! It's covered with fire ants and they can cause you a world of pain." Local residents were less afraid of wildlife and more distressed about their flooded homes. At the Family Assistance Center, clients from varied economic classes, races, religions, and ethnicities waited to meet with caseworkers, who would be able to arrange for damage assessment and provide them with immediate emergency funds for food, clothes, and lodging. The line was long, extending far outside. Some had to wait for hours in the blazing heat; some held children; some were in tears. Some were wet, and all were hot and miserable. Most mental health workers were inside the building. However, others were assigned to "work the line." This meant letting survivors in the queue know how long we thought the wait would be, and getting them water and snacks or small toys for the children. Most of what we did involved making contact and conversations, letting them know they were not alone—that we cared about them and what they were going through. We introduced ourselves, told them where we were from, gave them a bottle of water, and asked how they were doing. We did a lot of listening. Clients told us about belongings that were lost. They struggled to do a mental inventory of what would need to be replaced—and they talked about items destroyed that were not replaceable, such as wedding albums or photos of deceased relatives. Many were*

thankful that they and their family members were not injured, but most were upset and frustrated with family members, nature, luck, and God. Many were upset with themselves for not having enough home insurance, or not protecting their property, or keeping valuables in the basement, or living in an area that tends to flood.

When you respond to a disaster, you leave the familiar and ordinary world and many of the props and structures of routine work and clinical practice. There's no couch or comfortable chair for the therapist, no office and no waiting room. You enter a world where assumptions have been shaken or shattered. We live our lives thinking that the earth doesn't shake so violently it brings down buildings, that rainstorms end without creating chaos, and that planes don't crash. Yet when you enter the disaster scene you need to expect the unexpected. You might be doing counseling on a bench out in the cold. There are no scheduled appointments. There are no insurance forms. Counseling can last for a few minutes or a few hours. The practice of disaster mental health (DMH) is unpredictable. There can be unusual sights, sounds, and smells. You might be underwhelmed one day, overwhelmed the next. It's not unusual for you to go to a Disaster Response Center (DRC) or Family Assistance Center (FAC) and find that there are far too many mental health workers on the scene. It's also quite possible that, when working in a shelter or DRC that has recently been set up, you'll need to be an expert at triage, deciding whom you should help first—an angry parent, a crying child, an upset volunteer, or an overworked kitchen staffer. The settings where you might work can be most unusual.

It should be clear from the case study that disaster mental health is quite different from traditional practice, and it requires helpers to remain flexible and open-minded. Disaster mental health is not for everyone, and even if you are right for it there may be times when you shouldn't be doing this work. If you're under unusual stress, are grieving yourself, or if you think you're not quite fit for duty, it may be best to postpone working at a disaster. If there's one thing you can count on, it's that there will be another disaster at some point in the future. The emotional hazards of this work and the importance of self-care will be discussed in Chapter 11. Although it's reasonable to be careful and circumspect when you're deployed to a disaster, with training and experience you have the opportunity to be very helpful to people who are very much in need.

A BRIEF HISTORY

The study of disaster mental health begins with the study of trauma, which, according to Judith Herman (1992), has a history of investigation followed by denial or forgetting. Herman wrote that three times in the twentieth century a particular form of trauma surfaced into consciousness.

The first was hysteria. Sigmund Freud initially listened to patients as they told him horror stories of sexual abuse, rape, and incest and deduced that the trauma led to a double consciousness or dissociation. His colleagues despised him for insisting on the sexual nature of the cause of hysteria. Later, Freud could simply not believe that so many women had been subjected to sexual trauma. He concluded that the symptoms were not the result of an unbearable or traumatic situation but, rather, an unacceptable impulse—an inappropriate desire for sex that the ashamed patient repressed, leading to the emergence of hysterical symptoms as the urge struggled for conscious awareness. Freud's inability to accept the reality of the commonness of trauma set the field back for decades.

The second time trauma came to the fore was through the study of the combat veterans from the First World War through the Vietnam War. Although the back wards were filled with veterans suffering from "shell shock" after the First World War, once again no one wanted to think or to know about trauma. Their psychological symptoms were blamed on physical exposure to shelling, long past the point at which evidence contradicted that explanation, or on personal weakness or cowardice. Self-advocacy and a refusal to suffer in silence by veterans of the Vietnam War inspired long-term studies of the trauma from war. In the 1970s Vietnam veterans offered comfort to each other in "rap groups." They not only told their stories of the horror of war but also forced the American Psychiatric Association (APA) to legitimize their distress with a new diagnosis: Posttraumatic Stress Disorder (PTSD), which was first included in the third edition of the APA's *Diagnostic and Statistical Manual* (DSM-3), in 1980.

The third recent trauma focus is on sexual and domestic abuse. Not until the 1970s did the women's movement bring to awareness that the most common horror causing traumatic symptoms was not the impact of war on combatants but abuse of women in civilian life, which previously had been viewed as a private matter that wasn't worthy of acknowledgment. This history of not recognizing trauma reminds us that there can be a powerful motive to not see the emotional pain of disaster survivors. We might have to remind officials and others that disasters cause more than physical injury and property damage, and result in emotional and psychological wounds as well.

Looking specifically at disasters, in 1883 Herbert Page was one of the first to recognize and study disaster survivors in the aftermath of railway accidents as this new technology spread after the Industrial Revolution, exposing people to dramatically higher speeds than they had ever traveled at before, and to more damaging accidents when trains crashed. The symptoms he observed and reported—emotionality, sleeplessness, heightened startle response, re-experiencing, and hypervigilance—are in fact the symptoms of PTSD. Page's colleagues assumed there must have been damage to the brain or spine and coined a new diagnosis: "railway spine." However, Page viewed the cause of the symptoms as a shock to the whole person rather than to any particular organ, which was groundbreaking (Brewin, 2003).

Despite some early efforts, such as Page's work, and the crisis counseling that Erich Lindemann provided to survivors and bereaved relatives of victims of the Cocoanut Grove nightclub fire in Boston that killed 492 people and injured hundreds more in 1942, it wasn't until the 1970s that disaster mental health came into its own, as a result of a broad network of mental health practitioners responding to disasters (Morris, 2011). Their DMH work was reported in the press, and soon counseling services were included in the Disaster Relief Act, passed in 1974. In the early 1990s the American Red Cross established disaster mental health as a function not only to help disaster survivors but to support impacted staff and volunteers.

The field then expanded quickly, in parallel with the growing need created by disasters of increasing frequency and intensity. By 1995 hundreds of counselors were deployed after the Oklahoma City bombing and thousands of DMH workers responded to the attacks on September 11, 2001. At present in what is now an established field:

- DMH is practiced by some 5,000 licensed mental health volunteers working with the American Red Cross.
- Most states and counties have disaster mental health teams.
- Professional organizations, including the National Association of Social Workers, the American Psychological Association and the American Psychiatric Association, have statements of understanding with the American Red Cross to provide DMH.
- The Disaster Distress Helpline provides mental health assistance to disaster survivors 24/7 via phone and texts.
- University-based programs, such as the Institute for Disaster Mental Health at SUNY New Paltz, offer both academic programs and professional trainings.
- The Council for Accreditation of Counseling and Related Educational Programs (CACREP) now requires that counselors, as part of their core curriculum, "study the effects of crisis, disasters, and trauma on diverse individuals across the lifespan" and learn the "skills of crisis intervention, trauma-informed, and community-based strategies, such as Psychological First Aid" (CACREP, 2016).

Although disaster mental health is a relatively new field, it has become an essential part of helper education as well as the post-disaster response to survivors' needs.

THE ROLE OF THE HELPER

Let's begin by noting what disaster mental health is *not*. DMH helpers do not provide any type of analytic therapy, prolonged exposure therapy, cognitive processing therapy, or eye movement desensitization and reprocessing therapy. No traditional therapy is appropriate because helpers don't approach clients as patients suffering from a psychopathological disorder. Instead, helpers approach disaster survivors with the attitude that they're under extreme but understandable stress resulting from their recent experience and are not disordered.

Counselors do use their clinical skills and assist survivors in this most difficult time because, as mental health professionals, they're experienced at working with people who are suffering. They're trained to be calm in the face of pain and in trying circumstances. It's also helpful that social workers, psychologists, and counselors all receive training that each case is unique and that one size does not fit all.

Remember that, when assisting disaster survivors, flexibility is most important. In one situation and with one client the helper might need to be very *active*. For example, after an earthquake there could be aftershocks, but survivors will want to check their homes and remove some valuables. Helpers might need to tell them forcefully that they're in an unsafe place and need to get to safety. Similarly, a counselor might say to an older client who is furiously shoveling mud out of his house that he needs to be more careful not to overexert himself. However, the next client, in the house next door, might not need such direct guidance, but only warmth, support, and empathy. In this home, the counselor might need to listen for a long time as survivors talk about their lost photograph albums that were stored in the basement.

In traditional counseling, most therapists work with some eclectic combination of exploration, insight, and action. In disaster work, the orientation and emphasis must be very adaptable. At one Disaster Response Center, a couple were very distraught because they weren't sure where they and their children would sleep that night. A counselor sat sympathetically and comforted them, explaining that everything would work out and that the situation was only temporary. However, a more effective response would have included exploring possible practical solutions by checking with the clients to see if there were friends or family who might help out, or, as many agencies are at a DRC, the counselor might have identified the appropriate agency for assistance and walked with the client to the desk. At the same DRC another client was very distressed that a family member had been hospitalized. This time, effective help meant providing calm reassurance, and helping the client to obtain support from those who cared about her.

These vignettes remind us that our allegiance is to our clients, not to any particular counseling approach, and that we have to be very adaptable when doing disaster work—sometimes providing direct guidance and sometimes providing active listening. These cases also remind us that one size does not fit all. This is one reason why Critical Incident Stress Debriefing, an early approach to providing post-disaster mental health assistance that is discussed in Chapter 5, is no longer recommended for the general public. The practice of DMH requires too much flexibility to think that any one protocol or structure of clinical intervention is the best way to help all disaster survivors.

"I DON'T NEED MENTAL HEALTH"

In the aftermath of the most horrific events it's possible that a DMH supervisor may experience difficulties communicating with a government official or emergency management official regarding the need for mental health services. Why? The officials might not understand or see the importance of mental health services because they're focused on catching the bad guy who perpetrated the attack, or they're busy thinking about how to get the roads open and the injured to hospitals. Bear in mind that government officials, first responders, and emergency managers may be traumatized themselves but are too busy to identify or acknowledge their distress. Additionally, there continues to be a stigma associated with the need for mental health services among some responders and survivors, though that's generally improving. The responsibility of DMH leadership is to assess and provide help to the impacted community—and for DMH workers to acknowledge that we may not always be welcomed with open arms by officials or community members.

If a DMH worker is assigned to help at a shelter or DRC and sits at a desk in front of the room with a sign that says "Mental Health," it's unlikely that he or she will get much business. If a counselor is making home visits and asks if anyone needs "mental health," the answer is likely to be "No." Upset, stressed, and anxious survivors are usually not looking for a "shrink," psychologist, or social worker. They're often reluctant to ask for or accept professional services. What they are looking for is human contact and support. Counselors shouldn't hide the fact that they're mental health professionals, but they do not need to shout it. In most cases counselors shouldn't introduce themselves as Dr. Smith or Social Worker Jones. Instead, they can explain that they're working with the state or county (or Red Cross, or other affiliation) and are experienced in helping people with stress or loss or grief, or in helping families deal with disaster. It may be best for helpers to introduce themselves without titles, make a connection, and build on that connection to establish trust and provide DMH help.

WHO PROVIDES THE MENTAL HEALTH RESPONSE?

Given the potential for extreme distress and lasting psychological reactions following a disaster, it's essential that people with appropriate professional training provide the mental health response. Different organizations involved in the formal response have specific standards to ensure proficiency, but you should be aware that mental health helpers often show up after a disaster as "spontaneous volunteers" who are not affiliated with a particular organization, meaning that their credentials haven't been vetted. To protect the safety of both survivors and responders, these well-meaning volunteers should be turned away by the mental health lead and encouraged to seek DMH-specific training to ensure they understand the specific demands of this kind of response.

State or County Mental Health Responders and American Red Cross

Most state and county DMH responders possess advanced degrees in a mental health discipline and/or a Credentialed Alcohol or Substance Abuse Counselor degree, and/or have significant experience as a psychiatric nurse. In many states there are criteria and credentialing requirements. If there is a nationally declared disaster, there will be an entity in the state that's responsible for the overall program implementation and oversight of the Crisis Counseling Program (CCP), a program of disaster mental health services funded by the Federal Emergency Management Agency (FEMA).

The American Red Cross has over 5,000 DMH volunteers. To be eligible, these DMH workers must have at least a master's degree and be registered or hold a license from any US state or territory as a social worker, psychologist, professional counselor, marriage and family therapist, or psychiatrist (any level license/registration, including non-clinical licenses such as Licensed Master Social Worker, or LMSW); or currently be a school psychologist or counselor with a master's degree and license or certification. Registered psychiatric nurses who have a state license and work in a psychiatric setting are also eligible, as are some retired mental health professionals who used to hold a license and are in good standing. Graduate student teams from mental health programs are also eligible if a licensed professional supervises them. All DMH workers must take specific Red Cross DMH trainings. If you're interested in doing some DMH work, check with your local Red Cross chapter for additional information (American Red Cross, 2013).

Other Agencies Involved in Disaster Response

Different states have different agency structures, but many have some version of an Office of Children and Family Services or the Office of Temporary
and Disability Assistance, which play a vital role in helping survivors recover
from a disaster. At multiple disaster settings (such as shelters, DRCs, FACs)
you can expect to see representatives from many governmental and non-
governmental agencies, such as local and state emergency management,
Departments of Health and Mental Health, the Small Business Administration (for disaster loans), the Internal Revenue Service (tax counseling
and assistance), the Department of Labor (information and assistance for
individuals applying for unemployment insurance benefits and disaster
unemployment insurance), the National Transportation Safety Board, FBI
victim services, domestic and foreign airlines, disaster chaplaincy services
and other spiritual providers, the American Psychological Association, the
National Association of Social Workers, the Office for Victims of Crime, and
local and state equivalents (if the disaster was a crime), and the National
Guard. You can also expect to see representatives from Voluntary Organizations Active in Disaster (VOAD), a coalition of non-profit organizations
that respond to disasters as part of their overall mission. They provide anything from cleanup kits to food to donated goods and labor. The coalition's
membership includes Catholic Charities, United Way, the Salvation Army,
the American Red Cross, and numerous other faith-based and voluntary
organizations. Most of these agencies are described by abbreviations and
their staff often use acronyms to describe services, policies, and procedures.
Don't be hesitant to ask them the meaning of these abbreviations.

Spiritual Care in Disaster Response

The United States of America is a very religious country. A vast majority of
Americans pray regularly, and most pray every day. Psychotherapists and
psychologists are far less religious than the public in terms of religious affiliation, attendance, membership, and perceived importance. Although psychologists are less religious than other academics, most believe that being
religious is beneficial to mental health (Delaney, Miller, & Bisonó, 2007).
This is fortunate, because as a disaster mental health helper you'll likely be
working alongside disaster spiritual care workers who will be involved in
planning and response. Survivors regularly turn to clergy and their faith
communities for direction, care, and meaning. Disaster spiritual care providers often do not share a faith tradition with the people and communities
they serve and they understand that some care recipients may not belong
to any faith community or may be atheists. Their goal is to provide pastoral

care, and to restore faith, hope, and meaning. Chaplains and spiritual care providers are often among the first to respond to disaster and stay involved the longest. They provide a range of vital services. Some faith communities are beginning to get more involved in preparedness by developing social networking tools in advance of emergencies (Aten & Topping, 2010). Relationships between mental health and spiritual care providers should be established well ahead of a crisis to allow for effective referrals, and this relationship should be reciprocal so as to address all of a survivor's needs. Spiritual care providers should refer a depressed or suicidal client to a mental health professional, who in turn should refer clients who complain that they have lost faith in God for spiritual care.

SETTINGS

Disaster mental health can take place at more locations than we can list. It could be delivered on a boat or bus, taking survivors to or from memorials. It could occur on a park bench not far from where a neighborhood was destroyed by flood or fire, at a morgue, in a church, in front of a home that was destroyed by a tornado or hurricane. The following is a list of some of the sites where counselors might be deployed within their own community, in another state, or even in another country:

- disaster site
- Disaster Recovery/Assistance Center
- Family Service Center or Family Assistance Center
- medical Point of Dispensing (POD)
- outreach team
- headquarters/emergency operations center
- shelter
- school or hospital
- memorial service
- telephone call center.

These unusual settings raise issues for practitioners that are not found in an office setting. If you're outside or in a shelter, for example, and speaking with a survivor, there are privacy issues. It might be best if possible to walk away from the crowd and try to find a more quiet or discreet setting. At a memorial, if you're speaking with a survivor when another mental health practitioner recognizes you, doesn't realize you are engaged in counseling, and calls out and intrudes on the conversation, you might have to tell the colleague that this is a private conversation and you'll catch up with them later. If you're part of an outreach team, checking on survivors whose homes have been badly damaged, you might have to consider whether or not the home you're about to enter is safe. We'll discuss issues and challenges of physical safety further in Chapter 11. If survivors are moving back into an impacted neighborhood, you might encounter reporters badgering a survivor. Your most helpful intervention might be to provide some psychoeducation to the reporters by asking them to be gentler with survivors, to appreciate the enormous stress survivors are under, and to please give them the space they need now.

The diverse and unique settings in which disaster mental health is practiced always make for significant challenges for the practitioner. Assignments to shelters, DRCs, and FACs are more common than most, so we will describe these settings in more detail.

Shelters

When there's an impending disaster and an evacuation is necessary, or if power is out during a freeze or heatwave, or if victims are unable to return to their homes because they were destroyed or damaged, shelters provide a safe haven for those who can't stay with family or friends or in a hotel. These shelters, typically staffed by American Red Cross or government housing services personnel, are usually in community centers, churches, or schools where arrangements have previously been made.

The atmosphere in a shelter is often hectic and stressful as residents worry about possible damage in the case of impending disaster, or think about their known losses in the aftermath of one. The conditions in a shelter are often crowded. There is little privacy, often with rows of cots placed in large space to accommodate as many displaced people as possible. There can be many more people sharing a bathroom or TV than most are accustomed to. When shelter residents have to wait for long periods of time to use the bathroom, or children are misbehaving, or someone is snoring loudly, tension grows. Pre-existing racial or cultural issues can be exacerbated. Also, there are rules and procedures intended to ensure safety and maximize the comfort of all, but these can be upsetting for some residents: no tobacco, alcohol, or illegal drugs; no pets; lights out at a specific time. All of the Psychological First Aid and other interventions we'll be discussing are likely to be used when assisting in a shelter.

Disaster Recovery Centers

Disaster Recovery Centers are established to provide information and referral services to individuals and families affected by a disaster. They run as a joint operation between FEMA and state agencies. Many state and federal agencies as well as volunteer organizations will be present, offering both information and immediate assistance across a wide range of areas, from submitting insurance claims to FEMA registration to housing. DMH responders support the DRC operation by ensuring that clients and or staff at the center are provided immediate emotional support if it is needed.

There may be two supervisors or managers a counselor needs to report to. There will be a **DRC site manager**, who coordinates all activities at the Recovery Center. If you're assigned to one and it's your first day on the site, locate and check in with the site manager and let them know who you are. In addition to the site manager, someone will be the **lead** or **chief disaster mental health worker**, who will provide direction, specific assignments, and supervision.

If you're assigned to a DRC, one of your first objectives there should be to introduce yourself to the other workers at each table at the center. Let DRC staff know who you are, what your primary role at the center is, and that they can look to you for assistance should someone they're working with appear to be in need of emotional support. You should plan to stay mobile when not working directly with an individual or group, circulating throughout the center to identify situations that might benefit from your assistance. If someone appears to be in distress, assess the situation and provide necessary assistance. In some DRCs there is a discreet and private counseling area that is available should you need such space. If not, you might look for a space that's set off, or, if weather permits, even consider walking outside to find a more secluded space.

Family Service Centers or Family Assistance Centers

A service center, similar to the DRC, is where clients come for support and to apply for aid. In the aftermath of large disasters, the federal, state, or local government may set up a Family Assistance Center so that clients can come to one centralized place to receive the services from all of the public and private organizations active in disaster recovery. In Red Cross service centers, mental health workers often have an assigned area, usually adjacent to health services, where they can meet with clients. The area is not private or closed off and is not a typical counseling setting. Other staff members might interview clients to determine their eligibility for aid. Mental health workers keep a close watch on these interviews to monitor stress and distress.

In all of these response settings, counselors should bear in mind that, although they're responding to a crisis, there is no circumstance where they should be unsafe. If you feel in danger or threatened, leave the scene and/ or call on-site security forces or 911. In keeping with DMH principles, you should not address acute psychological symptoms but be prepared to refer such clients to local outpatient services or a hospital if necessary. Referrals or the need to contact emergency services should be coordinated with the site manager. The environment at shelters, DRCs, and FACs may be chaotic, especially in the first days after the disaster. You can assist the staff and volunteers by providing a calming presence while checking in with them about their own situations and responses to the event, and educating them about self-care.

THE DMH ROLE OVER TIME

In all of these response settings, staff can refer clients to DMH workers if the client is highly distressed or agitated. Sometimes a staff member signals he or she needs help from a DMH worker during an interview. Sometimes it's clear without such a signal that a staff member or client could benefit from a mental health intervention. If the operation is crowded there can be lines of clients waiting for services both inside and outside the center. Disaster mental health practitioners "work the crowd," making supportive contact with survivors, engaging in conversations with those who are waiting, providing brochures to adults, and giving toys, coloring books, and crayons to the children. The role of DMH workers in these circumstances is to maintain calm by lowering the arousal level through these simple actions, and through outreach that offers modest but cumulatively helpful stress relief.

In service centers and DRCs, DMH workers also provide assistance to stressed workers. One way to accomplish this is to spend time with workers, socializing in the kitchen or break room, joining them for lunch, and lending a hand with all of the tasks and chores that need to be done to keep a center operating. DMH workers may make sure that there's toilet paper in the bathrooms and that light bulbs are replaced quickly. This is helpful for the obvious reasons of keeping the bathrooms usable and the lights on, but it also builds a sense of trust and camaraderie with the workers whom DMH is there to support, should they need assistance. Counselors monitor the staff for stress, encourage them to take breaks and time off, and advocate for an environment that's conducive to mental health. Many assistance centers also have meetings either before opening in the morning or after closing. These meetings are an excellent time for DMH staff to address the group about mental health issues, including self-care.

Settings typically change over time. In the immediate aftermath of a disaster, you might be asked to take calls at a helpline, or assist in a shelter. It can take some time to set up a DRC, where you might be assigned days or weeks after the disaster. If survivors had to evacuate, you might go door to door helping them with the adjustment of moving back home. There are also very different challenges depending on how long after the disaster you're deployed. In the earliest stages, there's often little information available, survivors are more likely to be in shock, it's more likely there will be media present and more general hubbub, and it may be harder for you to be grounded. Later in the response you might see more despair or depression among survivors, including sadness and difficulty understanding why the press and the public are no longer paying attention to their plight. Staff members' needs evolve, and the strain of an extended deployment or the cumulative stress of being the target of survivors' frustration take a toll. Planners and responders can be sufficiently drained and exhausted if the long-term needs of the community are not adequately addressed (Séguin et al., 2013).

As you can see from the unusual settings and circumstances in which you might be working, DMH workers need to be aware of practical considerations. Preparedness is important not just for potential survivors but for helpers as well. You may need to be ready to respond with little advance notice. This means keeping IDs handy, along with a "go bag" with clothes and supplies for several days. Helpers also have to be very mindful of how to dress, and to give consideration to the weather. We'll return to these logistical issues in Chapter 11.

WHO ARE YOUR CLIENTS?

Let's begin by considering how we best refer to people affected by disaster. Early in the history of trauma work, clients were referred to as *victims*—victims of abuse or violence or disaster. However, *victim* connotes weakness, vulnerability, and powerlessness and does not do justice to clients' strengths and their ability to bounce back from adversity. It then became more common to refer to those impacted by disaster and other traumatic events as *survivors*, a word that connotes strength and resilience. However, keep in mind that someone who was injured or who just lost a loved one in a disaster may not appreciate being called a *survivor*. As Yael Danieli discussed in her extensive work with Holocaust survivors, many react negatively to being called *survivors*. They did not recover and they felt more like victims.

Perhaps one way to help us all feel better and more optimistic is to overemphasize the recovery and downplay the pain and suffering of trauma clients by calling them "survivors." Or perhaps both points of view have some real merit: those impacted by disasters are likely to have both vulnerabilities and strengths, with "victim" emphasizing the damage and "survivor" emphasizing the ability to recover. There is no word that perfectly describes the complex reactions of those who have been impacted by disaster—but even without a perfect label you can still supply much-needed help.

Everyone impacted by the disaster is someone who could potentially benefit from your assistance, but consider that not everyone is looking for therapy or counseling. You need to balance being more proactive than is typical in your primary work setting and yet not be too intrusive or overbearing. As a supportive presence you make connections and set the stage for help you or others might provide later on. However, although you can be helpful to all who are involved with the disaster, do not assume that everyone needs and is looking for your counseling. Some survivors really benefit most from the help and support they receive from family, friends, and clergy.

In traditional practice, when a client calls asking for help, their status as patient is often unambiguous. In disaster mental health, we typically do not "treat patients," as we're not often making diagnoses. Rather, we're assisting those impacted by the extreme stress caused by disaster. If you're assigned to a shelter you need to have a very wide lens as you assess whom to help. It might be clear that a parent needs help with a frightened child, or that a couple are arguing over what they forgot to bring to the shelter, or a shelter worker may approach you to say that a resident showing strong signs of distress needs help. However, if there are no obvious indicators, you can still provide considerable assistance.

- You might check with the shelter managers to determine if there are residents or staff members who could use support.
- You might walk around the shelter or DRC and introduce yourself to residents/visitors and let them know you're available if they need anything, or wander into the kitchen or break room so you can get to know staff members and build a sense of connection and trust in case they need help later in the response.
- You might also check to see if people are generally comfortable—decent lighting, food, and clean bathrooms.
- You can let people know that food is on the way, that toys are available for children, that the storm has passed, that the local sports team won the game.
- You might just listen to their complaints about shelter life or frustrations with response resources.
- You can check in with response leaders, reporters outside the operation, or first responders coming in for a break to see how they're doing and if they could use some DMH support. There are higher rates of PTSD and depression in firefighters and police officers and emergency management professionals than in the general public (LaFauci, Schutt, & Marotta, 2011). The exposure to trauma puts these groups at elevated risk, and other early responders, such as the 911 telecommunicators, also show distress (Lilly & Pierce,

2013). Some first responder departments have their own mental health support and some do not. Check in with first responder leaders to see if and how you can be of help. Bear in mind that they will not want to discuss mental health issues with you if there are other priorities.

As this overview of the logistics of disaster mental health shows, the circumstances vary in many ways from the more traditional practices most counselors and social workers train in. Still, while the settings and the specifics of the helping relationship are different, many of the skills you've learned can be adapted to the demands of the post-disaster environment. Now let's turn our attention to the wide range of disasters you're likely to respond to when you're called to assist during or after a complex emergency.

REFERENCES

American Red Cross (2013, November). Disaster mental health fundamentals [PowerPoint slides]. Washington, DC: American Red Cross, https://intranet.red-cross.org/content/redcross/categories/our_services/disaster-cycle-services/dcs-management/training/dcs-training-index.html.

Aten, J. D., & Topping, S. (2010). An online social networking disaster preparedness tool for faith communities. *Psychological Trauma: Theory, Research, Practice, and Policy*, 2(2), 130–4.

Brewin, C. R. (2003). *Posttraumatic stress disorder: Malady or myth?* New Haven, CT: Yale University Press.

CACREP (2016). *2016 CACREP standards.* Alexandria, VA: Council for Accreditation of Counseling and Related Educational Programs, www.cacrep.org/wp-content/uploads/2012/10/2016-CACREP-Standards.pdf.

Delaney, H. D., Miller, W. R., & Bisonó, A. M. (2007). Religiosity and spirituality among psychologists: A survey of clinician members of the American Psychological Association. *Professional Psychology: Research and Practice*, 38(5), 538–46.

Herman, J. L. (1992). *Trauma and recovery: The aftermath of violence—from domestic abuse to political terror.* New York: Basic Books.

LaFauci, J., Schutt, J. M., & Marotta, S. (2011). Personal and environmental predictors of posttraumatic stress in emergency management professionals. *Psychological Trauma: Theory, Research, Practice, and Policy*, 3(1), 8–15.

Lilly, M. M., & Pierce, H. (2013). PTSD and depressive symptoms in 911 telecommunicators: the role of peritraumatic distress and world assumptions in predicting risk. *Psychological Trauma: Theory, Research, Practice, and Policy*, 5(2), 135–41.

Morris, A. J. (2011). Psychic aftershocks: Crisis counseling and disaster relief policy. *History of Psychology*, 14(3), 264–86.

Séguin, M., Chawky, N., Lesage, A., Boyer, R., Guay, S., Bleau, P., ..., & Roy, D. (2013). Evaluation of the Dawson College shooting psychological intervention: Moving toward a multimodal extensive plan. *Psychological Trauma: Theory, Research, Practice, and Policy*, 5(3), 268–76.

Chapter 2

Describing Disasters

In July 2015 California state firefighters responded to almost 4,000 fires. Drought, high winds, and high temperatures created a much stronger risk of wildfires throughout the West and Northwest. One family, faced with an order to evacuate their home as fires raged nearby, packed their belongings while watching helicopters and air tankers fight the fire. They agonized over what to pack and what to leave behind. The family had no doubt they would bring most of the pets, but the parents drew the line on the aquarium. The fish, they explained to the children, would have to fend for themselves. Everyone was quite stressed when they arrived at a shelter about 30 minutes away, only to find out that the shifting winds now allowed them to return home. They were relieved but exhausted. When they got home they made calls to reassure relatives and got some rest. In the middle of the next night they were awakened by a police officer, who informed them that a containment line had been breached and they would have to evacuate a second time. The family drowsily got into their van and headed back to the shelter, with the expectation that this would be another false alarm. Although they loaded up the pets, they did not bring as much as a change of clothes. Tragically, this time there was no home to return to. The fire had destroyed the neighborhood, along with all their belongings. The parents were distraught and grieved the loss of photographs they had not saved. They blamed the boy who started the fire by playing with matches. They blamed the authorities for denying climate change that contributed to the drought and higher temperatures. They blamed their bad luck about having to evacuate at night, but most of all they blamed themselves for not taking their most precious belongings, being careless, and believing the evacuation order would just be another false alarm.

Consider the factors that made this disaster, like most, a unique event. Why would it be helpful for a mental health responder to have an understanding of the characteristics of this event before meeting with the family? As you read this chapter, think about how you could translate your understanding into providing more effective assistance.

This chapter focuses on disasters themselves, in particular on key event characteristics that tend to impact survivors' reactions. These characteristics directly affect survivors in terms of the length and nature of trauma they experience, which we will see are strong predictors of mental health reactions. In addition, these same characteristics often influence the logistical demands faced by emergency responders and community members before, during, and after disasters. Since the degree of success responders have in managing those demands impacts the resulting conditions in the community, these characteristics also indirectly influence individuals' reactions by shaping the recovery environment they'll live in while they adjust to their disaster experience and losses.

Before we describe those characteristics, let's consider a basic question: What constitutes a disaster? There's no single universally accepted definition, and, as we'll see, an event that's experienced as a disaster in one setting might be perceived as a routine emergency in another. As a general description, a disaster is "a natural or human-caused catastrophe that causes destruction, frequently including loss of life, with permanent changes to an environment and a community" (Halpern & Tramontin, 2007). We return to issues of causality and loss later; for now let's focus on the final part of this definition.

The main factor that sets disasters apart from more individual types of traumatic events is that they occur at the collective, community-wide level. While an experience such as a serious car accident or a sexual assault is traumatic, and certainly feels disastrous to the person who goes through it, generally we can assume that his or her natural sources of support—friends, family members, and neighbors—have not been directly affected, so they're available to provide comfort and assistance to the trauma survivor as he or she processes and recovers from the event. That's often not the case in disasters that impact an entire neighborhood or large group. If the neighbors who might offer shelter to a family displaced by an individual house fire has also lost their home to a wildfire, each family is left in need. Rather than helping each other out, both may need to rely on outside assistance in the form of, for example, an American Red Cross shelter, where their specific needs and preferences may not receive much attention amid the demands of housing and feeding all who have been impacted.

Compounding that collective impact, disasters often permanently reshape the communities in which they occur. Infrastructure may be damaged or destroyed, leaving people unable to get around, without hospitals and healthcare services, schools, and places of worship. This means that the recovery environment is disrupted and unfamiliar. The sense of community and stability most of us rely on is suddenly gone, and it may take considerable time to regain it. It's not uncommon to hear residents say things immediately after an event along the lines of "We'll rebuild and make it just the way it was before!" only to come to the painful realization that it will never be exactly the same again. Some community members may choose to move away rather than risk living through another weather event they now realize they're vulnerable to; some may not be able to afford to rebuild; some may have died. Although, ultimately, the community should be able to achieve some type of "new normal" (which may in some ways be better than the original), getting there involves accepting and mourning the loss of the old way of life.

So, while you will be able to apply your training in treating individual forms of trauma to your work as a disaster mental health helper, keep in mind how disasters shape not only survivors' actual experience of the event but also the context their recovery will occur in, especially the constrained ability to rely on their usual sources of support.

TYPES AND FREQUENCIES OF EVENTS

Think about the wide range of disasters we hear about in the news and prepare for professionally—from seasonal events, such as hurricanes and ice storms, to mass transportation accidents, such as plane and bus crashes, to terrorist attacks. Here's a far from complete list of events that can and do occur within the United States and worldwide:

- floods
- volcanoes
- mudslides
- oil spills
- toxic spills
- wildfires
- transportation disasters (plane, bus, train)
- bridge collapses
- nightclub fires
- mass shootings
- terrorist attacks
- bioterrorism
- pandemics/public health emergencies
- tornadoes
- hurricanes
- ice storms/blizzards
- extreme heat/heatwaves
- earthquakes

- tsunamis
- power outages/blackouts
- crowd stampedes/crushes
- violent public disturbances/civil disorder.

Unfortunately, many of these events are increasing in frequency and intensity. Acts of organized terrorism and episodes of violence by so-called "lone wolves" are on the rise; according to the FBI, an active shooter incident occurs about every three weeks on average in the United States. Forty percent of these incidents qualify as mass killings and they most commonly occur in the workplace and in schools—places we don't have the option to avoid—as well as in nightclubs, restaurants, and other "soft targets," where people gather to have a good time and where it's difficult if not impossible to limit access to those intent on doing harm.

At the same time that terrorism and acts of mass violence are on the rise, climate change is causing more frequent and extreme weather events worldwide as well as increasing the spread of many diseases, and creating general anxiety about food insecurity and other future effects (Food and Agriculture Organization, 2015). Compounding the problem further, population increases worldwide result in more people living (sometimes by choice, but often due to economic necessity) in areas that are prone to regular natural disasters such as wildfires, floods, or hurricanes, so more people may be impacted when an event does occur than in previous times.

All of this means that the need for mental health services for disaster survivors has never been higher. Fortunately, this growth in demand has been paralleled with both increasing recognition of the psychological toll disasters take and the development of more effective interventions for both short- and long-term reactions.

DISASTERS VERSUS ROUTINE EMERGENCIES

A brief point before we move on to the characteristics of disasters: From the response perspective, what qualifies as a major disaster in one setting could be less disastrous in another if there are adequate resources to respond to it. Every community has first responders who are equipped to deal with some level of "routine emergencies"—firefighters, emergency medical technicians (EMTs) and paramedics, and law enforcement agents who respond to car accidents, house fires, and other emergencies. But when an event's demands exceed that local capacity in terms of personnel, skills, and equipment, so that additional support needs to be brought in from the outside, suffering is likely to increase during the response, which means that subsequent emotional reactions are likely to be worse.

For example, imagine a serious bus accident in a large city versus a rural setting. Even if the number and severity of injuries were identical, in the urban event quick access to skilled responders with adequate rescue equipment who can rapidly transport victims to trauma centers throughout the city is likely to result in fewer casualties than in the rural setting, where victims may need to wait longer for help to arrive and then be flown to hospitals in multiple surrounding counties. Does the incident still feel like a disaster to those in the urban version? Of course it does, but having their needs attended to quickly is likely to at least mitigate emotional distress as well as physical suffering.

In a variation on this point, no one would consider the "Miracle on the Hudson," when pilots safely landed a commercial plane on the Hudson River in 2009, to be a routine emergency, but the successful evacuation of all 155 passengers and crew members was a direct result of where and when the event occurred: in the afternoon, on a cold but clear day, in a section of the river where commercial vessels were able to reach the scene and begin rescuing passengers within minutes. That point is in no way meant to undermine the remarkable performance of the pilots and cabin crew in landing the plane and organizing an efficient evacuation, but the outcome for the passengers might have been a lot less miraculous had it occurred in a different time or place.

Bear this in mind when you start to think about potential events in your own community and what resources might be available to address them. Will a certain incident be manageable like a routine emergency or will it overwhelm resources and turn into a disaster?

DISASTER CHARACTERISTICS

As we've seen, the variety of disasters is vast, and it would not be feasible to have a specific response plan for each particular type of event. Instead, emergency responders generally take an "all hazards" approach based on a general plan that can then be tailored to the specific type and timing of an actual event. We'll take a similar approach on the mental health side: Rather than teaching you how to help the survivor of, say, a hurricane versus a terrorist attack, we'll focus on certain key characteristics that research has identified as tending to influence survivors' psychological reactions to their experiences. As we'll see, what matters is less the specific type of disaster than factors such as event size, cause, and timing. Those patterns provide an important basis for understanding how a specific event is likely to affect people, but it's essential to keep in mind that survivors are individuals first.

Table 2.1 Predictors of survivor reactions: variables to consider.

Disaster characteristics	Individual characteristics	Response characteristics
• Was it human-caused or natural, or a combination? • Was there a warning period? • Was there a clear end point to the disaster, or uncertainty about it recurring or about its long-term health effects? • How widely was the community infrastructure damaged?	• If there was a warning period, did the individual take protective action? • How directly was the individual impacted (e.g., injury, loss of home, death of loved one)? • Did the individual have pre-existing strengths or vulnerabilities that might impact his or her response? • Does the individual have an intact support network to draw on? • Did the individual have previous disaster experience?	• Did the community have pre-existing resources to aid recovery? • How were survivors treated immediately after the disaster? • How were survivors treated in the longer-term recovery stages?

Specifically, each person you'll encounter had different pre-disaster strengths and challenges; each person had a different private experience of the event; and each person will have access to different resources to assist in his or her recovery. This may seem obvious, but it's easy to lose sight of when you're dealing with large groups of survivors after a major disaster. It can be tempting to adopt a one-size-fits-all approach to interventions— everyone went through the same hurricane, for example, so why wouldn't they all need the same response services? But that's likely to misallocate limited mental health resources by directing unneeded attention to some people who already have sufficient personal resilience or access to support, while depriving others of the full level of assistance they could benefit from. It's essential to bear in mind that any one survivor's reaction will be an **interaction between the characteristics of the disaster, the individual, and the response**.

With that caveat, there are some evidence-based correlations between disaster traits and typical emotional reactions. Let's now examine the characteristics that tend to influence survivors' mental health.

Specifically, relevant characteristics include categorizing disasters by **size**, by **cause**, and by whether they were **expected or not**. Additionally, the **timing** of the event can influence both its logistical and emotional impact. We'll examine each of these factors in detail.

Disaster Size: Scope, Intensity, and Duration

Scope, intensity, and duration all measure different aspects of the size of an event. In essence, they describe how **big**, **bad**, and **long** the disaster was. Note that there are no standard definitions for these characteristics (for example, there's no official number of fatalities that qualifies an event as low versus high in intensity), and that the available resources relative to demands certainly will influence the response.

Scope can be thought of as a measure of the breadth of damage caused by a disaster. It describes how extensively the larger community is impacted, including the rescue and support infrastructure, which in turn predicts how much help is available and how quickly recovery can proceed. As we said earlier, in an event with a large scope, survivors may be unable to turn to their normal support systems of friends, family, and neighbors as they would after a smaller-scale traumatic event, since those people may be dealing with their own recovery needs. This means that survivors may also feel guilty for not being able to help others in need because of the urgent demands they're facing to tend to their own families. Hospitals may be damaged or destroyed, leaving healthcare needs unmet. Children may miss school for extended periods, which impacts their emotional need for routine as well as their academic progress. Widespread damage to housing stock typically drives up rents in an area, further challenging those lower on the socioeconomic spectrum. After events that are very large in scope, such as Hurricanes Katrina and Sandy, or the 2010 earthquakes in Haiti and Chile, survivors may be forced to relocate permanently in order to find housing, work, and schools, which adds the emotional stress of resettling and losing one's community on top of the direct disaster losses. And, when the physical cleanup and rebuilding of communities are very protracted, residents face constant reminders of what they've lost, which many people find very distressing.

Intensity refers to the level of damage in terms of injuries and deaths—the event's human cost. As we've said, any serious injury or loss of life will feel tragic for those directly affected, but disasters that cause multiple losses can compound distress for everyone involved, including professional responders, who may suffer secondary trauma from exposure to many injured people or dead bodies. The effect of losing multiple loved ones goes beyond pure addition: Not only is someone whose child and spouse were both killed in a disaster grieving two deaths at once, but he or she may have lost what would have been the main source of comfort in grappling with the death of a child, as well as a chief reason to keep on going in coming to terms with the sudden loss of a partner. As a result, people who experienced multiple losses are at the highest risk of a difficult bereavement process and should be a focus of early mental health attention. We'll return to disaster-related loss in Chapter 6.

Scope and intensity are often linked, but not always. An event may be large in both, or large in one measure and small in the other. For example, a hurricane or ice storm may cause extensive property damage, but, if warnings were provided and complied with, the human cost may be minimal. In contrast, an event may be high in intensity but limited in scope. This was the case in the 2016 nightclub shooting in Orlando, Florida, when a terrorist shot and killed 49 clubgoers and wounded 53 more. It was the deadliest mass shooting by a single gunman as well as the deadliest episode of violence against the LGBTQ community, making it a terrible event in terms of intensity. However, only one building was damaged, leaving the rest of the community's physical infrastructure intact as it coped first with the need for emergency medical care for the wounded and then as survivors mourned the human loss.

Duration may be thought of in multiple ways. First, it can refer to the length of the disaster itself, which could range from seconds for an earthquake or explosion, to hours or days for a hurricane or blizzard, and even to weeks for a slowly advancing and receding flood. Or we can think of duration as the length of time people are affected by a disaster, including the recovery period as physical damage is repaired and losses are adjusted to emotionally. In the case of events that are very large in scope, that might take years, or might never be fully completed.

From the mental health perspective, the most useful way to think about duration falls somewhere between those two measures: It's the length of time until survivors begin to *feel safe* again. Real recovery can begin only when survivors believe that the imminent danger has passed (Hobfoll et al., 2007), but sometimes that point is not clear. In addition to the threat of additional physical harm, ongoing uncertainty about whether an event is truly over can greatly compound distress, since survivors never know when they can let their guard down. Survivors of earthquakes often sleep outside for fear of aftershocks. Terrorist attacks are often organized simultaneously or in sequence, leaving survivors wary of repeat attacks. Exposure to biohazards may cause great anxiety about long-term health effects. In any event, without a clear end point, survivors may remain in a state of heightened vigilance that interferes with their ability to recover emotionally from the initial experience.

Scope, intensity, and duration also tend to be correlated with the degree of impact on professional and community response systems: Are there enough emergency responders to contain damage and rescue survivors? Can area hospitals handle the number of injured people? Can schools and workplaces reopen quickly? Are people displaced for extended periods of time?

While the resulting logistical difficulties are obvious, there's also a clear mental health connection: All three measures tend to predict survivors' reactions in what is referred to as a "dose–response relationship," meaning the bigger the dose of disaster a person experiences, the worse his or her psychological reaction tends to be. Therefore, in assessing mental health needs post-disaster, survivors whose disaster experience was particularly intense or long-lasting or whose recovery environment is highly disrupted are likely to require more support than those who received a smaller dose of trauma.

Disaster Cause

While the relationship between dose and response is fairly clear-cut (more = worse), the impact of a disaster's cause is more nuanced—as is the division between causal categories. The most basic way of classifying disasters is as natural or human-caused. However, this is a more complex divide than might be evident, since natural events can trigger secondary technical disasters (referred to as na-tech events), and human-created conditions can limit or increase damage resulting from natural events. For example, in Hurricane Katrina the storm was obviously natural, but the flooding of New Orleans was caused by the failure of levees due to human error and neglect. In Japan in 2011 a natural earthquake and tsunami led to the meltdown of a nuclear power plant that displaced hundreds of thousands of residents.

We noted earlier the impacts of climate change and population growth. A large wildfire in an unpopulated region might have little human impact; only after people decide to build in these areas does the potential for property damage and injury or death exist. Should that be considered natural or human-caused? Should increased flooding caused by higher sea levels as the atmosphere warms and polar ice melts be considered natural or human-caused?

Another factor that blurs the line between causes is differences in building practices. The massive devastation and death toll of over 230,000 caused by the magnitude 7.0 Haitian earthquake in early 2010 was largely due to the use of unstable building materials and designs, resulting in the collapse of countless structures. In contrast, the 8.8 magnitude Chilean earthquake six weeks later was 500 times more powerful, yet the death toll was below 1,000, since strict building codes kept most buildings standing long enough for people to escape. Therefore, the built environment can affect the intensity of damage caused by a naturally occurring event. We should also note that there has not been a death due to fire in an American public school in over 40 years. This is because fire departments and the general public have demanded and achieved rigorously enforced fire codes in US schools. This is a triumph that could serve as a model for other efforts at prevention.

Another type of disaster, public health emergencies, can be either naturally occurring, such as pandemic flu, or intentionally caused, as in a bioterrorism attack. Even when they're natural in origin their psychological impact is closer to human-caused events given the anxiety they tend to produce. As these examples illustrate, there's not always a clear divide between causes. However, for those events that can be classified as natural or human-caused, research has identified certain typical emotional reactions. In particular, differences in anger and blaming are often seen.

Natural Disasters
In general, people tend to have an easier time recovering emotionally from natural disasters such as weather events. These events are recognized as unpreventable and not anyone's responsibility. There's no one to blame, except possibly God or a higher power, so adjustment is often facilitated because survivors don't typically have anger or a desire for revenge compounding their losses.

However, the negative side of that lack of preventability is the recognition that one is powerless to stop a similar disaster from happening again in the future. As a result, survivors of natural disasters may feel helpless and unable to protect themselves, which can be very distressing in a culture that tends to emphasize feelings of personal control. People may overextend this sense of helplessness well beyond the disaster itself, feeling as if "I'll never be able to rebuild, and if I do another hurricane will just come along, so why bother?"

Natural disasters may either strengthen religious people's faith or shake it. One person's response may be "God was really watching out for us because he only took our house but he kept us all safe," while another's may be "God must really have it in for us because he destroyed our house." For those whose faith is tested, the loss of a past source of comfort and sense of trust in a benevolent deity can be very upsetting, and enlisting spiritual care providers in a mental health response plan can help to address it.

It should be noted that, when a natural disaster is very large in scope or intensity, the relative protection of the cause tends to fade out and emotional reactions may be as strongly negative as for human-caused events. That exception aside, psychological reactions following smaller-scale natural disasters tend to involve less distress than responses to events that are clearly human in origin, with **helplessness** as the most typical troubling emotion.

Human-Caused Disasters
Human-caused events, such as transportation disasters, industrial accidents, mass shootings, and terrorist attacks, are generally associated with more psychological distress among survivors. Realistically or not, these events are often perceived as preventable, so many survivors experience **anger**, plus a

strong need to lay **blame**. They usually want to identify whoever is responsible and punish them, either through the judicial system or by seeking revenge or retribution.

The urge to blame can be extremely strong, and for some survivors it becomes a driving force, squeezing out any focus on adjusting to the original loss. This blaming often extends beyond actual perpetrators to include authorities that survivors perceive as having failed to recognize the potential threat and stop it. In hindsight it's often possible to pinpoint someone who truly might have done better at preventing a human-caused disaster, whether that could have been through legal action, such as the capture of suspected terrorists before they had a chance to act, or through the creation of safety policies to prevent transportation accidents. If such an official scapegoat is identified, survivors may feel betrayed by authorities that they believe failed to protect them, as well as by the person or people directly responsible for the event.

This can be viewed as a coping mechanism: Finding someone to blame and punish gives survivors a perception of control and a belief they can prevent the event from recurring, as well as a sense that someone can be made to pay for their losses. However, it can also lead people to become so fixated on their anger and need for justice that they don't come to terms with their disaster-caused losses and become stalled in their recovery process. And, if survivors perceive that justice isn't being done, they may lose faith in humanity in general and need to learn to trust again.

It's also essential to recognize that within the category of human-caused events there are different degrees of **intentionality**, from accidental to negligent to intentional, and this can clearly affect psychological reactions. We'll illustrate this with a quick thought experiment.

First, take a moment to imagine that you've just learned that a loved one has been killed in a plane crash that occurred shortly after takeoff when the plane hit a flock of geese, which stalled the engines. The pilots were unable to bring it down safely and all on board were killed. How do you feel? Terrible, most likely—shocked, saddened, full of regret that you didn't have the opportunity to say goodbye, and so on. Who do you blame? That's a bit harder to answer for most people. The geese are the real culprits, but you can't get much justice from them. You might blame the pilots (those other guys managed a safe emergency landing, so why couldn't these do the same?), but the pilots have died, so there's no way to punish them. You could stretch a bit and blame the aircraft designer for not creating bird-strike-proof engines, and you might blame airport authorities for not recognizing and dealing with the threat posed by the flock. But most people react to this as an accident—tragic, to be sure, but not really anyone's fault—so there is typically not a lot of anger in their response (again, except possibly at God).

Now imagine you've just learned that a loved one has died in a crash that occurred because the captain, who was newly licensed to fly this particular aircraft, overcorrected in response to strong winds while approaching landing, causing a spiral that couldn't be recovered from so all on board were killed. Additionally, the cockpit recorder indicated that the pilots were talking during the landing approach rather than maintaining the required silence at that time. How do you feel now? Your reaction to the death is probably pretty similar, but how about the anger and blame aspects? Most people express far more anger in this scenario. Even though the crash wasn't intentional it's easy to hold the pilots responsible, though, again, they can't be punished since they died in the crash. Many will then shift their anger to the airline authorities, demanding better training procedures and enforcement of safety rules. Some might pursue policy changes to make sure this never happens again to anyone else's loved one, while others might pursue legal proceedings against the airline.

Finally, imagine your loved one has died in a terrorist attack that brought down an airplane. Does that feel different? For most people, the anger and desire for justice are drastically more powerful than in the other scenarios. In this case the loved one was intentionally murdered, which will be far more difficult for most survivors to come to terms with. While events caused by accident or negligence may lead to blame of the individuals perceived as responsible, or to a demand for changes to systems that permitted the failure to occur, these responses are not likely to be as intense or long-lasting as those resulting from intentional malevolence. There are few things harder to accept than the idea that someone has intentionally harmed us or our loved ones, and knowing that one's suffering has given someone pleasure or advanced their political or personal goals can be devastating psychologically (Hassani, 2007).

Also, disasters caused by criminal behavior often necessitate legal proceedings against suspected perpetrators that can go on for many years. Research (for example, Madeira, 2012) has shown that these proceedings (arraignments, trials, sentencing, parole hearings) often bring about a resurgence of symptoms in survivors. Therefore, survivors of acts of terrorism or other intentional crimes should be viewed as being at high risk of serious posttraumatic reactions and targeted for early mental health interventions.

Public Health Emergencies
Whether they're caused by a naturally developing disease such as influenza, an accidental release of radiation or other toxins, or an intentionally introduced act of bioterrorism, public health emergencies create some specific stressors for responders and for those who have been exposed—or merely fear they might have been.

Above all, the **uncertainty** around this type of threat is extremely upsetting. In most disasters, whether natural or human-caused, we know immediately if we've been physically harmed. That is not generally the case with diseases that may have an incubation period of several days from exposure to the development of symptoms, and it's certainly not the case when exposure to a toxin may result in cancer, lung problems, fertility issues, or other health issues only years later.

For some people, the thought that they may have been exposed to something, but don't know for certain, can be terrifying, so public health emergencies often produce large numbers of "MUPS," or people with medically unexplained physical symptoms (formerly referred to as the "worried well"). These people may interpret the physiological expressions of their stress reactions (such as a pounding heart or shortness of breath) as symptoms of the disease they fear they're developing, and they may flood emergency departments or healthcare clinics that already have their hands full dealing with those who are actually suffering from the condition in question, as well as with their ordinary flow of patients (Neimark, Caroff, & Stinnett, 2005).

Mental health professionals may need to help respond to MUPS to prevent them from unnecessarily consuming medical resources, as well as to assist with managing crowd emotions and behaviors at settings such as Points of Dispensing for large-scale distribution of vaccinations or medications, or at decontamination sites. These experiences are unfamiliar to most people and may create concerns about additional exposure in addition to worries about side effects of the treatment. For example, during the 2009 emergence of the H1N1 influenza pandemic, many people resisted getting vaccinated because of media-fueled rumors that the vaccine was unsafe—even though it used the exact same technology as seasonal flu vaccine development and production. This kind of fear is an emotional reaction, but it can lead to very real health consequences if it causes people to avoid necessary prophylaxis or treatment.

Above all, remember that most people have limited understanding of disease processes or treatments. For example, many are uncertain about the difference between antibiotics, vaccines, and antiviral medicines. They also don't understand the difference between **isolation**, which separates sick people with a contagious disease from people who are not sick, and **quarantine**, which separates and restricts the movement of people who were exposed to a contagious disease to see if they become sick (see www.cdc.gov/quarantine). Therefore, public health emergencies tend to create both personal worry about becoming sick and a susceptibility to rumors or misinformation that will be compounded if accurate information is not provided in a timely, credible, and comprehensible manner. We mental health professionals may be limited in our ability to respond to the actual health threat but we can contribute by obtaining and disseminating accurate information, and by preparing for and intervening in the cognitive and emotional distress public health emergencies cause.

Expected or Unexpected

A third major factor associated with typical psychological reactions is whether a disaster was expected or unexpected. This factor primarily means whether the disaster allowed for a specific warning that it was approaching, but to some degree expectedness applies to simple recognition that a type of event is even possible.

Expected Events

Expectedness is partially correlated with causality. Many natural disasters offer a warning period, but some, such as earthquakes, do not. For those events that do allow warnings, the length of the warning periods varies widely, and as a result so does the type of protective action possible. Major storms can be predicted with reasonable accuracy days in advance, allowing for evacuation and the advance opening of emergency shelters, while tornado warnings might provide a few minutes' notice to seek safety.

This is a mental health issue because survivors generally demonstrate less intense emotional reactions to expected disasters. Of course, in part this is because warnings provide an opportunity to evacuate, seek shelter, or take other protective action and avoid or minimize the dose of trauma received. Apart from that obvious practical protection, receiving a warning also allows for some psychological adjustment to the idea that a threat is approaching, rather than blindsiding people, as an unexpected event does.

However, warnings are not without a downside. Essentially, receiving a warning places the recipient in an unpleasant decision-making situation: Will they comply with it or not? Choosing to comply means first acknowledging that a potential threat to life and property is approaching, which is not something most of us readily embrace. If we do accept the threat as legitimate, most recommended protective actions are onerous in terms of time, money, effort, and distress. As a result, the typical tendency after receiving a warning is to deny that one is at risk and to disregard it, or to wait to collect more information—sometimes until it's too late to take the most effective action (Vermeulen, 2014). We'll elaborate on this in the next chapter, when we discuss typical reactions by disaster stage.

If people receive a warning and they fail to take action, they're likely to experience guilt and shame later from the recognition that they could have avoided some losses, which of course is devastating if those losses include the deaths or serious injuries of loved ones. What could be worse than knowing that a loss could have been prevented if only you'd complied with the warning? Survivors may then have to cope with self-blame, as well as blame by others who question why they didn't heed the warning. These can be powerful emotions that complicate recovery, as survivors must learn to accept that part of their losses was due to their own decisions. However, vowing not to repeat that mistake and to follow subsequent warnings can provide them with some perception of control over the future.

It's also possible that survivors might take reasonable steps in reaction to a warning, only to discover that they were insufficient. For example, before evacuating in response to a flood warning, residents might place valuables in high locations within their home. If the floodwaters rise higher than expected and the items are destroyed, survivors might still engage in self-blame that is unreasonable—they *did* take precautions they believed would be appropriate—but nonetheless distressing. Residents in disaster-prone areas such as flood plains may also engage in self-blame because they know they made a choice to live in harm's way. In the case study described at the beginning of the chapter we saw that, after a false alarm concerning the approaching wildfire, survivors were less likely to take precautions when there was a subsequent warning. We can reassure them that their actions were typical and understandable, since false alarms often create an impression that warnings are exaggerated, which leads to less compliance with subsequent alerts. It is to be hoped that this will mitigate their self-blame without making it seem as if we are dismissing their reactions.

Unexpected Events
Most human-caused and technological disasters do not have specific warning periods; if they did, the events could potentially be averted, or at least the people in the area could be protected from harm. However, there may be recognition that an event is at least possible, which can allow for some logistical and psychological preparation. For example, those living near levees and dams probably have some idea that breaches are possible; those working in buildings that would be high-value terrorist targets may be aware of that vulnerability. This theoretical awareness can help people function more productively during a disaster than they might in response to a completely unforeseen event, but obviously it offers less protection than an actual warning period does.

Since people who experience unexpected disasters have no chance to prepare physically or psychologically, they're more likely to be overwhelmed during and after the event. They also may feel helpless or vulnerable to a recurrence: If a traumatic event occurred once with no warning and with nothing they could do to prevent it, that can happen again, and there's no way to protect oneself or one's family in the future. There *should* be less guilt in this group since there was no warning to respond to and so no need to blame oneself for failing to act. However, people often feel or express guilt over things they could not realistically have foreseen or controlled, such as "I should have seen it coming," "We never should have bought that house," "I shouldn't have let him get on that flight," and so on. People may also manufacture their own warning signs in hindsight: "I had a funny feeling that morning when she left for the airport," or "The animals were acting weird so I should have known there would be an earthquake." Even if these thoughts are implausible, they still cause very real pain to survivors, so mental health interventions might include gently correcting these distorted cognitions. We'll return to this point in Chapter 5.

Timing

A final characteristic to consider is the timing of the disaster, which can influence its severity, the speed and success of the emergency response, and the distress it produces.

Time of day obviously determines whether it's light or dark during the event and the immediate response and recovery efforts. Especially if electrical power is lost, darkness can increase the risk of injuries and complicate rescue activities. It can also cause disorientation and increase fear and anxiety as people try to help each other or wait for assistance. On the positive side, families are more likely to be together at night, whereas during weekdays they're typically apart, with parents at work and children at school. Being separated during a disaster causes tremendous anxiety and often results in parents rushing to locate children, potentially clogging roads needed by emergency responders and creating traffic flow problems at schools.

Time and day may impact other logistical factors, which in turn affect the dose of trauma survivors may receive. Does rush hour traffic slow the ability of survivors to escape a disaster site or of emergency responders to reach it? Are hospitals fully staffed or at nighttime personnel levels? In areas with volunteer fire departments and ambulance corps, are responders available to report to a firehouse or disaster scene quickly? Are children in transit on school buses and even more difficult for anxious parents to find? Does a shift change mean twice as many factory workers are present during an industrial explosion? These timing questions can influence the ability of responders to help out effectively, as well as the emotional impact of the experience.

Of course, season is directly connected with certain kinds of disasters (hurricanes, blizzards), but season and climate can also impact conditions, particularly sheltering needs, in the recovery period. For example, when a major earthquake struck in the mountains of northern Pakistan in October 2005, the combination of high elevation and approaching winter meant that providing warm temporary housing was essential to survival. In contrast, Haiti's tropical climate meant that emergency sheltering after the 2010 earthquake did not need to provide heat—however, the arrival of the rainy season three months after the disaster meant that tents and tarpaulins could no longer provide adequate protection for displaced survivors.

Weather can have other effects as well, positive or negative. The brutal heat following Hurricane Katrina certainly increased the suffering of those who were displaced or awaiting rescue and increased the number of casualties, especially among elderly people, who are very vulnerable to dehydration and hyperthermia. In contrast, as we noted, when US Airways flight 1549 landed in the Hudson River, the clear skies and daylight facilitated the rescue of the passengers, which might have been far less successful at night or during a winter storm.

Is this a mental health issue? As we'll see, the principles of Psychological First Aid clearly tell us that people's physical needs must be attended to before they can benefit from mental health interventions. If people are extremely hot or cold, feel physically unsafe, or lack adequate shelter, food, and clothing, they'll be unable to focus on anything beyond these immediate needs. Therefore, addressing the effects of these logistical conditions must be considered a first step in mitigating psychological reactions to trauma, which are discussed next.

REFERENCES

Food and Agriculture Organization (2015). *The state of food insecurity in the world 2015: Meeting the 2015 international hunger targets: Taking stock of uneven progress.* Rome: Food and Agriculture Organization of the United Nations.

Halpern, J., & Tramontin, M. (2007). *Disaster mental health: Theory and practice.* Belmont, CA: Brooks/Cole.

Hassani, B. (2007). Trauma and terrorism: how do humans respond? In B. Trappler (Ed.), *Modern terrorism and psychological trauma.* New York: Gordian Knot Books, pp. 1–13.

Hobfoll, S. E., Watson, P. J., Bell, C. C., Bryant, R. A., Brymer, M. J., Friedman, M. J., …, & Ursano, R. J. (2007). Five essential elements of immediate and mid-term mass trauma intervention: Empirical evidence. *Psychiatry: Interpersonal and Biological Processes,* 70(4), 283–315.

Madeira, J. L. (2012). *Killing McVeigh: The death penalty and the myth of closure.* New York: New York University Press.

Neimark, G., Caroff, S. N., & Stinnett, J. L. (2005). Medically unexplained physical symptoms. *Psychiatric Annals,* 35(4), 298–305.

Vermeulen, K. (2014). Understanding your audience: How psychologists can help emergency managers improve disaster warning compliance. *Homeland Security and Emergency Management,* 11(3), 309–16.

Chapter 3

Disaster's Impact: Typical Reactions

Like his father and brother, Ron had always wanted to be a firefighter. His young adult life was just beginning and he was very happy that he had just joined the force and had an engagement party on Labor Day, 2001. On the morning of 9/11 he woke up with his fiancée. It was a lovely sunny morning, but soon nothing would normal again. He was an early responder to the attack and saved several people by assisting them in escaping from World Trade Center One. He saw people leap from the towers to their death to escape the fires. As the first tower collapsed he and some other firefighters escaped the debris by finding their way into a neighborhood restaurant and slamming the door as everything turned black. After what seemed like an hour they managed to get out and continue their rescue efforts. None of Ron's family was injured but he, like all New York firefighters, lost "brothers" on that day. He worked long shifts but said he was in "an altered state" and did not talk much about it at the time. Weeks later he was considered a hero, though he did not feel like one. Still, he made several TV appearances including Saturday Night Live. *Companies called and offered him jobs, and women called and wanted to go out with him. About a year later he left the Fire Department and broke off his engagement. In 2009 Ron talked about how much he missed his fiancée and his job as a firefighter. He did not have significant symptoms but believed that he had made some bad decisions and that 9/11 had thrown his life off course. He did not quite understand how or why but said he had been profoundly damaged.*

As we discussed in the previous chapter on disaster characteristics, patterns of reactions to disasters tend to correspond to the event cause, size, expectedness, and timing. However, those group-level patterns are also impacted by the survivor's individual characteristics (such as pre-existing strengths or vulnerabilities), and by characteristics of the response (for example, how well survivors' needs were met in the short and long term).

Looking more closely now at what those specific individual reactions can include, this chapter will examine the wide range of responses you may encounter while helping disaster survivors. While you read this chapter remember that these are common, typical reactions that we expect to see in anyone who goes through a disaster, not disordered or clinical reactions. These reactions "make sense" after disaster exposure and therefore don't suggest that the individual is at risk for developing lasting emotional or psychological problems, but they're still deeply distressing and confusing for the person experiencing them (Halpern & Tramontin, 2007).

Surviving and recovering from a disaster is a new experience for most people, so a key role of the DMH helper is to demystify their emotions—which requires your familiarity with the full range of typical reactions you may encounter. Helpers and survivors alike may be surprised by how varied individual responses can be. Not only will each person experience a specific combination of reactions across a number of realms, so you'll see **inter-individual differences** between survivors, but those reactions also evolve as people adjust to what has happened to them and begin to absorb the extent of their losses, leading to **intra-individual differences** over time as well.

Both of these types of difference can complicate the recovery process for survivors, and complicate your ability to know how best to help them. One particular challenge is that you probably won't know how survivors functioned before the disaster hit. Without that kind of baseline understanding of individuals' usual manner it can be difficult in a brief interaction to assess whether their reactions seem in line with expectable distress or are indications they need more intensive support. For example, are they acting highly emotionally because that's their usual level of expressiveness or because they're overwhelmed by what they're feeling? Is another's silence consistent with a generally reserved style or a sign of dissociation?

Another factor is more internal to the client: At any point in time, survivors may compare and judge themselves or others for their disparate reactions, including within families. For example, one member of a couple who is still in acute distress may think "My partner just wants to put this behind us and move on—how can she be so unfeeling?" while the other thinks "My partner just keeps dwelling on what happened—why can't he try to put this behind us and move on?" That can increase stress, perhaps making one person feel weak or misunderstood and the other frustrated and impatient. This disparity limits the couple's ability to be present and caring for each other, undermining what would ordinarily be each partner's main source of emotional support.

Then, as an individual moves through the painful process of adjusting to the losses, new emotions can emerge. While, ultimately, the arc of this evolution typically moves towards recovery, the shifts along the way can be destabilizing for a survivor who has perhaps learned to manage a certain level of anxiety about his or her situation, only to have that emotion evolve into a new (likely temporary) sense of hopelessness about the future. You may be able to help prepare clients for this kind of shift and encourage them to view it as a sign of progress towards recovery in order to mitigate the stress that change often creates.

Further complicating the picture in the days and weeks after the disaster is the fact that early responses to extreme stress can look somewhat like Posttraumatic Stress Disorder or Acute Stress Disorder. People may develop a heightened startle response or be generally anxious and have problems sleeping. They may re-experience the event, especially when triggered by cues in the environment (for example, storm clouds after a hurricane, or loud noises after a bombing). They may try to avoid any reminders of the disaster that reawaken their distress. While these responses can be very disturbing for those experiencing them, the expectation is that, over time, these reactions will fade away for most people, becoming less frequent and less intense. The disaster becomes a normal if unpleasant memory, one that doesn't possess the immediacy of the original experience, so it doesn't reactivate the physiological arousal of the fight or flight response as it may have in the early days.

While that's the usual outcome, this natural recovery process doesn't occur for some individuals, who will go on to develop PTSD or other serious conditions that will be addressed in a later chapter. Still, the bottom line is that **virtually everyone who experiences a disaster will experience some type of posttraumatic reaction, but post-disaster traumatic stress does not equal Posttraumatic Stress Disorder**. One goal of mental health interventions after disaster is to assist survivors with the former in order to prevent the latter.

REACTIONS BY REALM

Post-disaster reactions are typically grouped into different areas of functioning: physical, emotional, cognitive, behavioral, and spiritual—and they can be intense. Some of these reactions are more internalized, such as depression and anxiety, while others are more externally directed, such as anger and blaming. As you read through the list, consider whether any of these would be particularly difficult for you to handle. Could you remain calm while talking to a client who is enraged, or numb, or sobbing, or expressing a loss of faith? Think about how you would respond to these diverse reactions.

Common Reactions of Disaster Survivors

Physical:

- jumpiness, edginess, agitation, increased startle response
- appetite change (general increase or decrease, craving for sweets)
- increased desire for caffeine, nicotine, alcohol
- cardiovascular symptoms (palpitations, breathlessness, rapid and shallow breathing, lightheadedness)
- gastrointestinal distress (indigestion, nausea, constipation, diarrhea)
- sleep disruption (fatigue, exhaustion, insomnia)
- general somatic symptoms (muscle tension or pain, headache)
- worsening of chronic health conditions.

Emotional:

- depression, sadness, tearfulness
- anxiety, fear
- guilt, shame, self-doubt
- apathy, emotional numbing
- feeling overwhelmed, hopeless, out of control
- panic
- irritability, impatience
- anger, hostility, rage, resentment
- emotional lability (mood swings).

Cognitive:

- disbelief, sense of unreality
- worry, rumination, preoccupation with situation
- difficulties with memory or concentration
- reduced ability to focus, solve problems, or make decisions
- confusion, slower processing speed
- cognitive misappraisals (inappropriately blaming self or others, all-or-nothing thinking).

Behavioral:

- avoidance of reminders of the disaster
- blaming (of self or others)
- change in sleep habits (sleeping too much or too little)
- change in diet (eating too much or too little, seeking comfort in unhealthy foods)
- numbing through alcohol or drugs
- hypervigilance, inability to relax

- social withdrawal, isolating oneself
- increased conflict with family and/or co-workers, outbursts of aggression
- immersing oneself in activity to avoid thinking about event
- crying easily
- trying to over-control relationships, bullying others
- change in sex drive.

Spiritual:

- change in relationship with God or higher power (increase in faith, questioning of faith)
- change in religious practices (increase or decrease in prayer, attending services)
- questioning of belief in a just world
- struggle with questions about reality, meaning, justice, fairness.

All clients will experience their own combination of reactions—which they may not even connect to the traumatic event. Generally, people expect the emotional and perhaps spiritual symptoms (though they may not expect their intensity or how long they can last), but they're often not prepared for the cognitive and behavioral changes. In particular, the impact on concentration and memory tends to take people by surprise. They'll say things such as "I must be losing my mind, because I just can't remember anything!" You can explain that this is common and understandable given how many changes and losses they're working to absorb at the moment. Also, note that in some cultures, especially many Asian cultures, expressing distress through physical symptoms is more acceptable than demonstrating strong emotions, so don't overlook somatic complaints in your assessment of mental health needs.

As we mentioned in the last chapter, spiritual changes can go in different directions. Some religious people may experience an increase in faith while others experience a blow to their faith. Many will wonder how a benevolent God or higher power could have allowed an evil act to occur, or caused a destructive weather event. Even people who don't practice a specific faith may struggle to accept that their universe is not always safe or fair, as the disaster has vividly demonstrated. These negative emotions can cause a kind of existential blow as survivors grapple with a changed understanding of their world, often without the comfort of their faith.

This broad range of expectable reactions underscores the challenge of assessment in post-disaster settings. As we noted earlier, unfamiliarity with survivors' pre-disaster functioning can make it difficult to differentiate an individual's reaction to the event from his or her typical manner of expression or interacting with others. Additionally, changing reactions over time make it difficult to determine how vulnerable specific survivors may be to more lasting psychological consequences. While this variability can make the practice of disaster mental health seem daunting, it also underscores the importance of providing a positive, safe, and supportive recovery environment so that all survivors have the best possible chance to bounce back from their disaster experience. Psychological First Aid and psychoeducation, described in later chapters, are both "universal interventions" that can and should be offered to everyone post-disaster in hopes of activating people's natural recovery and heading off any lasting effects.

That said, there are two key points we would like to make regarding these typical reactions.

First, although as mental health professionals we recognize that these effects are common and understandable in response to a particularly traumatic event, they're often shocking and overwhelming to those experiencing them. Survivors will often say that they think they're going crazy, they fear they'll always feel this way, they feel weak for not being able cope better, and so on. A common phrase in the field used to be "You're experiencing a normal reaction to an abnormal situation." While that underlying **message** is accurate, we encourage you not to use this particular **wording**, as the reaction probably feels anything but normal to the person in the throes of these intense emotions. Describing it that way risks sounding dismissive or insensitive to the survivor, undermining their trust in your ability to assist them.

Instead, it may be more helpful to describe these feelings as reactions that are painful but reasonable under the circumstances; to explain that many people experience similar feelings, and that most people feel better once some time has passed; and to provide information about finding someone to talk to if they're not starting to feel better soon or would like to speak to a helper now. This approach acknowledges and validates the person's current suffering while creating an expectation of recovery—and while providing resources to help in the event that additional assistance is indeed needed, now or later. We'll return to this point when we discuss Psychological First Aid.

Second, our professional recognition that these reactions are common and will most likely improve over time should not be used by response organizers as an excuse for ignoring or dismissing how much distress they may be causing survivors at that moment. A great deal of recent research in the field has focused on some people's innate resilience and others' ability to achieve posttraumatic growth after a loss, which will be described later in this chapter. While DMH helpers certainly want our clients to reach these positive outcomes in the long run, we should remain vigilant that an overemphasis on these results for some survivors isn't used as a reason to limit resources for mental health support in the short term. Although migraine headaches pass with time, healthcare professionals still provide assistance for the pain. Similarly, although most people recover from disaster stress eventually, we should still do all we can to mitigate this suffering.

REACTIONS BY TIME: THROUGHOUT THE DISASTER LIFE CYCLE

Disasters unfold over time, and most can be divided into phases, though there are some exceptions: Slowly unfolding threats, such as climate change, or chronic situations, such as ongoing civil unrest, may make it hard for people to identify a clear "before" and "after." However, more traditional events do have an identifiable impact phase, and you may discover that survivors divide their lives into pre- and post-disaster stages.

We referred earlier to intra-individual changes as a survivor's reactions evolve over time. Understanding the "disaster life cycle" may provide insight into some typical patterns of reaction, though, as always, the characteristics of the event, the individual, and the response will impact any given person's state at a particular time. That means that the following patterns are useful as a general guideline, but don't expect every person you help to follow them in a linear fashion (Miller, 2012). Individuals may diverge from this pattern at any given point, or they may cycle back and forth between phases as, for example, reminders of the event cause a recurrence of symptoms or new access to resources increases optimism and reduces negative emotions.

Disaster mental health workers are generally not present for the **pre-impact** and **impact** stages and usually work with survivors during the **post-impact** stage. However, in some cases of expected events, DMH workers are asked to provide pre-impact assistance in shelters in anticipation of an extreme weather event, or to provide immediate, on-scene mental health support, especially when there are fatalities or injuries, or when other disaster responders are understood to need psychological support (for example, in a disaster involving child victims).

Before Impact

As noted in Chapter 2, disasters with warnings allow people to prepare cognitively and emotionally, helping to jumpstart coping mechanisms. If there's little or no warning, there may be more initial shock, disbelief, and fear. However, even if there was a warning, there's a good chance that many people disregarded it. To understand why, let's look at the psychological state of arousal produced by mere exposure to a warning.

First, what is a warning? Of course it's a notice that a disaster or other threat is approaching, but, to be effective, it must contain not only information about the nature of the threat but also what receivers can *do* to protect themselves from it. Otherwise it offers no real protective value and may merely increase anxiety. The trick, though, is that a disaster warning has to persuade people to do something they usually don't want to do (Vermeulen, 2014).

In essence, receiving a warning creates a unique and unpleasant decision-making situation. To understand this, put yourself in the position of a parent learning that a hurricane appears to be heading towards your area and all residents are being urged to evacuate. What's your thought process? First, if you're going to even consider following the evacuation order, you have to accept the premise that a dangerous storm is coming your way and may cause extensive damage. That's not a very welcome idea. If you do accept that, you then have to think through what will be involved in evacuating your family. Where will you go? Do you have friends or family you can stay with? If so, how long will they welcome you and your kids? Will you have to go to an emergency shelter, where you'll be sleeping on cots surrounded by dozens or hundreds of strangers? What will you do about your pets? If everyone else in the community decides to go, how long will you be stuck in traffic? Will your vehicle hold up? How will you pay for everything? Will you lose your job if you can't get back right away?

As you can imagine, virtually every factor in this awful decision will point to *not* following the warning, as you know for a fact that evacuating will be disruptive, unpleasant, and expensive, but you don't know if it's actually necessary. As a result, if you're like many people, your immediate response to the warning could be denial—that the hurricane will reach your area at all, that it will be as bad as they say, that you and your family are at risk. Once you enter that state of denial you're likely to practice "selective exposure" to subsequent news, seeking out reports that downplay the threat and avoiding or ignoring those that emphasize it. Or you may tell yourself you're just waiting to make a decision until the storm's path is clearer. That's a rational response at first, but the wait-and-see stance often leads people into a kind of psychological holding pattern, in which they delay deciding until it's too late to actually take the recommended action.

While denial seems to be the default response to a warning for many people, some swing over to the other extreme and become hypervigilant, overreacting to the threat and underestimating their ability to protect themselves. This is most likely in people who have actually experienced the specific form of threat before, especially recently. In our example, if you'd had a bad experience in a hurricane a month ago you might become highly anxious when you receive the current warning—so anxious that you feel paralyzed and incapable of taking care of your family. Of course, in the desired middle ground are the people who receive the warning and choose to comply, either because of past experience or because the warning is so credible and convincing that they decide not to take any chances. As one Hurricane Katrina survivor said as she prepared to evacuate from New Orleans before Hurricane Gustav in 2008, "I'd rather play it safe than sorry because I know what sorry feels like" (Nossiter & Dewan, 2008).

To summarize, exposure to a warning about an impending disaster produces a uniquely charged decision-making situation that can lead to denial, hypervigilance, or compliance. The specific outcome is likely to involve a variety of factors, including past experience, current resources, trust in the warning source, social influences, and a kind of cost–benefit analysis of whether the unknown positives of acting outweigh the known negatives.

In terms of later mental health effects, if no warning was received, survivors may feel unsafe and vulnerable, fearing that an event may occur again with no warning and that there's nothing they can do to protect themselves. If there was a warning that they ignored, you can expect to see a great deal of shame, guilt, and self-blame later on. This is often exacerbated by other people blaming the survivors for not following warnings, as was seen with many New Orleans residents who didn't follow mandatory evacuation orders before Hurricane Katrina, leading to a lot of public judgments about residents' foolishness or irresponsibility (Boyd-Franklin, 2010). However, that victim-blaming failed to take into account the facts that many urban residents didn't have cars; it was close to the end of the month, so those living on fixed incomes couldn't afford to pay for public transportation; there had been a recent false alarm that many had evacuated for unnecessarily; and so on. The main point to remember is that people typically have valid reasons for the decisions they make, and as helpers we need to understand the situation from their perspective rather than judging them for the choices they now regret.

One small upside to this situation is that individuals may feel less vulnerable about future events because they can vow to follow the warning next time; whether or not they actually follow through after time passes and the memory fades, it does give them some current sense of control.

During Impact

The impact stage while the disaster is actually occurring is characterized by magnified arousal levels as the fight, flight, or freeze response is activated.

Survival is the goal. Contrary to stereotype, panic is rarely seen (the most common exception being when access to escape is perceived as insufficient, as in a rapidly spreading fire in an enclosed space). Instead, purposeful and productive actions are more the norm. If families are separated at the time of impact they're likely to experience great anxiety about each other's safety, particularly parents for children.

There's usually very little for mental health helpers to do during the impact stage (beyond staying safe ourselves). What's most important to remember about this time is that how competent or helpless people act and feel during the event can play a key role in how they'll process the disaster experience later, though in hindsight people often have unrealistic beliefs about what they could or should have done better at the time of impact that may need to be addressed.

Beyond Impact

The post-impact period can be broken out into the heroic, honeymoon, disillusionment, and reconstruction phases, indicating a progression of emotional reactions over time (Herrman, 2006). We won't suggest time-frames, as each of these stages varies from days to years depending on the scope, intensity, and duration of the catastrophe, as well as the resources available for recovery; just note that this is another area in which survivors may progress at different paces, potentially causing friction among family members.

The immediate aftermath of disaster often brings out the very best in people during the **heroic** phase, as those impacted attempt to assist each other, often before external help arrives. People struggle to help their neighbors, dig survivors out of rubble, provide first aid, and so on. Sometimes the lingering physiological arousal of the fight or flight response impairs judgment and the rush to help exposes survivors to additional harm. As in the impact phase, the focus here is generally on action while the emotional effects are just beginning to be absorbed; it's still usually too soon for mental health helpers to have much of a role.

Once the dust begins to settle, there's often an influx of attention, media, money, and personnel at the scene to help those directly affected. This leads (sometimes) to a **honeymoon** period, in which those impacted feel unified by their collective experience. Survivors often downplay the significance of physical losses in their elation at having survived, so you may hear statements at this time such as "Our house can be replaced, the only thing that matters is that we're all alive!" Community members are shored up by the assistance and attention they're receiving and optimistic that they'll quickly be able to get back to normal. Social barriers and other differences are minimized and a collective community spirit rules as neighbors vow to get through it all together.

Like any honeymoon, this phase does not last. With the inevitable reduction in attention and response resources as time passes and external interest wanes, the **disillusionment** phase descends. Also note that, in many events, survivors bypass a honeymoon and go directly to this phase, especially if there has been the death of a loved one, community members feel neglected by outside helpers, or other factors block the temporary optimism of the honeymoon period. This phase can be thought of as a kind of reality check: Realization of the full extent of losses and the barriers to recovery begin to sink in, and community members may feel abandoned by the media, the public, and the aid agencies that had previously been so helpful. The communal spirit begins to erode as disparities in damage and resources become apparent. This phase may be the lowest emotional point for survivors as they come to terms with the permanent impact of the disaster, recognizing and accepting what they've lost and what they must do to try to create a "new normal." This is clearly a time when mental health helpers should be available to assist survivors.

Eventually, the **reconstruction** phase typically begins as the community and its individual members accept that they must adjust to changed circumstances on their own. Depending on the scope of the disaster, this phase can last for months, years, or even decades. The tasks here may be quite intense depending on the extent of change and loss. While outside mental health helpers (for example, those deployed to an impacted region by the American Red Cross) may no longer be present for much of the reconstruction phase, local helpers can and should remain attentive to survivors' longer-term mental health needs, providing ongoing psychoeducation and support for those who are recovering as expected as well as identifying and assisting those in need of clinical help. Additionally, anniversaries and other ceremonies are often supported by a DMH presence, providing a chance for mental health professionals to monitor long-term reactions and do outreach to community members who may still be struggling with their reactions. We'll return to anniversaries and other ceremonies when we discuss loss and grief in Chapter 6.

This stage model affects DMH planning and practice by suggesting what survivors may experience at the different points in the process of recovery, allowing us to anticipate and prepare for upcoming mental health needs. Without this understanding, a helper might conduct a needs assessment during the honeymoon stage, conclude that the community is coping well, and depart before the negative reactions of the disillusionment phase emerge and services are most needed.

We also can educate survivors about what a lengthy process their recovery may be. For those who have not experienced a disaster before, perceptions may be largely shaped by media coverage of other events. Journalists love a disaster and often swoop in to provide 24/7 coverage immediately after one occurs. They show the physical damage, interview survivors, perhaps identify an organization where concerned citizens can make a donation— and then move on to the next disaster. They rarely show the frustration as residents are left to fight with their insurance companies to cover damages, or the squabbling about how donated funds should be distributed, or the sadness when the full extent of losses is finally absorbed. While we don't want to dwell on the negatives during our DMH interactions, we do want to provide survivors with a realistic sense of what to expect in the short and long term, so they can try to marshal the support they'll need and use productive coping methods that will help them survive the long haul of recovery.

While the disaster life cycle is a useful guide for DMH helpers, we can't emphasize strongly enough that **these phases are not universal**, so, as always, you need to understand where the individual you're assisting is in their personal adjustment process at that particular point in time.

REACTIONS BY LOCATION: PROXIMITY AND THE DOSE–RESPONSE RELATIONSHIP

Disasters exist in space as well as time, so you can think of any given event as residing in the center of a bull's-eye. Consistent with the dose–response relationship described earlier, those closest to this epicenter—the point of impact—typically demonstrate stronger emotional reactions and the most need for support. Naturally, most of the convergence of aid after a disaster occurs in the impact zone, so mental health services tend to be directed to those indicated by the dose–response guideline. However, it's important to keep in mind that even those some distance away from a disaster can experience strong emotional reactions, especially if they have close connections to survivors, such as a young adult living in a state other than their disaster-impacted family.

But even those without a direct connection can be surprisingly affected by a distant event. In fact, research after the 9/11 World Trade Center attacks suggests that simply watching an event on TV can induce PTSD-like symptoms, though these tended to be short-term in nature and were not associated with diagnosable PTSD a year later among viewers without a family psychiatric history and/or pre-attack trauma history (Neria et al., 2006). Similarly, the current official criteria for PTSD in the fifth edition of the *Diagnostic and Statistical Manual of Mental Disorders* (DSM-5) do not recognize media exposure as a triggering experience except in the case of certain professional roles, but that doesn't mean that this exposure can't cause short-term distress among those not directly impacted, particularly if they identify with the victims in some way. Encouraging people (including ourselves) to limit media exposure can help prevent this type of vicarious trauma.

Another group whose mental health needs are often overlooked in the focus on direct survivors are the helpers—particularly those who are not official first responders, like police, firefighters, and EMTs; since those professional groups are self-selecting, they respond to the disaster by choice, and they tend to receive protective training and post-event support. A good example of this is the loggers and heavy equipment operators who participated in rescue and recovery efforts in Oso, Washington, after the 2014 mudslide that killed 43 people. While these volunteers contributed essential technical skills to the rescue and recovery efforts, which lasted for four months until the final body was recovered, they did not have the training and preparation for dealing with the gruesome sights they encountered, nor did they have the needed support structure afterwards, and many experienced psychological distress (Lurie, 2015).

Returning to the attacks of 9/11, an analysis of workers enrolled in the World Trade Center Health Registry who were involved in on-site rescue and recovery efforts found significantly higher rates of probable PTSD two to three years later among those in occupations such that they were not likely to have had prior disaster training or experience (Perrin et al., 2007). While there was widespread recognition at the time of the impact on police and firefighters given the high rates of colleague casualties, this study found that probable PTSD rates were equally high for emergency medical workers (14.1 percent) as for firefighters (14.3 percent). Examining two generally overlooked groups, Perrin et al. found rates of 13.0 percent among sanitation workers, and a disturbing 20.8 percent among construction or engineering workers, particularly those involved in search and rescue activity in the collapsed buildings. They also found that unaffiliated volunteers had probable PTSD at triple the rate of those working through volunteer organizations: 24.7 percent versus 8.4 percent. The authors specifically point to the lack of access to mental health services among unaffiliated volunteers, construction/engineering workers, and sanitation workers as a likely cause of their higher rates of distress, compounded by a lack of public recognition of their efforts relative to professional first responders.

There's no shortage of other examples of groups whose needs have been overlooked in disaster mental health planning because they were not directly proximate to the event at the time of impact. Our main point here is that recognizing the dose–response relationship is important, but it's also essential to be on guard for those whose needs may not be recognized and not to "profile" those impacted by disasters. One of the most helpful attributes of a disaster mental health worker is having an open mind and making it safe for clients to allow their personal experience to unfold and to be treated as individuals, regardless of whether their distress would be predicted by the research on group-level reactions.

SURVIVOR GUILT, SELF-BLAME, AND SHAME

Many who survive disasters in which others have died or suffered terribly experience some form of self-judgment about their role in the event. Survivors often feel they didn't do enough to save or assist others at the time of a disaster, or that they're somehow unworthy of having been spared. These beliefs may be fueled by cognitive distortions or misappraisals, involving either overestimating what they could possibly have accomplished or underestimating how much they actually did or how heroically they acted. Indeed, being labeled a hero for one's actions may increase these negative perceptions and create a sense of inadequacy.

Guilt is a common post-disaster response and takes different forms. **Survivor guilt** comes from trying to understand why one lived when others died, or why one's losses were less severe than another person's. Since this involves comparing one's good fortune with the misfortune of others, it's characterized by an uncomfortable interplay between relief at one's own relatively positive outcome and compassion for others who weren't so lucky. Survivor guilt may be increased by a person's perceived similarity to victims, and can lead to spiritual or existential questioning, leaving people wondering "Why did God/chance let me live when others died?" Of course, there's no answer you can provide to that kind of question, but simply allowing the survivor to express the emotion can be a first step towards accepting it.

Performance guilt is the belief that one could and should have done better—been better prepared, acted more bravely, rescued more people, and so on. A variant can be found among those who were not present but feel that they should have been, and that if they had been there they could have protected others from the harm they experienced. Of course, in hindsight we can always think of *something* we could have done differently, so there's often some basis of reality underpinning this type of guilt. However, survivors will often distort or exaggerate perceptions of their performance via a kind of magical thinking ("I had a bad feeling that night and never should have let her go to that nightclub") or fantastic belief ("If I had just acted more bravely I could have disarmed the gunman before he shot anyone"). Some gentle reality testing can help the survivor understand the limits of what he or she could have done differently, alleviating at least the inaccurate elements of this type of guilt.

However, sometimes these emotions are realistic and can't be corrected or dismissed. In particular, as we've discussed, if someone's failure to heed a warning resulted in harm, guilt, self-blame, and shame are likely. **Shame** is a remarkably powerful emotion. Whereas guilt generally reflects self-judgment about an action one did or didn't take, feeling shame involves judging the core self as weak, worthless, or powerless in the eyes of others, unable to take action or protect oneself or loved ones (Raphael, Taylor, &

McAndrew, 2008). Herman (2007) describes shame as "a relatively wordless state, in which speech and thought are inhibited. It is also an acutely self-conscious state; the person feels small, ridiculous and exposed ... Shame engenders a desire to hide, escape, or to lash out at the person in whose eyes one feels ashamed. By contrast, guilt engenders a desire to undo the offense, to make amends." As this suggests, relieving a survivor's sense of shame is particularly difficult, as it reflects a fundamental devaluing of the self in relation to others—but, since shame is the result of a fractured social bond, restoring connectedness with a DMH helper can begin to help shamed survivors reconnect with others whose acceptance of their worth they rely on.

Although they can be quite painful, guilt and shame may serve a defensive or protective function against even more confusing feelings of powerlessness and the arbitrary randomness of events occurring beyond anyone's control. The underlying cognition is something like "The damage was my fault, so by changing my behavior I can make sure that never happens again." As a disaster mental health responder, you may be able to recognize cognitions that suggest the presence of shame or guilt, gently correct potential misappraisals, and help survivors work towards acceptance of what they did or didn't do—and what they can or can't control in the future. There will be more on this in Chapter 5.

RESILIENCE

As we discussed earlier, recovery is the norm for the majority of people who experience disasters or other traumatic events. Over time, and with appropriate support (which could be provided by mental health professionals, spiritual care providers, or simply by the person's normal circle of family and friends), most survivors return to their pre-disaster level of functioning. While some in the field refer to that as "resilience," others consider resilience to be distinct from recovery. Specifically, resilience is seen as the ability to *resist* developing serious negative reactions in response to traumatic experience rather than the ability to bounce back from negative reactions.

What makes some people resilient and others vulnerable is linked to an interaction between risk and protective factors (Southwick & Charney, 2012). George Bonanno (2004) identifies the personality trait of hardiness as being associated with resilience in the face of extremely adverse events. He describes hardiness as including three dimensions: a belief that one can influence one's surroundings and the outcome of events; the belief that one can learn and grow from both positive and negative life experiences; and being committed to finding meaningful purpose in life. Another major report (Norris et al., 2002), which combined results from numerous studies of disaster survivors, found that resilience was associated with the following characteristics:

- membership in the majority culture
- previous experience of a less serious disaster
- professional training
- stable, calm personality
- perception of social support
- belief in own coping capacity.

While the first four characteristics are not really subject to post-disaster intervention, the last two are. As a DMH helper you can try to help survivors recognize and draw on their existing sources of support, and you can try to increase their sense of self-efficacy by encouraging them to participate actively in recovery activities. You can also help support resilience at the community level, which we'll discuss further in Chapter 5.

To reiterate a point made earlier in this chapter, resilience has become something of a buzzword in the field, and in popular media coverage of disasters. While this emphasis on a positive outcome is understandable, and we want to do everything possible to support recovery, as mental health helpers we need to be on guard that exaggerated expectations about natural resilience aren't used as an excuse to not provide services to all who need them in the immediate and longer-term aftermath of catastrophic events.

POSTTRAUMATIC GROWTH

Moving even further into the potential positive effects of very negative experiences, there's growing recognition that some people don't just maintain or return to their pre-trauma levels of functioning but eventually experience an actual *increase* in functioning in one or more realms, resulting in what researchers and clinicians Richard Tedeschi and Lawrence Calhoun (1996) have dubbed posttraumatic growth (PTG). After assessing survivors of diverse kinds of distressing events, they identify five realms of possible growth:

1. relating to others
2. new possibilities
3. personal strength
4. spiritual change
5. appreciation of life.

They and other researchers have found that, over time, many (though by no means all) people experience improvement in one or more of these realms. However, this result is earned at a great cost, as achieving PTG appears to require a period of negative response before growth occurs. In one study of 9/11 survivors (Butler et al., 2009), it was found that growth was more likely to occur among people who experienced higher levels of initial global distress and higher levels (both positive and negative) of event-related changes in existential outlook. Interestingly, those who demonstrated more resilience initially were less likely to report subsequent growth; it appears that achieving PTG first requires an immersion in the suffering caused by the traumatic event, which then leads to a reassessment of core values.

While the concept of PTG is sometimes questioned or dismissed as a form of denial of the significance of an experience, Calhoun and Tedeschi (2013) point out that the phenomenon can be identified in literature across time, and in the teachings of numerous religions. Recent research has also empirically demonstrated it among members of diverse cultures in response to a range of events, including illness and traumatic bereavement as well as disasters. Since you're most likely to be assisting clients early in the response while their pain is still acute, it's clearly not advisable to assure them that they'll eventually grow as a result of the trauma. However, you might see signs of PTG that should not be dismissed—and these findings allow helpers to be realistically hopeful about survivors' long-term outcomes.

As this chapter has described, possible reactions to disasters are as varied and unique as the survivors themselves, and they fluctuate and evolve over time. Just as we as disaster mental health helpers need to be flexible in terms of settings in which we're prepared to work, we also must remain open to and accepting of the full range of effects we may encounter in those we're trying to assist. How we begin to do so is the topic of our next chapter.

REFERENCES

Bonanno, G. A. (2004). Loss, trauma and human resilience: Have we underestimated the human capacity to thrive after extremely aversive events? *American Psychologist*, 59(1), 20–8.

Boyd-Franklin, N. (2010). Families affected by Hurricane Katrina and other disasters: Learning from the experiences of African American survivors. In P. Dass-Brailsford (Ed.), *Crisis and disaster counseling: Lessons learned from Hurricane Katrina and other disasters*. Los Angeles: Sage, pp. 67–82.

Butler, L. D., Koopman, C., Azarow, J., Blasey, C. M., Magdalene, J. C., DiMiceli, S., …, & Spiegel, D. (2009). Psychosocial predictors of resilience after the September 11, 2001 terrorist attacks. *Journal of Nervous and Mental Disease*, 197(4), 266–73.

Calhoun, L. G., & Tedeschi, R. G. (2013). *Posttraumatic growth in clinical practice*. New York: Brunner-Routledge.

Halpern, J., & Tramontin, M. (2007). *Disaster mental health: Theory and practice.* Belmont, CA: Brooks/Cole.

Herman, J. L. (2007, March 10). Shattered shame states and their repair. Paper presented at 14th John Bowlby memorial conference, London, www.challiance.org/Resource.ashx?sn=VOVShattered20ShameJHerman.

Herrmann, J. (2006). *Disaster mental health: A critical response: A training curriculum for mental health and spiritual care professionals in healthcare settings.* Rochester, NY: University of Rochester.

Lurie, N. (2015, April 17). Mental health consequences of climate change. Keynote address at 12th annual Institute for Disaster Mental Health conference, New Paltz, New York.

Miller, J. L. (2012). *Psychosocial capacity building in response to disasters.* New York: Columbia University Press.

Neria, Y., Gross, R., Olfson, M., Gameroff, M. J., Wickramaratne, P., Das, A., ..., & Weissman, M. M. (2006). Posttraumatic stress disorder in primary care one year after the 9/11 attacks. *General Hospital Psychiatry, 28*(3), 213–22.

Norris, F. H., Friedman, M. J., Watson, P. J., Byrne, C. M., Diaz, E., & Kaniasty, K. (2002). 60,000 disaster victims speak, part I: An empirical review of the empirical literature, 1981–2001. *Psychiatry, 65*(3), 207–39.

Nossiter, A., & Dewan, S. (2008, August 30). Hurricane Gustav strengthens to category 4. *New York Times,* www.nytimes.com/2008/08/31/us/30cnd-gustav.html.

Perrin, M. A., Digrande, L., Wheeler, K., Thorpe, L., Farfel, M. R., & Brackbill, R. M. (2007). Differences in PTSD prevalence and associated risk factors among World Trade Center disaster rescue and recovery workers. *American Journal of Psychiatry, 164*(9), 1385–94.

Raphael, B., Taylor, M., & McAndrew, V. (2008). Women, catastrophe and mental health. *Australian and New Zealand Journal of Psychiatry, 42*(1), 13–23.

Southwick, S. M., & Charney, D. S. (2012). *Resilience: The science of mastering life's greatest challenges.* Cambridge: Cambridge University Press.

Tedeschi, R. G., & Calhoun, L. G. (1996). The posttraumatic growth inventory: Measuring the positive legacy of trauma. *Journal of Traumatic Stress, 9*(3), 455–71.

Vermeulen, K. (2014). Understanding your audience: How psychologists can help emergency managers improve disaster warning compliance. *Homeland Security and Emergency Management, 11*(3), 309–16.

Chapter 4

Early Interventions:
Psychological First Aid

On October 31, 1999, EgyptAir Flight 990 crashed into the Atlantic Ocean, kill-ing all 217 people on board. When loved ones were notified about the crash their first thoughts were almost exclusively about whether or not their loved ones might have survived. Later there was, and continues to be, controversy about the cause of the crash. Possible theories include pilot suicide, revenge, or mechanical error, and some Egyptians believe the plane was shot down by the United States. None of these theories were relevant when family members arrived at a hotel reception center close to JFK Airport in New York. Most were in shock. Responders, including mental health professionals, arrived on the scene to provide whatever support they could. Many Egyptian family members did not speak English, and one woman who had arrived early sat alone, crying. A Red Cross disaster mental health worker saw the woman, approached her, sat with her, held her hand, and brought her some water. She remained present with the survivor for over an hour until other family members arrived. When the volunteer went home she was upset about the tragedy, and she was also upset with herself for how little help she had been able to offer the survivor, as she could not speak Arabic. A few days later the volunteer got feedback from supervisors on the scene. They reported that the survivor told family members that, without the support of the volunteer, without her kindness, she did not think she could have endured. She said she would be eternally grateful for the help she received.

This case study illustrates a few key points about the nature of early inter-vention.

- In the aftermath of some disasters, there is little need for material support but a significant need for mental health support. Family members did not need temporary shelter or something to eat. They were not worried about damage done to their homes. They were in shock, grieving, and traumatized.

- Clients are often in extreme pain.
- The support that is offered is not traditional psychotherapy but involves being with someone who is experiencing extreme stress and loss and is in crisis.
- There is little or no time to develop a treatment plan, or any plan at all, in thinking about how you will help those impacted by the disaster. You have to be agile in deciding how to help.
- The help you provide is often basic and yet quite profound.
- You might think that you did not provide much assistance and yet clients will thank you. When they do, though they may not articulate it, they're thanking you for being present with them in an intensely painful time and showing your humanity and kindness.
- Providing a compassionate presence when horrific events occur can give survivors the strength to go on.

THE IMPORTANCE OF EARLY INTERVENTION

It has been said that when a disaster occurs there are really three traumatic events that take place. The first, of course, is the disaster itself, but the damage doesn't stop there.

The second traumatic event is the negative response that can be delivered by community members and bystanders. Some survivors of Hurricane Katrina were asked why they lived in New Orleans, an unsafe place, or why they didn't follow the warnings to evacuate. Some 9/11 survivors were asked why they worked in the World Trade Center, an obvious target for terrorists. These questions are actually accusations, allowing questioners to maintain a distance between themselves and survivors, and such questions and negative bystander reactions can be harmful to survivors. Being the target of such negative remarks, when added to the injuries caused by the disaster, is one predictor of long-term emotional consequences of disaster (Brewin, 2003).

The third trauma is the self-talk that can result from the first two traumas. For weeks, months, and even years after the original disaster, survivors can be critical of themselves. They can view themselves in unhelpful and distorted ways, seeing the self as inadequate or helpless or inferior. This negative self-talk is another long-lasting form of trauma.

Traditional mental health practitioners assist patients with this third level, helping survivors to view themselves with less self-blame and in more positive ways. Some have stated explicitly that they cannot help at the first and second stages of the traumatic events. Disaster mental health practitioners believe otherwise. We believe that it's helpful to offer assistance before disaster strikes, building resilience through preparedness. We also believe that we can provide assistance soon after the impact of disaster to ensure a **positive recovery environment**, by providing support to the survivors and making sure that they're not exposed to negative, blaming reactions of others. By doing this, DMH helpers believe survivors will have a more positive attitude towards themselves, leading to less need for help with negative self-talk and less need for long-term traditional therapy.

EVIDENCE-BASED PRINCIPLES OF EARLY INTERVENTION

The attitudes and actions we'll cover in this section stem from principles that have accrued broad empirical support from research on stress, coping, and adapting after potentially traumatic experiences. Led by Dr. Stevan Hobfoll (2007), a group of 20 international mass trauma experts write that, in order to improve the lives of survivors of disaster or mass trauma, there are a few basic principles that should be followed. Each of these recommendations is supported by research, though Hobfoll et al. note that not all of the research used randomly controlled trials.

The five essential elements for early interventions they recommend are as follows.

- **Safety**: The first steps after a disaster require the removal of actual or perceived threats to reduce the physiological responses to fear and anxiety.
- **Calming**: Anxiety and distress are common responses to disasters, but, once the immediate danger has passed, heightened anxiety or arousal can become dysfunctional.
- **Efficacy**: Promoting self-efficacy can begin with restoring one's ability to regulate negative emotions and solve practical problems. It can also include facilitating community activities such as mourning rituals, getting children back in school, or rebuilding economic infrastructure.
- **Connectedness**: Connecting children with parents, and neighbors with neighbors, provides social support and increases the chances for longer-term recovery.
- **Hope**: Hope is a belief that one's actions can bring about a positive outcome. For some, hope involves a belief that luck or the government will address needs. For many, hope arises through a belief in God (Hobfoll et al., 2007).

How can these elements be applied to assist disaster survivors? In essence, they provide the theoretical basis of the currently recommended early intervention, Psychological First Aid.

PSYCHOLOGICAL FIRST AID

The National Institute of Mental Health (NIMH, 2002) defines Psychological First Aid as:

> Evidence-informed and pragmatically oriented early interventions that address acute stress reactions and immediate needs for survivors and emergency responders in the period immediately following a disaster. The goals of psychological first aid include the establishment of safety (objective and subjective), stress-related symptom reduction, restoration of rest and sleep, linkage to critical resources, and connection to social support.

As you can see, this definition is consistent with the principles described above. PFA interventions are meant to address the interrelated practical, physical, and psychological needs of survivors. These interventions are universal, meaning they're appropriate for children, adolescents, adults, and entire families—anyone who has been exposed to disaster or terrorism, including first responders and other disaster relief workers.

PFA is distinct from therapy and counseling in that it:

- is short-term
- focuses on symptom reduction, not treatment
- promotes healing, not the opening up of past wounds
- focuses on interrelated practical, physical, and emotional needs
- deals in the here and now.

At its core, the practice of PFA is meant to remove any barriers to survivors' natural recovery processes—to provide the emotional equivalent of treating a small wound before it has a chance to develop into a more serious problem.

Theoretical Roots of PFA

The roots of PFA can be traced back to the work of two eminent psychologists, Abraham Maslow and Carl Rogers. Rogers (1970) maintained that, in order to provide effective assistance, a helper should provide unconditional positive regard, empathy, and genuineness. As applied to PFA, this means treating survivors not as victims in need of rescuing but as individuals who were most likely leading productive lives before the disaster, and who have the capacity to recover their pre-event level of functioning with a bit of well-timed support. Maslow's (1999) "hierarchy of needs" emphasizes the importance of attending to survivors' physical and safety issues first before they are able to benefit from interventions targeting more complex emotional responses. Disaster mental health counseling involves "working the Maslow hierarchy" from the bottom up (NIMH, 2002). First we address **biological and physiological needs**, such as food and water, dry clothing, and shelter. Then we address **safety needs**, helping survivors to avoid actual danger and to begin to feel as if the threat has passed. The next level targets **belongingness and love needs** by encouraging people to reconnect with positive sources of support. Maslow's two highest levels, **esteem needs** and **self-actualization**, are generally beyond the scope of DMH interventions, though they may arise in longer-term counseling. Working the hierarchy, of course, needs to be done with much flexibility, as these needs vary by situation and individual, and may often lie outside what mental health helpers typically address.

Elements of PFA

It should be noted that there is no standard list of PFA components, but that the various versions found in the literature and in practice are generally consistent in spirit. These include models proposed by a range of experts and organizations, including the American Red Cross (2012), the National Institute of Mental Health (2002), the National Child Traumatic Stress Network and the National Center for PTSD (2006), and Halpern and Tramontin (2007). Because it's believed that anyone, not only people with previous mental health training, can provide PFA, many of these models include some basic guidelines for supportive interactions.

Remember that the elements of Psychological First Aid are a blend of attitudes and actions on the part of the helper—less a process than a toolkit of components that can be drawn on as needed for each specific survivor. As a result, these elements are not presented in any order of importance, nor are they meant to dictate a sequence of how they should be utilized, since that will be determined by the post-disaster situation and by the client's specific needs. We also must note that elements such as providing empathy and staying genuinely engaged with traumatized survivors can put the helper at risk for vicarious trauma. Later we'll discuss the occupational hazards of this work and provide information so you can take care of yourself in order to keep taking care of others.

A final point before we outline the elements of PFA: When DMH helpers-in-training read through descriptions of practicing PFA, their first response is often along the lines of "Well, of course, these are things I would do for anyone in distress." It's true that many of the suggestions are quite elementary and involve commonsense actions that most thoughtful helpers would take automatically when trying to support any upset individual. However, when trying to address many people's needs at once in the intense post-disaster environment, it's easy to feel overwhelmed and disconnected from one's usual helping instincts. That's why studying and practicing PFA is so important to ensure that we retain our ability to respond effectively.

Psychological First Aid elements:

- being calm
- providing warmth
- showing genuineness
- attending to safety needs
- attending to physiological needs
- providing acknowledgment and recognition
- expressing empathy
- helping clients access social support
- helping clients avoid negative social support
- providing accurate and timely information
- providing psychoeducation and reinforcing positive coping
- empowering the survivors
- assisting survivors with traumatic grief.

The case study presented at the beginning of the chapter illustrates that you can provide considerable assistance if you are **kind, calm**, and **present**. Survivors who have recently been through a traumatic experience often need a reminder that the entire world isn't disrupted, and that others care about what they've suffered. Helpers can address this need in a number of ways.

Being Calm

Disasters can increase both physical and emotional arousal levels. One core aim of PFA is to reduce this globally heightened arousal level (NIMH, 2002), which may be best accomplished via the helper being calm. Harry Stack Sullivan (1940) noted long ago that emotions, and anxiety in particular, can be very contagious. By remaining calm the helper is modeling calm for the survivor. The presence of a calm and steady helper allows survivors to better master or regulate their feelings.

Providing Warmth

Unconditional positive regard or warmth means relating to clients with comfort and acceptance of what they feel and say (Rogers, 1970). This is not always easy—especially if the client is irritable, unreasonable, or angry. Clients can sometimes feel and express rage at politicians or officials for not doing enough to prevent the disaster, or at agencies for not responding quickly enough to their post-disaster situation. If they are not suggesting they will harm anyone, but only venting their frustration, the counselor does not need to debate the client about the reasonableness of his or her anger. Providing warmth and kindness, expressed as attentiveness, open posture, and a soothing tone of voice no matter what the client says, is important to the helping process.

Showing Genuineness

Warmth and empathy are useful only to the extent that they're real or genuine (Rogers, 1970). Clients can feel manipulated if we show them a fake smile or spout platitudes about courage or resilience. Because disaster work can expose us to terrible sights, sounds, and stories, we need to know our limits so we can stay genuinely empathically engaged. If you're working at a mass casualty disaster or in a very protracted response where you hear so much grief and anger that you begin to feel numb, it's wise to take a break or get some support so you can be genuinely present for the client.

Attending to Safety Needs

Along with the emotional distress they cause, disasters often generate a variety of physical threats and logistical demands that can feel overwhelming to survivors, especially in the early hours and days while they're still trying to absorb what they've just experienced. DMH workers can step in to help people whose judgment and decision-making ability is temporarily impaired in the following ways.

It cannot be overemphasized that, in order to begin their recovery after a disaster, people need to feel that they and their loved ones are safe. Helpers should protect survivors from any threat or danger from the ongoing disaster, especially those who may be so disoriented that they're not able to care for themselves (Raphael, 1986). Attending to safety needs may mean strongly encouraging a survivor to not enter a damaged home or one that may be filled with mold as a result of a flood. Sometimes survivors are reluctant to stay with family or friends or go to a shelter. Helpers should encourage survivors to reside in a safe place.

If it seems clear that the danger has passed, helpers should remind survivors that this is the case; remember that those who have been through a traumatic experience may be relatively safe but not *feel* safe. Helpers can further support client safety and stability by encouraging families to maintain their routines. This may not be feasible immediately, but children should be encouraged to go to school as soon as possible after the disaster, meals should be eaten at regular times, and so on.

Attending to Physiological Needs

Mental health professionals are sometimes reluctant to address medical needs. However, if we observe that a client is injured or ill, we must be sure that he or she is taken to receive medical attention. If there's any threat to the physical health of clients, we should attempt to address it immediately by obtaining proper medical care, connecting survivors with resources for restoring access to prescription medications, and so on (American Red Cross, 2012; Raphael, 1986). This can help to reduce anxiety as well as directly addressing physical needs. After one disaster, when there were tetanus bacteria in floodwaters, a mental health worker was observed attempting to calm a frantic survivor who was looking for tetanus shots for herself and her family. Although the calming was well intentioned, it would have been more effective if the helper simply assisted the survivor in locating where to get the tetanus shots.

On a less urgent level, helpers should also offer food, water, hot drinks, or blankets. People in distress often ignore their physical state and forget to eat or drink, so providing these services addresses a genuine need as well as demonstrating that the helper is present and cares about their well-being.

Providing Acknowledgment and Recognition

The experience of surviving a disaster is so new and unfamiliar for most people that they'll often find they can't access their feelings initially, or they may minimize them out of recognition that others have experienced worse losses than they have. DMH helpers should try to encourage survivors to recognize and accept their emotions.

While it's true that we don't want to intensify survivors' feelings by acting panicky or suggesting that their normal stress reactions are unusual, we also don't want to downplay the seriousness of the situation. Survivors require acknowledgment and validation that they have experienced a trauma (Raphael, 1986). If the significance of the trauma is downplayed, survivors may not take the necessary time to rest and recover (Litz & Gray, 2004). The presence of helpers shows survivors that the community is not indifferent to the disaster they have experienced. Media presence also validates survivors' experience that something unusual has happened and deserves attention (though this presence can also be perceived as insensitive or voyeuristic).

Expressing Empathy

Helpers should be prepared to listen to survivors describe what happened to them; they should concentrate and attend to all aspects of the client's communication at both the emotional and cognitive levels. The helper must be willing to enter the client's world of pain, loss, anguish, hopelessness, rage, shock, and despair (Weaver, 1995). We not only need to listen but also to convey to survivors that we've heard what they said (Rogers, 1970). If clients decide to tell their stories or to discuss extremely painful feelings, be certain to not leave them alone with unmanageable or uncontrollable feelings. Be sure they've calmed down or that trusted family and friends arrive before leaving the scene (Raphael, 1986).

Sample empathy statements:

- "So you feel …"
- "I hear you saying …"
- "I sense you are feeling …"
- "You appear …"
- "It seems to you …"
- "You place a high value on …"
- "So tell me if I am getting this right? You seem to be feeling that …"

Helping Clients Access Social Support

Encourage connection. It's widely recognized in the field that most survivors receive far more comfort from their existing support networks than from any kind of professional intervention, so helping to restore access to loved ones is an important element of PFA—with some caveats. Social support can be expressed in different ways, but all can help an individual cope with stress. **Instrumental** support is practical in nature, taking the form of money or help with tasks and chores. **Emotional** support provides an individual with warmth, caring, and a trusting relationship (House & Kahn, 1985). **Informational** social support can include advice or guidance that's intended to help someone cope with difficult circumstances (Cohen, 2004).

There's substantial evidence that perceived social support can be a significant buffer from stress, even if the support comes exclusively from one reliable person. If possible, survivors should be physically reunited with loved ones who can provide emotional support and security (Fullerton, Ursano, Norwood, & Holloway, 2003). Helpers should ask directly "Who might you contact that could help you at this time?" and "Do you need help in getting the phone number or do you need to borrow my cellphone?" Sometimes survivors resist contacting loved ones in a time of need because they don't want to be a burden; if this is the case, you might ask how they would react if the situation were reversed and a friend in need was hesitating to reach out to them for help.

Helping Clients Avoid Negative Support

Sometimes helpers make an unintended mistake by suggesting that survivors contact family and friends. We need to recommend that clients contact family and friends whom they can trust to be supportive. Remember that not all relationships are supportive; in fact, most of us are aware that some family and friends can be sources of stress and misery. When you encourage clients to contact their natural support system, first try to be sure that these contacts will not strain the client with additional stress. Ask: "Who will you call? Will that person be helpful and supportive?" A recovery environment that's impoverished, punitive, blaming, demanding, anxiety-filled, and invalidating is one that creates a risk for PTSD (Bolton, Litz, Glenn, Orsillo, & Roemer, 2002; Brewin, Andrews, & Valentine, 2000).

Providing Accurate and Timely Information

Accurate information is one important antidote for the uncertainty and anxiety that survivors experience following a disaster. Survivors may want to know exactly what happened, who was responsible, whether it is truly over, how extensive the disaster damage was, and when they'll be able to return home.

They're likely to have numerous questions about recovery resources, such as shelter locations. Information about financial resources is also important, as survivors need to know what assistance they're eligible for. This is a new experience for most people so they may need to be educated about, for example, the implications of the president declaring a national disaster, or what forms they need to complete to receive Red Cross or FEMA aid, or how to file a claim with their insurance company. Helpers should be aware of any up-to-date lists of available resources for victims, as addressing those practical needs can help minimize immediate anxiety (American Red Cross, 2012).

There's another category of information that has more urgency than any other: when survivors are missing loved ones. The Red Cross and other relief agencies often have special services that can assist survivors when loved ones are missing. Even when there's little hope that a loved one will be found alive, relatives still may want to know details about the recovery process (for example, will there be a continued search for bodies after a plane crash? Will all remains be identified? Will they be released after identification or held for possible criminal proceedings?).

Accurate information may not always be easy for helpers to access, but we must try. If you're deployed to a shelter or assistance center, there's often a morning briefing. Managers and leaders report on damage, the pace and progress of the response and recovery, and resources that may be available. This is the time to try to get answers to questions you anticipate receiving or were asked the previous day. You'll be seen as an authority by survivors so try to be as informed as you can be before starting the challenging day ahead.

Whether the information you're providing is about a missing loved one or a more mundane matter, it's important that all communication be framed in simple language. Remember that cognitive ability can be impaired after a disaster due to stress or trauma, so we need to be certain that the information we provide is received. You may need to summarize or review what is being said, or provide it in writing as well as verbally (NIMH, 2002).

Providing Psychoeducation

We'll discuss psychoeducation as an element of PFA, but bear in mind that it can be provided at any point in the disaster cycle, though the nature of the information is likely to change depending on timing and intention. Much psychoeducation in the immediate aftermath of disaster involves normalizing survivors' stress reactions and helping them to use positive rather than unhealthy ways to manage that stress.

People who have not previously experienced a traumatic event and the resulting typical reactions may be further distressed by their own emotions, so psychoeducation after a disaster often involves normalizing the experience of survivors and informing them about effective means to reduce and manage their stress. According to the National Institute for Mental Health (2002), most survivors don't actively seek out psychoeducation or other mental health services after a disaster, so as a key component of early intervention efforts it's important that mental health workers perform outreach, defined as an "array of disaster mental health services extended to survivors wherever they congregate, designed to increase understanding of common reactions, coping, and when and where to receive more in-depth help."

However, evidence suggests that helpers should not force information on survivors who aren't receptive, as some individuals may have a repressive coping style that functions best by avoiding stressful thoughts. For this group, information about potential unpleasant symptoms may produce more anxiety than it allays. The take-home point here is that it's usually not advisable to pressure survivors to talk or engage with us if that doesn't feel right for them at that time. A gentle, supportive, encouraging approach is the default.

As noted earlier, one of the most common disaster mental health interventions is to remind clients who may feel that their distress is extreme or unending that *they're experiencing an expectable or typical reaction to an abnormal or atypical event.* Survivors can be reassured that having trouble concentrating or being easily startled, for example, are common reactions to disaster and that they're not going crazy. Survivors can also be reassured that, for most people, this stress will eventually pass, but that if they don't start to feel better or they feel in need of speaking to a mental health professional now, help is available. Parents can also receive information on typical stress reactions of children so they can see that their children are acting in response to the disaster. Explaining that children often react to stress by regressing developmentally and becoming more needy or clingy than usual can increase the parent's patience and understanding that the child's demands are probably temporary. We'll expand on this in Chapter 8.

Acute stress can often increase the use of ineffective coping mechanisms. Survivors can be cautioned about the use of ineffective and self-defeating coping mechanisms that might provide momentary relief but will ultimately cause additional problems, and they can be encouraged to utilize more effective approaches that help them function better as well as helping them feel better.

Table 4.1 Common coping mechanisms.

Ineffective	Effective
• Overworking	• Getting enough sleep
• Not getting enough rest or sleep	• Taking breaks
• Binge eating	• Exercising
• Excessive television watching	• Eating a balanced diet
• Drinking and smoking	• Allowing yourself to receive as well
• Isolating oneself	as give
• Attempting to regain a sense	• Connecting with others
of control by becoming overly	• Using spiritual resources
controlling of others—bullying those	• Limiting TV exposure
around you	• Balancing work, play, and rest

Empowering the Survivor

Sometimes, with great loss, we may want to acknowledge the vulnerability of the survivor. However, since the vast majority of disaster survivors recover with time, sometimes quite quickly, it is equally important for us to acknowledge and support a survivor's strength, competence, courage, and power. This can allow the survivor to access his or her resilience and help to restore a sense of control.

We empower a survivor by reinforcing strengths and positive coping strategies. Helpers should allow survivors to determine the kind of assistance they receive, the pace of any kind of self-disclosure, and as many other aspects of the response process as possible. We can ask "How have you gotten through tough times before?" or "What skills do you have that will allow you to get through this?" These questions remind survivors that it's likely that they've bounced back from very stressful events before and that they can recover from the present one. One very useful approach is to ask survivors to participate in the relief operation. This can be especially helpful to parents, whose children can see them as in control or powerful. It can also be helpful to children, who can gain a sense of usefulness at a time when they are likely to be feeling helpless.

Assisting Survivors with Traumatic Grief

If a survivor has lost a loved one to disaster, the helper will be faced with grief, which can take very different forms. Sometimes survivors are quiet and numb and sometimes they're quite loud, wailing and even screaming. For many helpers, being with someone who has just lost a loved one can be the most challenging experience they ever face. On occasion there are practical problems a client faces, and we can help them with tasks such as identifying remains or making funeral arrangements. Most often at these times there are no problems to solve. Our role is to be a compassionate presence for the bereaved. We might say "I am so sorry for your loss," "Is there anything I can do for you now?" "Is there someone you would like me to call?" or "Do you need me to notify anyone?"

Helpers often wonder if it's okay to cry with a client. The answer is that as long as the client would not feel burdened by your expression of sadness and you're not indicating any need for help—that you're shedding tears *with* the survivor—it can be perfectly appropriate and may even be comforting to clients. The role of the helper is similar to the role of family and friends: to be available and to share the loss with those in grief. As a visible supportive presence we can offer comfort. This effort should not be minimized. In fact, we might want to remind ourselves that at these moments we need to do the opposite of the dictum "Don't just stand there, do something." We should follow the wisdom **"Don't just do something, stand there."**

Disaster mental health helpers also may be called upon to provide assistance at memorials, which may be held soon or some time after the disaster. The bereaved are often very thankful if mental health helpers provide a compassionate presence. The need for more intensive professional services at memorials is rare, as mourners are unlikely to decompensate or experience other psychological symptoms. If someone is in great distress, there are usually family and friends to provide support. Helpers can provide tissues and water, and can stand beside those writing messages on memorial surfaces as a calm presence. When survivors thank us for these services, they are thanking us for not ignoring their plight, for not being indifferent.

SOME CAUTIONS WHEN USING PFA

Even when you're using an evidence-informed practice, there are still cautions you should be aware of. Remember that when we provide disaster mental health, we're attempting to help survivors return to pre-disaster functioning. We might find a survivor struggling with many problems not related to the disaster. We should not be overly ambitious and try to solve issues that are unrelated to the disaster. Similarly, we should note that sometimes a disaster survivor could be suffering from more than one trauma, so the distress we observe could be a result of an altogether different event. In conversation with survivors we can ascertain what other life stressors they're facing. In this way we can be more certain that we're actually assisting with the impact of the disaster trauma.

Also remember that survivors of a disaster should not be treated identically. Individual needs and cultural differences must be respected when providing PFA or any other mental health service. Some survivors may prefer the comfort and support of peers or clergy, while others prefer to work their problems out alone or want support only from family members. Although we may offer assistance, we need to be careful to not intrude if the client isn't receptive. There's a fine line between helping and meddling.

In the same way that bandaging a wound can be practiced by those trained in first aid as well as by medical professionals, PFA can be taught to and practiced by clergy, teachers, parents, first responders and others, including mental health professionals. It's desirable to have as many people trained in PFA as possible so that, in the aftermath of a large disaster, community members can be more helpful in supporting one another. In contrast, the interventions described in the next chapter related to correcting self-cognitions, rumor control, assessment, and referral are beyond the practice of PFA and should be used exclusively by mental health professionals.

REFERENCES

American Red Cross (2012). *Psychological first aid: Helping others in times of stress: Instructor manual.* Washington, DC: American Red Cross.

Bolton, E. E., Litz, B. T., Glenn, D. M., Orsillo, S., & Roemer, L. (2002). The impact of homecoming reception on the adaptation of peacekeepers following deployment. *Military Psychology,* 14(3), 241–51.

Brewin, C. R. (2003). *Posttraumatic stress disorder: Malady or myth?* New Haven, CT: Yale University Press.

Brewin, C. R., Andrews, B., & Valentine, J. D. (2000). Meta-analysis of risk factors for posttraumatic stress disorder in trauma-exposed adults. *Journal of Consulting and Clinical Psychology,* 68(5), 748–66.

Cohen, S. (2004). Social relationships and health. *American Psychologist,* 59(8), 676–84.

Fullerton, C. S., Ursano, R. J., Norwood, A. E., & Holloway, H. H. (2003). Trauma, terrorism, and disaster. In R. J. Ursano, C. S. Fullerton, & A. E. Norwood (Eds.), *Terrorism and disaster: Individual and community mental health interventions.* Cambridge: Cambridge University Press, pp. 1–20.

Halpern, J., & Tramontin, M. (2007). *Disaster mental health: Theory and practice.* Belmont, CA: Brooks/Cole.

Hobfoll, S. E., Watson, P. J., Bell, C. C., Bryant, R. A., Brymer, M. J., Friedman, M. J., …, & Ursano, R. J. (2007). Five essential elements of immediate and mid-term mass trauma intervention: Empirical evidence. *Psychiatry: Interpersonal and Biological Processes,* 70(4), 283–315.

House, J. S., & Kahn, R. L. (1985). Measures and concepts of social support. In S. Cohen & S. L. Syme (Eds.), *Social support and health.* New York: Academic Press, pp. 83–108.

Litz, B. T., & Gray, M. J. (2004). Early intervention for trauma in adults: A framework for first aid and secondary prevention. In B. T. Litz (Ed.), *Early intervention for trauma and traumatic loss.* New York: Guilford Press, pp. 87–111.

Maslow, A. H. (1999). *Toward a psychology of being* (3rd ed.). New York: John Wiley & Sons.

National Child Traumatic Stress Network & National Center for PTSD (2006). *Psychological first aid: Field operations guide* (2nd ed.). Washington, DC: National Center for PTSD.

National Institute of Mental Health (2002). *Mental health and mass violence: Evidence-based early psychological intervention for victims/survivors of mass violence: A workshop to reach consensus on best practices.* Washington, DC: US Government Printing Office.

Raphael, B. (1986). *When disaster strikes: How individuals and communities cope with catastrophe.* New York: Basic Books.

Rogers, C. (1970). *On becoming a person: A therapist's view of psychotherapy.* Boston: Houghton Mifflin.

Sullivan, H. S. (1940). *Conceptions of modern psychiatry.* New York: W. W. Norton.

Weaver, J. D. (1995). *Disasters: Mental health interventions.* Sarasota, FL: Professional Resources Press.

Chapter 5

Early Interventions: Other Actions

Hurricane Katrina was the costliest natural disaster, as well as one of the most deadly hurricanes, in the history of the United States. Almost 2,000 people died in the hurricane and floods, most in New Orleans as the levee system failed. The courts judged the Army Corps of Engineers to be responsible for the catastrophic failure of the levee system but they were held to be immune from any financial liability due to the Flood Control Act of 1928. In November 2005 a team of health, mental health, and client services disaster responders visited households in a New Orleans parish devastated by the hurricane. Although it was months after the storm, the neighborhood still looked apocalyptic. Mud, dead trees, garbage, and even rotting animals could be seen in the streets. Tim and Fanny greeted the team at the door and invited them in. The house was moldy and it was unclear whether or not they were officially allowed to be back in this home. Tim said that they had weathered other storms so they thought they could take the chance that this one would pass them by. It didn't. As the storm grew worse they wound up in the Superdome, which turned out to be a nightmare. There was no place to sleep comfortably and not enough food and water. Although they were not diagnosed with dehydration, they were thirsty and worried that conditions could deteriorate. "Why is there no help?" they kept asking each other. The bathrooms did not function, resulting in very unsanitary conditions and horrific smells. They also heard stories about children being raped and babies being murdered, with their corpses laid next to human excrement. Although Fanny added that they now understood that those rumors were not true, conditions were so bad that they believed them at the time, making their stay at the Superdome even more miserable than it had to be. Now, months after the storm, the couple were still disgusted that they could not get the assistance they expected to receive. Why could they get no aid; why were the streets so filthy; why were dead animals not yet removed from the streets; and, most importantly, when would they get into some kind of temporary housing, which they heard was available to Katrina survivors? Fanny could not sleep and she was startled by loud noises. She wondered if she needed more professional help, and who would pay for it. They were both appalled with the performance of their political leaders—the mayor, the governor, and the president. "None of them really cares about people like us."

As you read through the post-disaster early interventions described in this chapter, consider how you might use them to help this family.

While PFA elements are likely to make up the majority of your DMH activities, you may need to draw on other clinical skills as you try to assist disaster survivors and other responders. The last early intervention we review, Psychological Debriefing, is no longer recommended for trauma or disaster survivors, but it is still sometimes used with first responders, and even the general public.

There is increasing attention being given to how we can help build resilience before disaster strikes, and some of your activities may involve helping communities to prepare and plan when there are no disasters on the horizon. It can be difficult to encourage preparedness when it is peaceful, but, since disasters are inevitable, building resilient communities may be one of our most important activities.

We conclude the chapter by describing effective ways to build individual and community resilience before disaster strikes, as an ounce of prevention is worth a pound of cure.

ASSISTING WITH PROBLEM-SOLVING

Survivors often face pressing decisions, which they could normally handle with ease but which seem insurmountable in their unfocused, distracted state shortly after a disaster. We might provide assistance in problem-solving as we aid clients in finding shelter, or as we help them to decide which friend or relative to stay with. This may involve being far more directive than we would be in more traditional forms of counseling, but should still strive to involve the client in any decision in order to begin to reactivate their usual capacity for autonomy.

Skills for Psychological Recovery (SPR), developed by the National Center for PTSD and the National Child Traumatic Stress Network (2010), is intended to promote adaptive coping in disaster survivors by encouraging the development of new skills, including **problem-solving, positive activity scheduling, managing reactions, helpful thinking**, and **building healthy social connections**.

Problem-solving begins with *information gathering and prioritizing* the client's needs and concerns. The goals at this stage are to get a clear sense of clients' concerns and priorities. You can ask clients what they are most concerned about or what their biggest problems are right now. If clients answer with a problem that can't be solved, you might be able to help them frame it in a way that can be solved. "My brother and sister are impossible and making me insane" could be redefined as a problem: "How can I keep my siblings from getting under my skin?" or "How can I get along better with my family?" If there are many problems, you need to help the client to prioritize. You might ask some version of "We've found a few important areas that we can address. Which one of these areas is bothering you the most that we can work on today?" Once you identify one problem to focus on, you can work together to define the goal and then brainstorm various solutions. Let the client know that you are not advocating for a particular solution but that sometimes it's helpful to think through and list many possible solutions, along with pros and cons for each option. Once you have a reasonable list, you and the client can evaluate them and choose the best solution. Some therapists or counselors believe that, unless they're working on deep emotional issues, they are not providing the most help. In post-disaster situations, working at a more basic level, helping to keep a survivor grounded, and solving problems are significant accomplishments (National Center for PTSD & National Child Traumatic Stress Network, 2010).

CORRECTING DISTORTED SELF-COGNITIONS

Sometimes the most distress comes not from a lack of action but from distorted thinking. As they try to process their experience, trauma survivors often think in ways that are inaccurate and not useful (Shapiro, 1995). You can help survivors to identify and change these unhelpful and often distorted thoughts. Any of the following thoughts or beliefs may be detected when speaking with a victim of disaster.

- It was my fault.
- I am shameful or inferior.
- I am stupid.
- I am weak.
- I cannot protect myself or my family.
- I am inferior to other people.
- I will never get over this.
- It will happen again.
- I am in danger.
- I cannot trust anybody.
- I want to get revenge.
- I want to make it undone.

As the list of examples shows, these typically cluster into two categories: thoughts about the inadequacy of the self, and overgeneralizations about the dangerousness of the world. Use of extreme words such as "always" and "never" is often a clue that this kind of distorted thinking is occurring and should be addressed.

Let's look at the following client statements based on actual case studies after the 9/11 attacks:

> If I had run faster downtown, I could have gotten to the 100th floor and saved my brother. He was my younger brother and he could always count on me to keep him out of trouble, but I failed him on that day.

> When my sister left the Midwest to work in New York I told her not to go. It's a dangerous city. I feel terrible that I did not try harder to keep her home and I also feel horrible that I argued with her. I should have been more supportive of her going.

> When the building collapsed, I began to run, and there are videos of me, a police lieutenant, running down the street. I will never get over the humiliation.

Counselors should attempt to help a survivor find a more helpful perspective that is consistent with reality. **Self-blame** is often a significant issue for disasters survivors and can be a focus for counseling, and **shame** can be a significant predictor of developing long-term problems (La Bash & Papa, 2014). A survivor who experiences self-blame and self-recrimination may be able to come to understand that, in truth, "I did the best I could." We can speculate that self-blame after trauma is common because survivors think that they can prevent the trauma in the future if they act and think more competently. In this way self-blame can contribute to regaining a sense of control, but it is most often distorted and only adds more pain and distress. It has been suggested that Posttraumatic Stress Disorder is as much a disorder of shame as of fear (Herman, 2013). Whether or not it is the most important emotional element in the development of PTSD, it is often present and is quite painful. We can gently help clients to perceive and think more accurately and help them to be gentler with themselves.

In some situations after a disaster has passed, a survivor may think: "I am still in danger." Although you can empathize with the survivor's heightened sense of danger or fear, it can be a result of a traumatic event that has passed (Marshall et al., 2007). It is true that the world isn't always a safe place, but it's not true that we are always in grave danger and need to be at a heightened state of vigilance to guard against a threatening world or dangerous people. After an earthquake you can't reassure a survivor that there won't be aftershocks, or that one hurricane will never be followed by another, but you can provide realistic reassurance that the threat is quite low. A counselor might help a survivor to restructure the cognition to "The danger has passed" or "It's over; I'm safe now" (Beck, 1995; Herman, 1992).

When we correct these distorted and unhelpful cognitions, we need to be careful to not be so reassuring that we ignore legitimate dangers or the responsibility that the client bears. If an active shooter has not been caught, the client could be in danger. If survivors of a flood believe they could have done a better job protecting their property, they might be right. Legitimate responsibility can't be dismissed, but it can be reframed to be less painful.

RUMOR CONTROL

Rumors are common in disasters, wars, public health emergencies, and other times of uncertainty as anxiety, stress, and a lack of reliable sources increase the chance of speculation and misinformation. A rumor's potential impact is related to its importance and its ambiguity: The more important and ambiguous the material, the more likely it will be spread. There are many reasons for the spread of rumors following disaster. Don't forget that, in our discussion of common post-disaster reactions, we mentioned that people who have been through a traumatic experience often demonstrate a diminished ability to think clearly and critically, which may cause them to pass along the most improbable tales (DiFonzo & Bordia, 2007).

Rumors can give people a hook to hang their fears and anxieties on. If survivors are still feeling fearful while being told they're safe, they may seize on a rumor about a continuing threat that justifies or explains the emotion they're already feeling. Rumors may also feed the desire to find someone to blame for a disaster, leading to ill-will and potentially even violence against members of certain religions, ethnic groups, or others selected as scapegoats. This issue is even more potentially harmful today than in past decades, as rumors can be broadcast instantly via the internet, texting, Twitter, and other forms of social media. After Hurricane Katrina the media reported that there were violent armed gangs running amok in the Superdome. There were also reports of gunshots coming from roofs of houses, which were interpreted by rescue workers as attacks on them rather than as cries for attention and help. These rumors of rampant violence, rape, and murder led to the suspension of some hospital evacuations and an emphasis on riot control rather than rescue, which significantly hampered the relief effort (Gheytanchi et al., 2007).

Therefore, as mental health professionals we must caution the population about the likelihood of rumors and misinformation. We should take a proactive position and urge officials to take a similar stance on rumor control. If there is dire but confirmed information, we should provide it, since failing to do so will undermine trust and open the door for rumors to fill in the information vacuum. Helpers and authorities should also be consistent in the information provided; messages should not contradict each other

(Vermeulen, 2014). This requires cooperation and coordination among authorities, media, and other information sources. Remember that in our discussion of PFA we discussed the importance of providing accurate information and orientation to services. In shelters or Family Assistance Centers, mental health providers can provide accurate lists of resources and other information, and also display another list clearly labeled "Current rumors" with explicit explanations of why each rumor is inaccurate.

CONFLICT MITIGATION

The frustration and scarcity caused by disaster can increase conflict. Sometimes survivors feel they need to compete for shelter space, cleanup supplies, recovery funds, and—most importantly—emotional support. Family members have more needs, and expect more from one another, than they have the capacity to deliver. Survivors' friends and neighbors may have also been impacted by the disaster, so they too are unable to supply the support that's most needed, leading to frustration, intolerance, and conflict. Survivors often feel that assistance does not come at the right time, or not quickly enough, or it comes in the wrong form—and sometimes they're right. Disaster workers also face their own conflict-escalating issues, most notably the burnout that can occur when they become emotionally, psychologically, and physically exhausted from coping with cleanup, recovery, long hours, worry, fear, and a lack of resources. The resulting stress and frustration may lead to friction among workers, or between workers and clients. The best way to handle conflict is to keep it from occurring in the first place by monitoring stress levels, encouraging workers to take breaks or take time off, and encouraging survivors to use healthy coping mechanisms. When you see conflict, you can step in as a neutral third party in order to help break through the self-perpetuating cycle that characterizes many conflicts, by reminding workers or survivors that everyone is under stress (Folger, Poole, & Stutman, 2001). You can support reciprocal empathy and assist in helping parties to work towards compromise.

ASSESSMENT, TRIAGE, AND SCREENING

In the practice of disaster mental health, we're always and continually involved in observation and assessment. This type of assessment should not be confused with making formal diagnoses. We need to appraise the current status of individuals, groups, and the overall affected community (NIMH, 2002). There should be ongoing evaluation of the characteristics of the recovery environment, including whether survivors' needs are being adequately addressed and what additional interventions and resources are required (Watson, 2004). Mental health workers should be asking themselves if the environment is suitable for psychological recovery. Is it physically safe? Is it unnecessarily noisy or chaotic? Is information being provided regularly? Even such practical issues such as making sure the food being served in a shelter is appropriate to residents' cultural and dietary preferences can provide comfort and a sense of being seen and valued as human beings at a time when survivors may feel they have little control over their circumstances. Helpers should continually assess whether more workers are needed and ask for such resources if necessary.

As the relief operation proceeds, there should be ongoing monitoring of the stress level of the affected population as well as those working on recovery needs. Helpers need to decide if a follow-up visit to the home of a survivor is needed or if a client needs a referral to a community mental health center for additional help. Other types of assessment might include:

- whether spiritual support is needed
- if additional information should be made more accessible to more members of the community
- if the community is by and large angry or disappointed in response efforts and/or in political leaders
- if disaster workers need to take breaks or be rotated out and replaced
- whether medical or psychiatric referral is warranted.

In addition to this more general *needs assessment*, individual mental health assessments should be considered. As we've discussed, after a disaster most people recover on their own or with support from friends and family, so early interventions should make sure there is a positive recovery environment (Bonanno, 2004; Norris, Friedman, & Watson, 2002). This is the intent of Psychological First Aid. However, some people will need more than basic help. How do we best identify these survivors and ensure that they get the additional assessment and treatment they need? **Triage** is "the process of evaluating and sorting victims by immediacy of treatment needed and directing them to immediate or delayed treatment. The goal of triage is to do the greatest good for the greatest number of people" (NIMH, 2002). Our efforts at triage, to identify those who most need help, can take a number of different approaches, focusing on experiential factors, observable behaviors, or endorsement of symptoms.

Experience-Based

One approach to triage focuses on evidence-supported risk factors that are characteristic of the individual or his or her experience. The National

Institute of Mental Health (NIMH, 2002) takes this approach, which suggests the following groups are considered to be at high risk and deserving of special attention, namely those:

- who have acute stress disorder or other clinically significant symptoms stemming from the trauma
- who are bereaved
- who have a pre-existing psychiatric disorder
- who require medical or surgical attention
- whose exposure to the incident is particularly intense and of long duration.

Clients with several of the risk factors listed above should receive additional attention and care. Assessing most of these risk factors is usually not too difficult. If a client is injured or bereaved or missing a loved one or is showing extreme distress, it is often apparent. It may take some conversation to discover that the survivor had a long or intense exposure to the disaster. It also may be more difficult to ascertain if the client has a pre-existing psychiatric disorder. One possible way to determine this is to ask if the client took medications that got lost in the disaster that need to be replaced.

You can develop your own checklist of risk factors for survivors of disaster and check to see which clients have one or many of them. Survivors with flooded basements are at a lower risk than those who lost their homes, or those who lost homes and have neither friends nor family nor home insurance. And let's not forget that, for many people, pets are family members, so if they are missing or dead the family has lost a loved one. Injured survivors who have lost loved ones are clearly more at risk than those who can't get back to their homes for a few days due to a mandatory evacuation. We know that this sort of triage or prioritizing sounds like common sense, but, as with the practice of PFA, in the hubbub and stress of a disaster, common sense is not always so common.

Behavior-Based

The need for referral for individual assistance is often demonstrated through survivors' actions. We won't cover mandated reporting here, but, if you observe or suspect the possibility of child or elder abuse or maltreatment, you must comply with the law, which requires it to be reported. Similarly, you must report any imminent attempt to injure self or others.

Beyond reporting any threat of harm, you should be on the lookout for behaviors that indicate problematic psychological responses. We've noted that much of the distress that we observe in disaster survivors is an expected or typical reaction to unexpected or atypical events. However, if a survivor

Table 5.1 Screen and treat trauma-screening questionnaire.

Survivors are asked if they have experienced the following at least twice in the previous week.

1. Upsetting thoughts or memories about the event that have come into your mind against your will
2. Upsetting dreams about the event
3. Acting or feeling as though the event were happening again
4. Feeling upset by reminders of the event
5. Bodily reactions when reminded of the event
6. Difficulty falling or staying asleep
7. Irritability or outbursts of anger
8. Difficulty concentrating
9. Heightened awareness of potential dangers to yourself and others
10. Being jumpy or being startled at something unexpected

Answering "Yes" to more than six items indicates the need for additional assessment.

Source: Brewin et al. (2002).

tells you he or she is getting messages about the disaster from outer space or is thinking that life is no longer worth living, these should *not* be considered typical reactions but indications that additional attention is needed.

If you notice significant cognitive impairment, such as psychotic symptoms, major memory disturbance, an inability to make simple decisions, substantial disturbance of memory, obsessions, or dissociation, a referral for further assessment is indicated. If you notice serious withdrawal or repetition of ritualistic behaviors, or aggressive behavior (screaming, slander, threats), a referral would be in order. Although very intense reactions, such as hysteria or panic, are not uncommon following traumatic experiences, they may indicate the presence of Acute Stress Disorder, which needs treatment. Also be on watch for signs of dissociation (a lack of connection in a person's thoughts, memory, and sense of identity), another indicator of possible Acute Stress Disorder that can be easy to overlook. Sometimes it's not the person yelling or sobbing who most needs help but the one sitting quietly on his or her cot, depressed and dissociated, completely disengaged from the surroundings.

Symptom-Based

Chris Brewin and his colleagues (2002) have developed another approach to triage or screening by taking the direct route of asking survivors about their symptoms. They developed a simple test that can be administered to quickly identify those survivors for whom a more in-depth evaluation for PTSD is merited. This ten-item instrument (see Table 5.1) is intended to tap into the hyperarousal and re-experiencing symptoms associated with PTSD. When it was first used to screen the survivors of a train crash, the researchers found that, of those who answered "Yes" to six or more questions, 86 percent were found to have PTSD based on extensive clinical interviews. In contrast, among those who endorsed five or fewer items, only 7 percent were found to have a clinically diagnosable reaction. Brewin and his colleagues used this "screen and treat" approach on a larger scale in the aftermath of the 2005 London subway and bus bombings (Brewin et al., 2008). It proved to be a sensitive and specific way of identifying survivors for whom a more intense diagnostic interview was indicated, allowing clinical resources to be targeted effectively.

The screen and treat approach emphasizes the importance of outreach and targeting limited resources to those who most need them. While this assessment tool is very promising, keep in mind that using it requires an ability to refer those who are identified as being at risk to an appropriate provider or facility that can treat the client with evidence-based practices. Therefore, it should be implemented only if there is an overall plan that allows for outreach and long-term treatment following the screening, since it would be unhelpful and unethical to communicate to survivors that they are at risk for PTSD if there is nowhere to send them for treatment (NIMH, 2002). Practitioners are therefore cautioned not to use this approach if there is not a clear system to ensure effective referral.

REFERRALS FOR LONG-TERM CARE

However those in need are identified (and they may well self-identify as wanting more intensive assistance), there will be times when it is necessary to make a referral for long-term treatment. As part of preparedness and planning, a disaster mental health worker should know before a disaster strikes where and how to make a referral for follow-up care. There should be collaboration with local and neighborhood agencies and organizations to ensure continuity of care. As part of this planning, helpers should be able to let survivors know if there will be a fee and, if so, how much it is; or if there is a wait list for receiving services and, if so, how long. As part of coordination and collaboration before a disaster strikes, DMH workers should establish relationships with local mental health associations and county or government mental health organizations so that follow-up treatment can be as seamless as possible.

PSYCHOLOGICAL DEBRIEFING: CRITICISMS AND CAUTIONS

Now we turn our attention to an early intervention that *we do not recommend*: Psychological Debriefing. We list it here because it has been a significant part of the disaster mental health literature and is undoubtedly still being used (Halpern & Vermeulen, 2011), albeit in modified form, sometimes among the first responder community and sometimes with the general public (McNally, 2004).

Since the mid-1980s psychological debriefing has been used to assist first responders and others impacted by disaster in an attempt to reduce the risk of developing PTSD (McNally, 2004). One of the most popular forms of debriefing was developed by Jeffrey Mitchell (1983) and called Critical Incident Stress Debriefing, which was intended to be used as one component of a broader Critical Incident Stress Management program meant for groups of emergency professionals who trained together and responded to a particularly stressful event together, such as an event involving the deaths of colleagues or children. In a group debriefing session, which takes place shortly after the incident (typically 24 to 72 hours later), participants describe the event and their thoughts, feelings, and symptoms, and leaders provide information on how to reduce stress. A similar model was taught to disaster mental health workers by the American Red Cross through the 1990s, but this has since been discontinued as research has shown that the practice does not decrease the likelihood of developing PTSD (Rose, Bisson, Churchill, & Wessely, 2001).

Specifically, studies consistently show that participants like debriefing sessions, but they don't actually benefit from them in terms of the prevention of serious or lasting reactions to traumatic experiences. There is also some evidence that debriefings can be harmful when used for individuals or groups (such as office workers) who are not trained first responders and who may have had very different experiences of a disaster. If participants are already in a heightened state of arousal and then feel pressure to enter further into the traumatic experience, they could be at even greater risk for developing symptoms. They may feel pressured to share their experience before they're ready to, increasing rather than soothing emotional reactions. They may later regret displaying strong emotions in front of colleagues. And they may experience (or inadvertently cause) vicarious traumatization by exchanging personal accounts with varying degrees of traumatic exposure. According to the NIMH (2002):

> There is some Level 1 evidence suggesting that early intervention in the form of a single one-on-one recital of events and expression of emotions evoked by a traumatic event (as advocated in some forms of psychological debriefing) does not consistently reduce risks of later developing PTSD or related adjustment difficulties.

Since the evidence shows that debriefings are not helpful and there is some evidence that they might actually be harmful among the general public, it is advisable to use other methods. Remember the maxim "First, do no harm."

AN OUNCE OF PREVENTION …

In Chapter 3 we spoke about resilience, or a resistance to experiencing negative reactions to disaster. In this final section we'll return to practices that can foster resilience—not only as part of our early post-disaster interventions, but also through preventative pre-disaster efforts we can encourage in our communities.

Building Individual Resilience before Disaster Strikes

Early interventions, including PFA, are intended to create a positive recovery environment to ensure that survivors are not retraumatized and to promote a natural capacity for resilience and recovery. DMH workers can also minimize traumatic reactions by encouraging the community to plan and prepare for disaster as a means of prevention and resilience building. If community members have working smoke detectors, there will be fewer fires and less need to mitigate negative mental health outcomes. It might appear that assisting in a smoke detector campaign doesn't look like a traditional mental health intervention, but preventing disaster, or the more severe aspects of disaster, improves the mental health of the community. Most Americans don't have a disaster plan, nor are they taking sufficient precautions towards mitigating disaster. Prevention and preparedness could be seen as the most effective and important means of building resilience, and as the "earliest interventions."

Resilience has been defined as "the process of adapting well in the face of adversity, trauma, tragedy, threats, or even significant sources of threat" (see www.apa.org/helpcenter/road-resilience.aspx). Although there is not one standard definition, they all tend to emphasize **hopefulness** and the **ability to adapt**. Operationalizing the concept in more detail, people who score high on the Connor–Davidson Resilience Scale (Connor & Davidson, 2003), a 25-item scale, believe they can "adapt when change occurs;" that they can "deal with whatever comes their way;" that "past successes give me confidence in dealing with new challenges and difficulties;" that "I believe I can achieve my goals, even if there are obstacles;" that "even when things look hopeless, I don't give up;" and that "during times of stress/crisis, I know where to turn for help."

Most researchers and clinicians believe that resilience can be enhanced. This can be done if the population learns to be more resourceful, more confident, and better prepared. When you consider the commonness of trauma and disaster, the notion of preparing people before disaster strikes is a pre-emptive approach to crisis. People feel more confident and more resilient if they have a disaster plan. You can work with community leaders, faith communities, schools, Red Cross chapters, and other stakeholders to hold "citizens' preparedness meetings." These should emphasize that any emergency is easier to handle when you have prepared ahead of time. It's also important to emphasize that there's a big difference between worrying and planning. Citizens should be able to make a plan, review it once or twice a year, and live their lives.

There are many planning and preparedness websites on which you can find strategies to help individuals and families prepare, including detailed lists of recommended emergency supplies.

The Department of Homeland Security offers free "Ready" emergency preparedness publications to individuals and organizations that can be ordered or downloaded. You can obtain brochures on family emergency plans, emergency supply lists, materials for pet owners, seniors, people with disabilities, commuter emergency plans, materials for parents and kids, and tribal materials as well. All of these brochures are available in many languages (see www.ready.gov).

Similar and even more detailed materials are available through the American Red Cross. You can find checklists and materials in many languages on planning for events from chemical emergencies to winter storms (see www.redcross.org/prepare/disaster-safety-library).

Some cities have preparedness materials custom-made for their localities. For example, in New York City there is an Office of Emergency Management public education campaign intended to encourage residents to learn about the hazards they may face, and to prepare for all types of emergencies by writing an emergency plan, choosing a meeting place, gathering supplies for their home, and preparing a Go Bag in case they need to leave their home in a hurry. Brochures and workbooks are available in English, Spanish, Chinese, Russian, Arabic, Bengali, French, Haitian Creole, Italian, Korean, Polish, Urdu, and Yiddish (see www1.nyc.gov/site/em/ready/guides-resources.page).

Building Community Resilience

Resilience can also be supported at the community level. This is the major aim of the Federal Emergency Management Agency's "whole community" approach to emergency management, which involves engaging diverse representatives in planning and response, including members of social and community service groups and institutions, faith-based and disability groups, academia, professional associations, and the private and nonprofit sectors, as well as government agencies that may not traditionally have been directly involved in emergency management (see www.fema.gov/whole-community). In essence, this approach considers all members of the community to be part of the emergency management team—including local mental health professionals, who can contribute essential insight in planning for and responding to the range of disasters that could impact their area.

Community resilience describes the ability of a community to endure and survive crisis situations. It encompasses the community's adaptability to changing circumstances and its capability to respond effectively. Community resilience can be measured and enhanced (Leykin, Lahad, Cohen, Goldberg, & Aharonson-Daniel, 2013). Think about and talk with colleagues about how to build resilience in your community. In order to accomplish this you would be taking on the role of a community or organization psychologist rather than a traditional counselor.

The components of community resilience include:

- leadership
- collective efficacy
- social trust
- place attachment
- preparedness.

Leadership

Communities bounce back from disaster if the people have confidence in their leaders. Community members need to think that leaders are prepared to deal with crisis situations and can make the transition from routine to emergency management. They need to be confident in their leaders' ability to provide services fairly and to be highly cognizant of the needs of children in the community. More and more we expect our politicians to be able to manage crisis situations and to comfort stressed or grieving families. If the tragedy is local, town officials and mayors need to inspire confidence. National disasters and tragedies require the "consoler in chief" (the president) to be involved. As mental health professionals we can educate our local officials so that they understand the importance of their role and are prepared to offer effective assistance before, during, and after a disaster. We've all seen reports of high-ranking officials flying over a disaster site, looking concerned from a safe distance. Community resilience requires confidence in our leaders, and survivors are not inspired by very brief visits or fly-overs.

Collective Efficacy

Communities are resilient when people care for one another and believe that there's mutual assistance, when they have faith that their community can recover, and when survivors believe they can count on their neighbors. This dimension intersects with leadership, as leaders often need to convey this sense of community strength to residents. Optimism and confidence are protective when they are rooted in the knowledge that there's a powerful motive to bounce back.

Social Trust
In communities in which diverse groups get along, there's likely to be an easier recovery from disaster. If residents believe that their neighbors can be trusted and that their neighbors trust them, recovery will be easier. If people are worried that if they leave their home it might get looted or that neighbors are only out for themselves, the community will more likely have a long and painful recovery. Social trust and collective efficacy appear to be related, and are not easy to build during a crisis if they don't exist. It's important for all community leaders, teachers, clergy, and others to think about how to build these key qualities.

Place Attachment
Pride in place is a significant predictor of community resilience. New Orleanians after Hurricane Katrina, New Yorkers after 9/11, Bostonians after the Marathon bombing, and New Jersey residents after Hurricane Sandy all demonstrated a sense of pride in the distinct nature of their communities, with rallying cries such as "Boston strong" and "Jersey strong." When people are proud to announce where they live, they're demonstrating attachment and commitment to recovery. Similarly, when disaster survivors report that they would be very sorry to leave the town in which they reside they're demonstrating place attachment, a predictor of community resilience. Consider how you might build place attachment in your community. Perhaps preparedness events in community centers or places of worship could bring citizens together to brainstorm ideas and share a meal, leading to greater place attachment.

Preparedness
Communities bounce back when they're prepared for an emergency situation and if residents and officials are aware of their roles in an emergency situation. Are there planning meetings in your town or community? Do residents know where the shelters are in case of emergency? Are there enough shelters and are they properly equipped? Has the community done all it could to make sure that there are smoke alarms in every home? It's tempting to cope with threat or danger through denial or procrastination. As mental health professionals involved with disaster, one of our most important jobs is to persistently and positively remind the community of the importance of preparedness—not with scare tactics but with calm encouragement. We can work with emergency management officials, Red Cross or the Salvation Army, or local spiritual care leaders to sponsor preparedness

events, and we can encourage local elected officials to inform the community how the town is prepared and how citizens can prepare their households and homes. Perhaps our most effective interventions are the ones we make before disaster strikes.

REFERENCES

Beck, J. S. (1995). *Cognitive therapy: Basics and beyond.* New York: Guilford Press.

Bonanno, G. A. (2004). Loss, trauma and human resilience: Have we underestimated the human capacity to thrive after extremely aversive events? *American Psychologist,* 59(1), 20–8.

Brewin, C. R. (2003). *Posttraumatic stress disorder: Malady or myth?* New Haven, CT: Yale University Press.

Brewin, C. R., Rose, S. C. Andrews, B., Green, J., Tata, P., McEvedy, C., ..., & Foa, E. B. (2002). Brief screening instrument for post-traumatic stress disorder. *British Journal of Psychiatry,* 181(2), 158–62.

Brewin, C. R., Scragg, P., Robertson, M., Thompson, M., d'Ardenne, P., & Ehlers, A. (2008). Promoting mental health following the London bombings: A screen and treat approach. *Journal of Traumatic Stress,* 21(1), 3–8.

Connor, K. M., & Davidson, J. R. T. (2003). Development of a new resilience scale: The Connor–Davidson Resilience Scale (CD-RISC). *Depression and Anxiety,* 18(2), 76–82.

DiFonzo, N., & Bordia, P. (2007). *Rumor psychology: Social and organizational approaches.* Washington, DC: American Psychological Association.

Folger, J. P., Poole, M. S., & Stutman, R. K. (2001). *Working through conflict: Strategies for relationships, groups, and organizations* (4th ed.). New York: Addison Wesley Longman.

Gheytanchi, A., Joseph, L., Gierlach, E., Kimpara, S., Housley, J., Franco, Z. E., & Beutler, L. E. (2007). The dirty dozen: Twelve failures of the Hurricane Katrina response and how psychology can help. *American Psychologist,* 62(2), 118–30.

Halpern, J., & Vermeulen, K. (2011, June 5). Assisting disaster survivors: Are practitioners using evidence-informed practices? Paper presented at 12th European Conference on Traumatic Stress, Vienna.

Herman J. L. (1992) *Trauma and recovery: The aftermath of violence—from domestic abuse to political terror.* New York: Basic Books.

Herman, J. L. (2013, June 6). PTSD as a shame disorder. Paper presented at 13th European Conference on Traumatic Stress, Bologna.

La Bash, H. L., & Papa, A. (2014). Shame and PTSD symptoms. *Psychological Trauma: Theory, Research, Practice, and Policy,* 6(2), 159–66.

Leykin, D., Lahad, M., Cohen, O., Goldberg, A., & Aharonson-Daniel, L. (2013). Conjoint Community Resiliency Assessment Measure-28/10 items (CCRAM28 and CCRAM10): A self-report tool for assessing community resilience. *American Journal of Community Psychology,* 52(3), 313–23.

Marshall, R. D., Bryant R. A., Amsel, L., Suh, E. J., Cook, J. M., & Neria, Y. (2007). Relative risk appraisal, the September 11 attacks, and terrorism-related fears. *American Psychologist,* 62(4), 304–16.

McNally, R. J. (2004, April 1). Psychological debriefing does not prevent posttraumatic stress disorder. *Psychiatric Times,* www.psychiatrictimes.com/ptsd/psychological-debriefing-does-not-prevent-posttraumatic-stress-disorder-0.

Mitchell, J. T. (1983). When disaster strikes: The critical incident stress debriefing process. *Journal of Emergency Medical Services*, 8(1), 36–9.

National Center for PTSD & National Child Traumatic Stress Network (2010). *Skills for psychological recovery: Field operations guide.* Washington, DC: National Center for PTSD.

National Institute of Mental Health (2002). *Mental health and mass violence: Evidence-based early psychological intervention for victims/survivors of mass violence: A workshop to reach consensus on best practices.* Washington, DC: US Government Printing Office.

Norris, F. H., Friedman, M. J., & Watson, P. J. (2002). 60,000 disaster victims speak, part II: Summary and implications of the disaster mental health research. *Psychiatry*, 65(3), 240–60.

Rose, S. C., Bisson, J. L., Churchill, R., & Wessely, S. (2001). Psychological debriefing for preventing post traumatic stress disorder (PTSD). *The Cochrane Database of Systematic Reviews*, 2002(2), CD000560, DOI: 10.1002/14651858.CD000560.

Shapiro, R. (1995). *Eye Movement Desensitization and Reprocessing.* New York: Guilford Press.

Vermeulen, K. (2014). Understanding your audience: How psychologists can help emergency managers improve disaster warning compliance. *Homeland Security and Emergency Management*, 11(3), 309–16.

Watson, P. J. (2004, January 1). Behavioral health interventions following mass violence. International Society for Traumatic Stress Studies, www.istss.org/education-research/traumatic-stresspoints/2004-winter/behavioral-health-interventions-following-mass-vio.aspx.

Chapter 6

Disaster Loss and Grief

On December 14, 2012, Adam Lanza killed his mother, drove to the Sandy Hook elementary school in Newtown, CT, killed 20 children, aged five to seven, and six adult educators, and then took his own life. The first priority for counselors was to protect families from exposure to unwelcome sights and sounds, as well as the extremely intrusive press. Counselors provided as much calm and safety as possible and encouraged thoughtful conversation to elucidate and clarify what families hoped to gain by telling their stories to the media and the public. They provided support when authorities (state crime victim advocates and FBI counselors) informed families about benefits, reminded survivors to connect with trusted friends, family, and clergy, and gave permission to family members to make choices that were self-protective—including keeping unwelcome others at a distance. In the face of this traumatic grief, counselors encouraged and supported a strategy that placed trusted friends between themselves and what was at times an unhelpful and intrusive community. Parents asked very difficult and challenging questions. Some were versions of the heartbreaking query "How could this happen to my six-year-old child?" These were not really questions but cries of anguish, expressions of shock and grief. For these questions, a compassionate presence was the only response.

However, often parents sought advice and counsel, asking questions such as how the events should be explained to a surviving sibling, and if it was okay for children to watch the description of events on television or be interviewed by the press, or attend funerals or see an open casket. Counselors emphasized the importance of caregivers providing reassurance, safety, routine, and honesty while shifting back and forth between offering a compassionate presence—simply bearing witness to intense grief and suffering—and providing more direct advice, counsel, and psychoeducation. One parent was disturbed to hear from a friend that seeing the open casket would be helpful to her young surviving child in order to experience "closure." She did not feel comfortable allowing the child to witness this sight but was afraid she might be thwarting a healthy grieving process. The counselor was able to reassure her that such exposure was not a necessary part of the healing process. Husbands and wives needed each other more than they ever had in their lives, yet many spouses were unhappy with each other because they were each lost in their own grief, and the expression of that grief was disturbing to the other partner. One wife said her husband had no feelings, while the husband said he was doing the best he could to contain his grief because his wife's shrieks were driving him crazy. Family members were encouraged to tolerate each other's patterns and styles of mourning and understand that there is not a right or best way to mourn. Counselors also reminded parents that grief has a ripple effect. Surviving children have not only lost a sibling, but their parents and grandparents are grieving and are less available to console them. Family members were therefore encouraged to expand their support system of trusted friends, family, and clergy. Parents and members of the community needed to talk about death, meaning, and the afterlife, and counselors needed to be culturally competent to have these conversations while helping family members to access spiritual care providers.

In this chapter we'll discuss how you can help survivors cope with the worst type of losses disasters can cause: the death of loved ones. While the circumstances of the Sandy Hook massacre presented counselors with just about the most intense disaster mental health response needs imaginable, even less extreme events often cause multiple fatalities that are traumatic in nature, so it's important to be prepared for the powerful grief reactions you may encounter among survivors.

It's now understood that mourning is an ongoing process, and its goal is not to reach an end point after a series of stages. It may be more useful to think of the outcome as *adjustment to the loss* rather than recovery from it—a rebuilding around the missing piece that can never be replaced. A core task of this adjustment process requires bereaved people to re-establish the self amid their changed place in the world, including accepting alterations in their identity and social interactions. For example, a widow may need to find a new social circle that isn't based on getting together as a member of a couple; a father who focused his identity on providing for his family may need to find a new source of motivation if his family is killed. This process is deeply painful and often takes far longer than people expect it to, especially in a culture that continues to promote the myth of "closure." And, as we'll see, when those losses result from disaster there are likely to be many compounding issues that complicate this adjustment process.

Although we focus primarily on death in this chapter, you can apply much of what's included here to help people through other tangible as well as symbolic disaster-related losses. Tangible losses include pets and property (one's home, vehicles, clothing, treasured mementoes, important documents, assistive medical devices, and much more). Less obvious but no less real losses can include a sense of personal invulnerability, self-esteem or identity, and trust in God or protective powers. Disasters can also rob people of their health or occupation. All of these losses must be mourned as part of the adjustment process. Failing to do so may lead to more psychological or emotional problems over the course of time, especially when future losses occur.

REACTIONS TO LOSS

Like the range of reactions to disaster we discussed in Chapter 3, typical reactions to loss are often grouped into different realms of functioning, with each individual experiencing his or her own combination of symptoms that evolve over time (Stroebe, Hansson, Schut, & Stroebe, 2008).

Affective:

- depression and despair
- anxiety
- guilt
- anger
- hostility (towards the deceased, and/or towards those seen as responsible for the death)
- anhedonia (an inability to experience pleasure)
- loneliness
- relief/emancipation (because the deceased is no longer suffering, because the survivor is freed from caregiving responsibilities, or because the deceased was abusive or cruel; these feelings of relief are often mingled with guilt or self-blame).

Behavioral:

- agitation
- fatigue
- crying
- screaming, wailing
- social withdrawal
- disorganization
- self-injuring (hitting self, pulling own hair).

Cognitive:

- preoccupation with thoughts of the deceased
- lowered self-esteem
- helplessness and hopelessness
- a sense of unreality
- problems with memory and concentration.

Physiological/somatic:

- loss of appetite
- sleep disturbances
- energy loss and exhaustion
- somatic complaints (headaches, stomach aches, muscle pain)
- physical complaints similar to those the deceased had endured
- changes in drug/alcohol intake
- susceptibility to illness and disease.

These reactions are not disordered in any way, but are all expressions of **grief**, the universal response to the loss of someone or something we've formed an attachment to. You can picture this attachment like two trees whose roots have grown together over time. When one tree dies and that attachment is torn away, it leaves a hole not only next to the remaining tree but within its very foundation, causing a deep shock to its system. Eventually the surviving tree may be able to resume growth around the missing pieces, but it will never be intact in precisely the same way again.

While grief is a universal experience, the ways in which we express our grief and mark a death through rituals are strongly tied to personality, gender, and culture, which we'll discuss later in the chapter. Also keep in mind that some survivors will demonstrate little reaction to a death. This could be due to the fact that the relationship was not particularly meaningful or intimate, or it might be a result of a hardy personality or reserved emotional style that prefers to mourn privately. This should not be viewed as a sign of pathology.

CHARACTERISTICS OF DISASTER-CAUSED DEATHS

While any significant loss causes grief, disasters often complicate the situation for the bereaved person. Consider the following factors the bereaved person may be facing.

Survivors may have experienced the disaster personally and be dealing with traumatic memories of the event, and possibly with physical injuries, while trying to process the loss. They may even have witnessed the death of the loved one directly.

Survivors may be dealing with multiple deaths at once, and/or with other losses, such as their home or pets, that would normally have provided stability and comfort. While human beings are generally able to adapt to individual losses, this kind of cumulative anguish can lead to "bereavement overload" that overwhelms our normal coping capacity.

On the other hand, recognizing that other survivors of the same event had more extensive losses sometimes leads people to downplay their own distress rather than accepting their need—and right—to mourn. They may need to be reminded that, for example, it's true that they lost only their pet while others in the community lost family members, but that doesn't mean their own loss is insignificant.

Disaster-related deaths are almost always sudden and unexpected, so there is no chance to say goodbye or resolve issues with the deceased, or to prepare emotionally or practically for the loss. This often leaves survivors blindsided and stunned. They may express regrets about the final interaction with the victim. They may be faced with urgent major decisions, such as where to live and how to support their family. Even smaller challenges can be intensely stressful. For example, if the person who died was in charge of household finances, the remaining spouse may not know what kind of insurance they had just when it's most needed. That's a minor issue relative to the death of the partner, to be sure, but it's both a practical headache that must be dealt with and a reminder that the survivor is now on his or her own.

If the event was human-caused, there's likely to be anger, blame, and a desire for justice or vengeance that can interfere with the adjustment process. Survivors may have to get involved in legal or criminal proceedings that can keep reawakening the grief at each new stage, sometimes for years. This pursuit of justice can be a source of comfort if the outcome is satisfactory, but there are no guarantees that a perpetrator will be held accountable, or that a criminal sentence will seem fair or appropriate to the survivor (Madeira, 2012). In cases in which the perpetrator has evaded capture or is dead and can't be punished there may be a sense that the person "got away with it," accompanied by distress at the fact that justice can never be served.

If the survivor received and ignored a warning that could have prevented the loss, self-blame, guilt, and shame are common and powerful. If the deceased person received and disregarded a warning or committed some other action that may have contributed to his or her death, the survivor may feel anger, even rage, towards the victim, expressing emotions along the lines of "Why didn't she listen?" or "How could he have been so stupid?" This anger is often intertwined with guilt, as it's not socially acceptable to be critical of the deceased.

Media attention to disasters means survivors may be forced to do their mourning in public, or face constant reminders of the loss. This is not typical of more private kinds of losses. In many cases survivors find themselves, willingly or not, in the role of spokesperson, or hero by association. Think of the pressure put on parents of the children killed in the 2012 Sandy Hook school shooting to speak out about gun violence, or on the widows of first responders killed on 9/11 to be the public face of the nation's despair. Whether they liked it or not, these bereaved people became public figures, with all of the pressure and loss of privacy that entails. Some disaster survivors appreciate the media coverage, as it validates their loss and reminds the public that their loved one once existed. For example, after the Sandy Hook massacre some bereaved parents chose to address television cameras to discuss their murdered children (Applebome & Stelter, 2012). Some of these parents also went on to transform their personal tragedy into political action and advocacy to reduce gun violence. For others, journalists are perceived as intrusive and insensitive, and the risk of accidentally encountering coverage that will trigger traumatic memories causes them to avoid all media. This threat can go on for years, especially when a similar event or anniversary inspires a new wave of coverage. An extreme example of this: Two years after her astronaut husband was killed in the space shuttle Columbia disaster of 2003, Evelyn Husband was with her children in a restaurant, where a television was showing news about the upcoming launch of the Discovery shuttle on the first flight since the earlier disaster. The story then showed the Columbia crew walking towards their doomed shuttle, followed by footage of the craft breaking up on reentry. As she commented to *The New York Times*, "We just cannot escape it. Has anybody else had to watch their husband die on television over and over? I know that it's public and I know that it's national, but it's so private for me" (Kershaw, 2005).

(We should also note the negative psychological impact that covering disasters can have on the journalists themselves, a group whose risk of vicarious traumatization is often overlooked (Muller, 2010). There is an exceptional organization that educates journalists and students about the science and psychology of trauma and the implications for news coverage. The Dart Center, affiliated with the Columbia University Journalism School, advocates ethical reporting of trauma; compassionate, professional treatment of victims and survivors by journalists; and greater awareness by media organizations of the impact of trauma coverage on both news professionals and news consumers. For more information, see www.dartcenter.org.)

Finally, disrupted post-disaster conditions, or situations such as the inability to recover remains, often mean that survivors are unable to complete customary rituals, discussed next. As you can see from the lengthy list of complicating factors, disaster-related deaths often carry multiple stressors that compound the loss itself, which DMH helpers may need to attend to while supporting a bereaved survivor.

PRIVATE RITUALS

When someone dies under normal (meaning non-disaster-related) conditions, there are two basic needs that must be addressed: What do we do with the remains of the deceased, and how do we comfort the living? Every human culture (and many animal species as well) has developed specific ways to meet these needs through **funeral rituals** that determine how the remains are handled, while **mourning rituals** support the survivors. Many cultures have established procedures for the timing and method of preparing and displaying or concealing the body before burial, cremation, or another form of removal. Almost all cultures engage in a gathering of family and friends, which reminds survivors they're not alone. Sometimes that gathering is brief, just for the day of the service, or it may be extended for an established length of time, such as the Muslim mourning period or Jewish Shiva. In either case, there are, essentially, rules for how long the extended community is expected to be physically present with the family, and scripts for what to say and how to behave in a time that can feel destabilizing and isolating.

These customs are incredibly important to people. They can be a tremendous source of comfort and support when all goes well, but, if they're disrupted or there's any kind of disconnection between the ritual and an individual survivor's needs, they can cause added distress. That, unfortunately, is often the case after large-scale disasters. Friends and neighbors in the community who would usually provide practical and emotional support following a death may be preoccupied with their own disaster-related needs, depriving the bereaved of the comfort of traditional mourning rituals. Those from farther away may be unable to travel to the impacted region for some time. And funeral rituals often can't be followed due to the condition of bodily remains and the general post-disaster conditions.

- There may not be a body at all, such as after a plane crash when the wreckage hasn't been located, a flood that washed bodies away, or a fire that destroyed them.
- Remains may be recovered but so damaged that DNA is required for identification, delaying their release to the family.
- In the case of a criminal act, remains may need to be retained for some time as evidence, and they may require an autopsy or another procedure that's culturally inappropriate.

- During a public health emergency such as a pandemic flu, social distancing rules will ban gatherings such as funerals, so bodies may be stored or placed in temporary mass graves until the danger is over, then relocated.
- In enormous events, such as the Haitian earthquake and Indian Ocean tsunami, mass graves of unidentified victims may be permanent, and survivors may never know where their loved ones were buried.
- For members of any faith, their place of worship may be destroyed, or it may currently be used as an emergency shelter so they can't have their usual service.

The absence or damaged condition of remains creates three additional stressors for these survivors. First, many cultures practice some form of viewing the body in an open casket or other setting (though other cultures find that custom off-putting). If that isn't possible and the tradition isn't followed, people may fixate on the thought that the body was so damaged that it's not fit to be viewed. This can be a horrible thought about a loved one, but it may be true after a disaster or other traumatic cause of death. There's little empirical research to serve as guidance on whether it's better for family members to view very damaged remains, but, anecdotally, DMH professionals have found that many family members prefer to view and have access to remains, regardless of the condition of the body. Not having access (or at least the choice) may be more problematic, leaving people to imagine the condition of the body as worse than the reality.

Second, without physical evidence, survivors may be unwilling or unable to believe that a loved one has actually died in the disaster, which makes it hard to begin the process of mourning. In the words of Beverly Raphael, an expert on both bereavement and disaster mental health, in her book *The Anatomy of Bereavement*, "The experience of seeing and saying goodbye to the dead person as a dead person makes it possible for the bereaved to develop an image of the person dead, different and altered from the living image. This image may then be held alongside the living image in the process of separation and mourning" (Raphael, 1985). This need for undeniable confirmation of the death is why responders and medical examiners put so much effort into recovering and identifying all of the body parts recovered from World Trade Center after 9/11. Even when those remains were too damaged to be visually recognizable, some families could at least receive DNA evidence confirming that their relative did truly die in the event, allowing them to stop holding out some shred of hope that the victim was still alive somewhere. In contrast, survivors continued to search for their loved ones many years after the 2011 earthquake and tsunami in Japan. After searching along the beaches and in the mountains and forests, some have even become well trained scuba divers in their attempts to locate a body or any personal item, such as a wallet or jewelry, that would identify a loved one (Percy, 2016).

Third, once conditions are stabilized enough to resume holding rituals, when and how should a family commemorate a death in the absence of remains, especially if there is some hope that they'll eventually be recovered? This question is difficult enough to consider, but the decision is often complicated further by family members' different preferences. Some may want to proceed with some kind of memorial service without any remains. Others will want to hold out until a service can include any physical part of the deceased, but the reality is that they may never receive any trace of remains and must decide if and when to stop hoping for it; the family of one New York Fire Department chief killed in the attacks on 9/11 waited a full 15 years before giving up on receiving any remains from the World Trade Center and deciding to hold a funeral (Wilson, 2016). And what happens if a service is held and then remains are identified some time later, as happened to many other 9/11 victims' families? It's an excruciating dilemma for the bereaved, because it's so outside the norm of our customary ways of marking a death. You may be able to help survivors consider their options, perhaps in consultation with their spiritual care provider. You might also work with a family member whose personal needs are not met by whatever the group decision is to help that individual develop alternative rituals that provide some comfort (Landau & Saul, 2004).

All of these issues can prevent survivors from performing their final duty for the loved one. This can lead to guilt about failing to uphold their responsibility to the deceased, especially if religious beliefs about the person's afterlife are tied to proper observation of rituals, so it increases distress for the bereaved at the same time as it deprives survivors of the customary recognition and social support from family and friends provided by mourning rituals (Imber-Black, 2004). Think for a moment about what it would be like to be in this situation: Remember a time when you missed some important ritual, such as being unable to attend a holiday celebration with your family, and how that made you feel at the time—perhaps guilty, sad, or isolated. Now extrapolate that to something as significant as being unable to hold a funeral for a loved one. How would you react? Unfortunately, that is the situation that survivors may face after disaster-related deaths, and it can absolutely be a secondary trauma for them. This is why bringing in assistance from outside the affected area can be beneficial. Since DMH helpers aren't personally affected by the disaster, their attention to survivors' grief can at least provide some essential support until missing rituals can (we hope) be completed.

PUBLIC RITUALS

While disasters often impede survivors' ability to complete normal private death rituals, these events often inspire public rituals that include not only those directly impacted by the event but the broader community as well (Walter, 2008). In addition to funerals and public memorial services, these can include:

- spontaneous memorials, to which people bring candles, flowers, teddy bears, and other tokens of sympathy
- candlelight vigils, at which groups gather to sing, pray, and remember the victims
- religious services
- protest rallies (for example, against gun violence after a mass shooting)
- online and social media tributes.

All of these activities provide community members with a way to provide emotional support for those impacted and to express solidarity with victims—to do something at a time when they may be feeling helpless and grief-stricken (Doka, 2003). As time passes these ceremonies continue to demonstrate that those who died and their survivors have not been forgotten.

However, we should note that, despite their community-building potential, public memorials can have a number of negative effects as well as. First, the sheer amount of emotion present at these events can traumatize some people above and beyond their reaction to the disaster itself. It can be overwhelming to be surrounded by such a volume of grief, even if one hasn't been touched directly by the tragedy. Second, related to the earlier point about bereaved survivors of high-profile events sometimes feeling forced into a public role, those same survivors may be faced with expectations of making what are usually private rituals open to the public, or of feeling as if they have to appear at an event and fulfill the expectations of how they're "supposed" to act.

These events are often covered by the media, which means they're highly attractive to politicians who may attempt to dominate the narrative, detracting attention from those who are personally impacted or from others' goal of showing solidarity for victims. On the other hand, some grieving family members may welcome the presence of a sincere and comforting leader. A mayor or governor or president can reassure survivors and provide material and emotional support by meeting with mourners or speaking at memorials. How memorial events evolve or end can also become deeply politicized. Who decides when the items left at spontaneous altars should be removed and what should be done with them? How do authorities balance the desires of families who want annual name-reading ceremonies to continue indefinitely against the desire of other families or citizens to move on and scale back anniversary events? How should the design of permanent monuments be chosen? DMH helpers may be able to play a role in making these decisions, and/or in framing them in ways that will be acceptable to survivors.

We're also often asked to provide support at public memorial events, both shortly after the disaster and later at anniversary ceremonies. In this role, you may feel overwhelmed at the scope of emotion encountered, between the number of participants and the intensity of their anguish. However, there may be little for you to actually *do* beyond providing a calm and supportive presence, and being open to listening to those who want to talk about their loss. Most people at these events will be accompanied by friends or family members whose support is more welcome than an unknown mental health helper's. You might keep an eye out for and check in with someone who is alone. Still, however little you might feel you do at such an event, mourners may thank you for providing support and for simply being there. Your participation in the memorial reaffirms trust and reminds those present that people are not indifferent to their suffering.

SUPPORTING THE BEREAVED

As a disaster mental health helper, your awareness of the complexities of disaster-related deaths will enable you to support survivors who still may be struggling to understand the extent of their losses. As a guiding principle, remember that grief is not a disorder; it's a painful but natural process. Your role as a helper is not to fix a problem or take the pain away but to support the survivor as he or she moves through what are sometimes referred to as the tasks of mourning.

One misperception you're likely to encounter among members of the public, and often among helpers as well, is that bereaved people need to pass through five stages of grief—denial, anger, bargaining, depression, acceptance—in order to recover. These stages, identified by Elisabeth Kübler-Ross (1969) in her work with terminally ill hospice patients, were never meant to describe the experience of accepting the loss of a loved one, yet they've somehow been embraced as a playbook for bereavement. Sometimes people will actually blame themselves for not mourning "correctly" if they're not moving through the stages in order. You can disabuse them of this misunderstanding and point out that there is no single stage model that captures the unique experience of bereavement. They should not feel bad if their own journey is following a different path from what others expect of them.

A more nuanced description of this process that some people find helpful is the "dual process model of coping with bereavement" (Stroebe & Schut, 1999). According to this model, following the death of a loved one, adjustment to the loss occurs at two levels: **loss-orientation** and **restoration-orientation.** Loss-orientation refers to the affective or emotional side, focusing on the bond with the dead person, while the restoration-orientation process focuses on the reality of dealing with a large number of changes and stressors resulting from the death. Bereaved people experience both of these demands simultaneously, though one will be more salient at any particular point: At one moment the survivor may be crying over the loss, and at the next he or she may be worrying about how to support his or her family. As a helper, you can pay attention to which process is dominant and meet the client there, responding with a compassionate presence if he or she is in loss-orientation mode, and by helping to talk through practical demands if he or she is in restoration-orientation mode. It also can be useful to explain this model to the survivor so that he or she understands that what can feel like unpredictable mood swings is really an oscillation between different essential processes.

Other ways you can help include the following.

- It's very common for bereaved people to want to talk about the deceased loved one, so you can at least partially compensate for any missing social support by listening as they describe the person's life as well as their death.
- They may want you to look at pictures of the deceased. Do so respectfully and solemnly, but don't be afraid to smile at a picture and make a complimentary comment about the deceased. The survivor's desire is for the victim to be seen and acknowledged.
- Be prepared that bereaved people may feel more comfortable admitting less-than-perfect aspects of the dead person to you as a neutral helper than they might to family members. In a culture that tells us "Don't speak ill of the dead," people sometimes feel obligated to gloss over any problems, but it's important to acknowledge the totality of the relationship as part of the adjustment process. An invitation such as "Tell me all about him" can tacitly give permission to the bereaved person to move beyond an idealized description and to acknowledge any issues in the relationship that they need to address as part of their mourning process.
- Similarly, people sometimes feel a sense of relief or emancipation after a death, especially if the deceased person had been very sick or troubled. Your accepting attitude can give the survivor the permission to acknowledge that feeling and can alleviate his or her guilt about it.

- Sometimes survivors don't want to talk; they just want to know that someone is present with them. Remaining silent but attentive can be challenging, but resist the urge to fill up the silence with distracting chatter.

What to Say—and What *Not* to Say

If they want to talk, what should you say? Let's start with what *not* to say (and this is true whether you're interacting with a client or a friend).

- You'll be alright.
- You must be strong for your children/parent.
- This too shall pass.
- At least you had __ time together.
- At least he/she is no longer suffering.
- At least [anything].
- I know how you feel.
- It could have been worse.
- He/she is in a better place now.*
- It was God's will.*

Most of these statements will be perceived as insensitive, condescending, and generally not helpful, however well-intentioned the speaker is. Note that the final two are marked with an asterisk. If you absolutely know for certain that the person you're speaking to will find these sentiments comforting you could use them, but proceed with caution. Even if people usually take great comfort in their faith, they may not do so at this particular moment given their loss, so it's generally better to avoid invoking religious appeals.

Instead, it's hard to go wrong by saying something such as the following.

- I'm so sorry for your loss.
- I can't imagine what you're feeling right now, but I will be here to help you however I can.

These statements are somewhat generic, but if expressed sincerely they're unlikely to offend anyone. Also, many of us have an automatic habit of saying "Let me know what I can do to help." Usually we genuinely mean it and would welcome the opportunity to do anything asked of us. The problem is that newly bereaved people often don't actually know what they need, since they're still absorbing the loss and trying to figure out how to move forward. Instead, it can be useful to ask a specific question or offer a specific service, which might then activate recognition of what would be more helpful. For example, saying something along the lines of "I want to help you however

I can. How about if I look after your kids this afternoon so you can work on funeral plans?" might trigger a response such as "Hmm, my mother is going to watch the kids this afternoon, but it would be really helpful if you could go to the mall and pick up clothes they can wear to the funeral."

"Did My Loved One Suffer?"

This may be the most challenging question you'll ever be asked in your role as a disaster mental health helper. The sad reality is that most disaster-related deaths are violent (even those not caused by intentional violence), and, while they're sudden relative to death from an illness, many would involve enough time for the victim to understand what was happening. This means it's likely that the loved one did indeed suffer, at least briefly, from fear as well as pain.

This is obviously a horrific thought for the survivors to confront, so, when they ask you whether their loved one suffered, they're really look-ing for reassurance that the person did not. The easy route for the helper would be to say something such as "No, I'm sure it was instantaneous and they didn't know what was happening"—but you can't say that unless you're sure it's true. This may be the case if victims were shot at point-blank range or lost in a building collapse or explosion. It could possibly be the case in a disaster such as a plane crash when the cabin oxygen supply was suddenly destroyed, causing passengers to lose consciousness quickly, or a fire in which smoke inhalation overcame sleeping residents before they ever woke up. But, generally, you can't honestly state that the victim didn't suffer.

So how do you answer this impossible question? The best guidance is to tell the truth, while providing as much assurance as possible, and taking into account the age and perceived needs of the client. For better or worse, it's highly unlikely that you would know any details about the nature of the death that are not also available to the survivor, though he or she may have chosen not to learn full details at any point, or may have heard them but not yet be ready to confront them. On the positive side this means that you aren't faced with moral or ethical decisions about keeping any secrets from survivors. On the negative side, this means that they have some sense of the answer to their own question, so any attempt to provide comfort by dismiss-ing their concern is likely to backfire.

Instead, this is a classic "meet the clients where they are" situation. If they want to discuss what the victim may have experienced you should follow them there, but there is no need to volunteer details they may find distress-ing, and you certainly shouldn't speculate ("Well, I imagine in that situation people would feel …"). Most survivors, especially in the early days after the loss, really don't want to explore the details, as they're just too painful to confront, so when they ask you "Did my loved one suffer?" depending on the disaster, appropriate responses could be "We can't know with certainty but it was probably over very quickly" or a simple "I hope not."

ANNIVERSARY REACTIONS

While most individuals will naturally remember the anniversary of a loved one's death, and many religions have specific ceremonies for marking these milestones, disaster anniversaries are also likely to inspire public commemoration ceremonies and, often, a resurgence of media attention. By prompting memorial rituals (whether private or public), anniversaries provide a structured time to pause and reflect on those lost, and to recall one's own experience of the disaster. They also provide an opportunity for reflection on how far one has—or has not—come since the disaster.

Milestone anniversaries tend to take on extra significance for survivors, with the first year usually seen as most noteworthy. By the end of the initial year people have lived through the full range of "firsts"—the major ones they know will be difficult, such as the first round of holidays and birthdays without the deceased, as well as the seemingly minor milestones, which often pack an unexpected emotional punch, such as the first baseball season opener or a child's recital the dead person missed. By the end of that first year people may feel relieved that no more big surprises should be in store, though subsequent milestones, such as graduations and weddings, are likely to elicit a wave of pain over the absence.

As we've discussed, recovery from trauma and loss is typically a slow, incremental process, and people are often unaware of how far they've actually come. Anniversaries may inspire survivors who are adjusting to their loss over time to think back to their initial raw pain and recognize how much less acute their grief is now. However, our society often promotes unrealistic ideas of how quickly people should be able to recover from serious loss, so individuals may judge themselves harshly for not "getting over it by now." Even those who are coping reasonably well can expect to experience a spike in distress as the anniversary reawakens memories that have become less all-consuming over time. Psychoeducation can prepare people for these "anniversary reactions," so they know they're likely to be transient. Sometimes survivors will be concerned that they've had a complete relapse and need to begin the adjustment process all over, so reassuring them that it's generally a temporary setback can be very comforting. Public anniversary activities such as memorial services also provide you with an important outreach opportunity to reconnect with survivors and responders to see how they're functioning, and to reach people who are suffering in silence in order to educate them about available resources.

Advising survivors to be thoughtful about participation in public anniversary ceremonies is also appropriate. Some people may welcome the opportunity to gather with sympathetic community members, while others may prefer to mark the occasion privately. Media attention at public memorials is also a bit of a double-edged sword. Media coverage and political attention can remind survivors that the event hasn't been forgotten, but it may feel shallow or voyeuristic—especially if it contrasts with a perceived lack of real long-term assistance, increasing resentment or bitterness towards authorities. On the other hand, a lack of attention may leave survivors feeling forgotten or abandoned, as if their losses don't matter. In general, it can be helpful to encourage survivors to avoid media coverage if it makes them uncomfortable.

A final point on disaster-related loss: After a traumatic death, the interaction between posttraumatic stress and grief raises specific treatment implications. The current consensus is that, when you note significant posttraumatic symptoms, addressing stress reactions takes precedence over treating bereavement.

REFERENCES

Applebome, P., & Stelter, B. (2012, December 16). Media spotlight seen as a blessing, or a curse, in a grieving town. *New York Times*, www.nytimes.com/2012/12/17/business/media/newtown-has-mixed-feelings-about-the-media-horde-in-its-midst.html.

Doka, K. J. (2003). Memorialization, ritual, and public tragedy. In M. Lattanzi-Licht & K. J. Doka (Eds.), *Living with grief: Coping with public tragedy*. New York: Brunner-Routledge, pp. 179–89.

Imber-Black, E. (2004). Rituals and the healing process. In M. McGoldrick & F. Walsh (Eds.), *Living beyond loss: Death in the family* (2nd ed.). New York: W. W. Norton, pp. 340–57.

Kershaw, S. (2005, July 10). As shuttle returns, emotions tug Columbia families anew. *New York Times*, www.nytimes.com/2005/07/10/science/space/as-shuttle-returns-emotions-tug-columbia-families-anew.html.

Kübler-Ross, E. (1969). *On death and dying*. London: Macmillan.

Landau, J., & Saul, J. (2004). Facilitating family and community resilience in response to major disaster. In M. McGoldrick & F. Walsh (Eds.), *Living beyond loss: Death in the family* (2nd ed.). New York: W. W. Norton, pp. 285–309.

Madeira, J. L. (2012). *Killing McVeigh: The death penalty and the myth of closure*. New York: New York University Press.

Muller, D. (2010). Ethics and trauma: Lessons from media coverage of Black Saturday. *Australian Journal of Rural Health*, 18(1), 5–10.

Percy, J. (2016, August 2). I have no choice but to keep searching. *New York Times*, www.nytimes.com/2016/08/07/magazine/the-lost-ones.html.

Raphael, B. (1985). *The anatomy of bereavement: A handbook for the caring professions*. New York: Routledge.

Stroebe, M. S., Hansson. R. O., Schut, H., & Stroebe, W. (Eds.) (2008). *Handbook of bereavement research and practice: Advances in theory and intervention.* Washington, DC: American Psychological Association.

Stroebe, M. S., & Schut, H. (1999). The dual process model of coping with bereavement: Rationale and description. *Death Studies,* 23(3), 197–224.

Walter, T. (2008). The new public mourning. In M. S. Stroebe, R. O. Hansson, H. Schut, & W. Stroebe (Eds.), *Handbook of bereavement research and practice: Advances in theory and intervention.* Washington, DC: American Psychological Association, pp. 241–62.

Wilson, M. (2016, June 16). A funeral for a fire chief, 15 years after he died on 9/11. *New York Times,* www.nytimes.com/2016/06/17/nyregion/a-funeral-for-a-fire-chief-15-years-after-he-died-on-9-11.html.

Chapter 7

Disaster's Impact: Extreme Reactions

On September 11, 2001, when the first plane slammed into the World Trade Center, people were shocked but not sure what to make of it. For many, it was only when the second plane hit that they began to realize the country was under attack. No matter the cause or the extent, this was a big story, and journalists flocked to the site. Gillian had been working for a local TV affiliate of a major network for six years. Her good looks and personality helped her to be well thought of in on-camera interviews and stories in the Big Apple. Before coming to New York she had done crime reporting in Detroit, so she knew how to follow sirens and response vehicles. She and her small crew made their way downtown and arrived shortly after the second plane hit. They were setting up only blocks away when the first tower fell. Gil and her crew were not just reporting; now they were also victims. They dropped their equipment and ran for their lives, which was not easy for Gil, as she had to pull off her high heels as she ran. What she remembered quite clearly as the dust and debris engulfed her was that for a few seconds she could not breathe, and she thought: "I am going to die." She remembered feeling almost numb until she was pulled out of the rubble by two New York City firefighters, who saved her life. Her crew was also okay, though the equipment was destroyed. They went back to the studio, cleaned up, and quickly went back to cover the story. For Gil and her crew it was the story of a lifetime. That night, when she got home, her mother called and begged her to return home. "If you're lucky enough not to get mugged in New York you'll get blown up in a subway," her mother said. Her husband's reaction was more troubling. He said she was "out for the glory." He complained that he had tried to reach her all day and didn't think she made him enough of a priority. Although Gil was disappointed in the reactions from her mother and husband, she continued to cover the story. She was on camera with residents who could not return home and worried about their pets, and with firefighters who lost their brothers. She interviewed New Yorkers who lived far enough away from Ground Zero to take in strangers who could not get home. These citizen neighbors provided showers, towels, meals, beds, and comfort to their fellow New Yorkers. Gil's stories had consistent themes of tragedy and resilience. Two months after the attack she was walking down the street when an ambulance passed, with sirens wailing. She startled, began to cry, and couldn't stop shaking. Then she couldn't sleep, didn't want to go downtown, and eventually was reluctant to leave her apartment. She thought that sleeping pills mixed with alcohol might help, but when that recipe failed she saw a psychotherapist, who diagnosed and treated her successfully for Delayed-Onset Posttraumatic Stress Disorder—PTSD.

As we've discussed in earlier chapters, even when acute stress reactions resulting from disaster experiences are severe, they typically dissipate over time. However, a portion of disaster survivors do not recover. Some, in fact, can develop symptoms that last for decades (Holgersen, Klöckner, Boe, Weisaeth, & Holen, 2011), severely impairing their ability to work, sustain relationships, feel safe, and generally function in life. There is an important distinction between *disaster distress* and *psychiatric illness*, and we must be sure that we identify those with more extreme problems and provide them with evidence-based best treatments to try to cure these often debilitating reactions. In this chapter we'll examine key elements of these extreme reactions.

This chapter requires a bit of a shift in focus from our earlier emphasis on posttrauma reactions being unpleasant but understandable and typically transient responses to disasters. That is indeed the norm, but not the rule. Some percentage of disaster survivors won't recover but will go on to develop a clinically diagnosable mental illness. However, because disasters leave so many more distressed than disordered, the field of disaster mental health tends to overlook those who develop a diagnosable illness. For example, the federally funded Crisis Counseling Assistance and Training Program mostly provides assistance for survivor distress but offers little assistance for those with a psychiatric diagnosis. Yet these are the people who are in fact suffering well after the disaster has passed—and, given the collective nature of disasters, there are a lot of them. Take, for example, a hurricane that impacts 50,000 people. Even if only 5 percent of the survivors go on to develop PTSD or another disorder, this means that 2,500 people will develop serious and lasting reactions that require professional mental health care. Most of the literature and research in the field is appropriately devoted to assisting the majority of survivors with disaster distress, but we must be certain that those with psychiatric illness are identified, referred for, and receive evidence-based long-term treatment (North & Pfefferbaum, 2013).

RISK FACTORS FOR PTSD AND OTHER ILLNESSES

Norris, Friedman, and Watson (2002) did a great service when they summarized the results from 160 studies on 102 different events, which included "floods, hurricanes, earthquakes, wildfires, nuclear and industrial accidents, an array of transportation accidents on the ground, in the air, and at sea, terrifying sniper attacks, and bombings that caused unthinkable destruction." Some of the over 60,000 survivors studied experienced some stress and distress while others developed significant impairment. A large majority of disaster survivors were shown to be quite impacted by disaster, with only 11 percent minimally impaired, 50 percent moderately impaired, 21 percent severely impaired, and 18 percent very severely impaired. These findings make it clear that disasters cause considerable psychological harm, and there is a critical need for thoughtful planning to deliver mental health support, not only in the acute phase of the recovery but over time as distress evolves into illness for some.

Severity of the outcome and the need for mental health services have a lot to do with the disaster itself. A heavy rain leading to basement flooding throughout a community is less likely to cause a psychiatric illness than sniper attacks that result in severe injuries, threat to life, or loss of loved ones. Norris and colleagues' summary (2002) found that, when a disaster has at least two of the following four characteristics, there will be acute and long-lasting impairment in a substantial proportion of the population:

1. The disaster was large in scope, causing extensive damage to property.
2. The disaster created significant and ongoing financial hardship for the community.
3. The disaster was caused by human intent.
4. The disaster resulted in significant trauma: injuries, life threat, death.

If you consider these four characteristics of disaster, it is no surprise that an event such as the attack on the World Trade Center resulted in a high rate of mental disorder in the impacted population. In a study of survivors of the World Trade Center attacks, 35 percent of those directly exposed to the danger met the criteria for PTSD (North et al., 2011a). Keep in mind that New Yorkers who were out of town or lived far from the site were not impacted in the same way as someone was who worked in the area, lost a job, was injured, or lost a loved one. Yes, people outside New York City were upset after the attacks (Silver, Holman, McIntosh, Poulin, & Gil-Rivas, 2002), and those who spent a lot of time watching television coverage showed more symptoms, but they did not meet the official diagnostic criteria for PTSD (Schlenger et al., 2002). As we all know, the attack on the World Trade Center was not an act of nature or an accident. It was caused by human intent, and, as such, contributed to the increased trauma and impairment among those directly affected.

In addition to the nature of the event and disaster characteristics, Norris et al. (2002) identify four categories of risk factors for distress and illness following disaster: stress and trauma, survivor characteristics, family characteristics, and resources. Some findings seem obvious while others are more surprising. Although more recent studies help to explain these patterns of risk factors, more research is still needed to help us understand what makes some survivors more susceptible to extreme reactions.

Stress and Trauma

Norris and colleagues found that those who are **directly exposed** to the event are more at risk. New Yorkers who were sleeping at home when the buildings collapsed were at less risk than those who fled the World Trade Center, or who witnessed bodies falling from the buildings. But keep in mind that exposure to the disaster also includes being emotionally close to those who were severely impacted. Months after the Virginia Tech shooting, the highest posttraumatic stress symptoms (suggesting probable PTSD, though this was not formally diagnosed) were found for students who were unable to confirm the safety of friends or who experienced the death of a friend (Hughes et al., 2011). Those who live in a **neighborhood that is disrupted** or traumatized are more at risk, so survivors living in neighborhoods that are chaotic and undergoing repairs for months and even years are more likely to have lasting reactions. **High secondary stress** also predicts greater impairment. If a survivor's family member gets sick, loses a job, or has a dysfunctional marriage, he or she is more at risk. And, reinforcing the points we made in Chapter 3 about proximity and the dose–response relationship, people at the **epicenter** of the disaster may receive more aid, supportive services, and attention, but their exposure predicts the most serious psychological consequences. The higher the dose and the greater the exposure, the more likely not only that a survivor will have strong initial reactions, but that he or she will also develop psychiatric illness.

Survivor Characteristics

Norris and colleagues' (2002) second risk category involves the personal traits of those impacted. **Children** are the most vulnerable; we'll review why and how to assist them in more detail in Chapter 8. Within the adult population, **females** are more vulnerable than males, and **middle-aged adults** are more vulnerable than either young or older adults. This finding is somewhat surprising, since we often think of the elderly as vulnerable and more at risk, and this can be true for those with physical or cognitive problems. However, older adults who are healthy and mobile, who have survived many challenges over their lifetimes, and who are less responsible for the well-being of small children might be better thought of as a resource after a disaster than as a group needing special assistance. Survivors of any age or gender are more at risk for long-term problems if they have **little experience coping with disaster**, so it hits them out of the blue; if they belong to an **ethnic minority** or a **lower socioeconomic class**; or if they had a **predisaster psychiatric history**. Earlier traumas are also a risk factor for developing post-disaster mental illness. College women exposed to the Virginia Tech shooting were more likely to report depression and PTSD two months and one year after the event if they had a history of sexual abuse or sexual trauma (Littleton, Grills-Taquechel, Axsom, Bye, & Buck, 2012). There seems to be a cumulative impact of multiple trauma experiences. There are also general **personality factors** associated with risk and resilience. Some of the personality characteristics that have been linked to distress and symptoms after a disaster include emotional instability, negative affect, lower sense of self-control or self-efficacy, being prone to rumination, lack of ability to engage in self-serving biases, lack of hardiness, and lack of adaptive flexibility (Bonanno, Brewin, Kaniasty, & La Greca, 2010).

Family Characteristics

Norris and colleagues also found patterns of vulnerability related to the survivor's family. A poor post-disaster mental health outcome is more likely for an adult if **children are present** in the home, if the adult is **female**, and if **a husband is present**. A child is most at risk when there is **parental distress,** and everyone, child and adult alike, is at risk if a **family member is present who is significantly distressed** or if there is **interpersonal conflict or lack of supportive atmosphere** in the home. These findings remind us of the importance of family systems. For example, in one study of very young children (five years or younger) in New York City after the attacks of 9/11, children who were directly exposed and whose parents were more in conflict and parented less well had more trauma symptoms (DeVoe, Klein, Bannon, & Miranda-Julian, 2011), reflecting the ripple effect of trauma through families. Although children might receive post-disaster attention and support at school, it's probably more important that their parents receive the attention and support they need to function effectively as caregivers. Mothers may experience the most stress and pressure, feeling responsible for the well-being of the entire family, and therefore are most at risk for developing symptoms. It might be surprising to readers to see that the presence of a husband is a risk factor for women, but perhaps, when there is a crisis, he becomes another person for a wife to worry about. A family systems perspective also reminds us that one very distressed survivor or conflict in the home can have a significant impact on everyone else. These findings suggest that referrals for couple or family therapy should be a treatment option, even if only one member of the family has symptoms.

Resources

The final risk factor Norris et al. (2002) identify concerns resources, both material and social. When a disaster is imminent, those with more resources are better off. They can buy supplies to protect their property. They can evacuate and stay with friends, relatives, or at a hotel. If work is disrupted they can withstand interruptions in pay and they're more likely to have home insurance. In contrast, people with fewer economic resources are more likely to live in disaster-prone areas and in less sturdy housing. This was apparent in the aftermath of the 2010 Haitian earthquake, which killed hundreds of thousands as buildings collapsed on residents, in part due to low construction standards and no building codes.

All disaster mental health interventions are intended to replace resources as rapidly as possible. When disaster strikes and survivors lose possessions or the temporary or permanent use of their homes, it's more difficult to count on neighbors, friends, and relatives, who may also have been hit hard and have little to offer. If survivors begin to **lose belief in their ability to cope** and control outcomes, they're at risk for poor mental health outcomes. If they feel that they have **few or deteriorating social supports**, they're also at risk. This is why it's important for helpers to arrive on the scene quickly and provide reassurance before survivors lose hope. Survivors are also more resilient if they draw on their own strengths, resume normal activities as soon as possible, understand that they're in a community of people struggling with similar issues and problems, and share experiences, challenges, and solutions with their friends and neighbors. As outsiders and professional helpers, much in the same way that we can help individuals who are suffering by working with the family system, we should do what we can to support community members assisting one another.

TRAJECTORIES FOLLOWING TRAUMATIC EVENTS

People react to trauma and disaster in very different ways. Bonanno (2004) identifies four distinct patterns of disruption in functioning after traumatic events. There is one subset of trauma survivors who show symptoms at the outset and continue to struggle over months and years (the "chronic" group). Another group of survivors are stable at the outset and remain psychologically healthy ("resilience"). The other two groups change over time. There are those who "bounce back" over time ("recovery") and those who initially function well but whose condition worsens over time ("delayed").

In one study of individuals who were highly exposed to the 9/11 attacks, researchers (Bonanno, Rennike, & Dekel, 2005) found 29 percent with symptoms that stayed elevated over time ("chronic"); 35 percent who showed little impairment throughout ("resilience"); 23 percent whose symptoms declined ("recovery"); and 13 percent whose symptoms got worse over time ("delayed"). These self-reported findings were confirmed by ratings from close friends and family members who evaluated participants on adjustment both before and after 9/11. We get some clues as to what can account for these differences from a study of trajectories of scores for PTSD among more than 16,000 rescue and recovery World Trade Center workers (Maslow et al., 2015). PTSD in this responder population was studied over eight to nine years. Members of the higher-risk groups were associated with:

- exposure, including the duration of their World Trade Center work
- witnessing of horrific events
- being injured or perceiving threat to life or safety
- bereavement
- job loss.

High PTSD within each group was associated with lower social support, divorce, separation, widowhood, and unemployment. Another study of trajectories of PTSD among 17,000 lower Manhattan residents and workers following the World Trade Center attacks demonstrated the impact of severe exposure, lack of financial resources, and treatment barriers (Welch et al., 2016).

Overall, there is considerable variability about how people fare immediately and in the long term. They can be minimally, moderately, or highly symptomatic at the outset and recover a short time later, or symptom-free initially with delayed onset months later, as in the case study at the beginning of this chapter. These findings demonstrate that there is a need to screen disaster survivors immediately after the event and then at regular intervals to ensure that we don't miss individuals whose reactions take some time to develop.

POSTTRAUMATIC STRESS DISORDER IN ADULTS

The gold standard for diagnosing PTSD is a structured clinical interview such as the Clinician-Administered PTSD Scale (CAPS-5). Later we present the PCL-5 20-item questionnaire, which corresponds to the DSM-5 symptom criteria for PTSD and can be used for screening. First we'll review and summarize the criteria for a PTSD diagnosis according to the current edition of the *Diagnostic and Statistical Manual*, DSM-5 (APA, 2013).

Clients, the general public, and even professionals can overuse or extend the concept of trauma in a manner that risks minimizing its true impact. If you spill coffee on your computer or hear that your office may be beginning a series of job layoffs, you have a problem or stressor and you might be troubled or anxious, but you have not been traumatized. Still, the type of trauma that does qualify for a PTSD diagnosis is, unfortunately, all too common. Such an event occurs when the survivor feels his or her life or physical integrity is threatened or witnesses the serious injury or death of another. Over nine in ten Americans experience this kind of traumatic event in their lifetime (Curtois & Gold, 2009) due to disaster or another kind of distressing experience, and most research on the effects of disaster agree that PTSD is the disorder most often associated with exposure to disaster trauma.

Although trauma involves a threat to physical integrity or the perception of threat to one's life, it could also be said that trauma is a threat to cognitive or psychological integrity. The sight of a fragment of human tissue on one's sleeve hours after an explosion could be so grotesque, or imagining what a loved one suffered while confronting an active shooter so horrifying, that it presents a severe challenge to a survivor's understanding of the world and his or her place in it. Traumatic events, by definition, overwhelm our ability to cope. They shake and sometimes even shatter basic assumptions. We're forced to reconsider how benevolent, predictable, and controllable the world is. Derived from the Greek word for "wounded," trauma impacts our sense of vulnerability and self-esteem and leads to a cognitive reassessment (Calhoun & Tedeschi, 2013). Another way of looking at traumatic reactions is that they create a turning point in the life narrative, the watershed event that divides life into "before and after" (Janoff-Bulman, 2010). For some people, the "after" stage remains fixed on the loss or traumatic memory.

Summary of Criteria for a Diagnosis of PTSD

To qualify for an official PTSD diagnosis according to DSM-5, clients must meet a number of criteria regarding their experience and symptoms.

Criterion A necessitates **exposure to trauma**. This means exposure to actual or threatened death, serious injury, or sexual violence through one of the following:

- direct exposure
- witnessing the trauma to others in person

- learning of direct trauma exposure of a close family member or close friend
- repeated or extreme exposure to aversive details of trauma, such as handling dead bodies or body parts, or child protective workers being repeatedly exposed to details of child abuse.

Note that exposure via media does not count as a qualifying experience, except under certain professional conditions (for example, a law enforcement professional who must view images of child pornography in the course of investigations).

Criterion B describes **intrusive symptoms** that must include one of the following, beginning after the traumatic event:

- recurrent involuntary and intrusive memories of the traumatic event
- recurrent distressing dreams in which the content and/or affect of the dream are related to the traumatic events
- dissociative reactions, such as flashbacks, in which the individual feels or acts as if the traumatic event were recurring
- psychological distress at exposure to reminders of the trauma
- physiological reactions to reminders of the trauma.

Criterion C involves **persistent avoidance of stimuli** associated with the traumatic events, beginning after the traumatic event and is evidenced by at least one of the following:

- avoidance of or efforts to avoid distressing memories, thoughts, or feelings about or closely related to the traumatic event
- avoidance of or efforts to avoid people, places, conversations, activities, objects, situations that arouse distressing memories, thoughts, or feelings about the trauma.

Criterion D involves at least two of the following **negative cognitions and moods** associated with the trauma:

- inability to remember an important aspect of the traumatic event(s)
- persistent and exaggerated negative beliefs or expectations about oneself, others, or the world
- persistent distorted cognitions about the cause or consequence of the trauma that lead to self-blame or blaming others
- persistent adverse emotional state, such as fear, horror, anger, guilt, or shame
- diminished interest or participation in significant activities
- feelings of detachment or estrangement from others
- persistent inability to experience positive emotions.

Criterion E involves **alterations in arousal and reactivity** beginning or worsening after the trauma with at least two of the following symptoms:

- irritable behavior and angry outbursts
- reckless or self-destructive behavior
- hypervigilance
- exaggerated startle response
- problems with concentration
- sleep disturbance.

Duration of the disturbance must be for more than one month and cause significant distress or impairment in social, occupational, or other area of important functioning and must not be attributable to substance use or a medical condition.

It's difficult to convey how debilitating PTSD can become for some people as the symptoms strengthen and reinforce each other in a true vicious circle. Not only are the intrusive memories and dreams unpleasant, but they trigger the autonomic stress reaction—the fight or flight response—as if the threat is still present. To shield oneself from this pain, the patient learns to avoid reminders of the traumatic experience. At first this is a very effective way of reducing distress. The problem is that it tends to become increasingly generalized. Initially people may avoid, say, going to the building where they survived an attack. Then they start to avoid the entire neighborhood, because there might be reminders present. Then they start to avoid leaving their home at all, or watching television that might include news about the event. At the same time they feel hypervigilant and are always on guard for the threat to return. They begin to view the world as unsafe, and become consumed by blaming themselves or others for what happened. They don't sleep. Ultimately they withdraw from social and family relationships. Over time it can become more and more difficult to treat PTSD as the symptoms become entrenched. This is why early diagnosis and treatment need to be a focus of our DMH response.

Screening and the PTSD Checklist

A diagnosis of PTSD can't be made until one month after the traumatic event and requires a full clinical assessment. This means that rates of PTSD following a disaster can be underestimated, as survivors don't utilize mental health treatment (if it's available) and it's not practical or realistic to provide all survivors with full clinical evaluations. However, brief and uncomplicated screening tools can be very useful to ensure that survivors who need the most help get it. Screening locations could include work, school, community, and primary care settings. If survivors show a positive screen result they should be guided to full clinical assessment and treatment (North & Pfefferbaum, 2013). This approach was used quite successfully after the London subway and bus bombings in 2005 (Brewin et al., 2008), as we mentioned in Chapter 5.

One of the most commonly used screening tools, the PTSD Checklist for DSM-5 (PCL-5), is a 20-item self-report measure that assesses the symptoms of PTSD:

1. repeated, disturbing, and unwanted memories of the stressful experience
2. repeated, disturbing dreams of the stressful experience
3. suddenly feeling or acting as if the stressful experience were actually happening again (as if you are actually back there reliving it)
4. feeling very upset when something reminds you of the stressful experience
5. having strong physical reactions when something reminds you of the stressful experience (for example, heart pounding, trouble breathing, sweating)
6. avoiding memories, thoughts, or feelings related to the stressful experience
7. avoiding external reminders of the stressful experience (for example, people, places, conversations, activities, objects, or situations)
8. trouble remembering important parts of the stressful experience
9. having strong negative beliefs about yourself, other people, or the world (for example, having thoughts such as "I am bad," "There is something seriously wrong with me," "No one can be trusted," "The world is completely dangerous")
10. blaming yourself or someone else for the stressful experience or what happened after it
11. having strong negative feelings, such as fear, horror, anger, guilt, or shame
12. loss of interest in activities that you used to enjoy
13. feeling distant or cut off from other people
14. trouble experiencing positive feelings (for example, being unable to feel happiness or have loving feelings for people close to you)
15. irritable behavior, angry outbursts, or acting aggressively
16. taking too many risks or doing things that could cause you harm
17. being "superalert," or watchful, or on guard
18. feeling jumpy or easily startled
19. having difficulty concentrating
20. trouble falling or staying asleep.

Each symptom is followed by a self-report rating scale of 0–4, with a rating of "not at all," "a little bit," moderately," "quite a bit," and "extremely." Patients can complete the PCL-5 in approximately five to ten minutes (see www.ptsd.va.gov/professional/assessment/adult-sr/ptsd-checklist.asp).   A provisional PTSD diagnosis can be made by treating each item rated as 2 ("moderately") or higher as a symptom endorsed, then following the DSM-5 diagnostic rule that requires at least one criterion B item (questions 1–5), one criterion C item (questions 6–7), two criterion D items (questions 8–14), and two criterion E items (questions 15–20) (see www.ptsd.va.gov/professional/assessment/adult-sr/ptsd-checklist.asp for details on scoring).

For screening to be effective, the exposed population needs to be contacted in order to be sure that all people at risk are evaluated. This is not always a simple or easy task. After some disasters, survivors evacuate temporarily, while others leave the area for long periods of time or do not make themselves easily available for mental health screening. Also, some survivors may be symptom-free at one month after the event but could screen positively months or even years later. A systematic and thorough screening of exposed populations should take all of these considerations into account in order to maximize the chances of getting care to people who most need it.

MAJOR DEPRESSIVE DISORDER

Although PTSD is more common and a more frequently researched extreme reaction, disasters also consistently produce higher rates of Major Depressive Disorder (MDD). It's also more likely that a survivor might have a pre-disaster history of MDD than of PTSD, putting him or her at somewhat higher risk of relapse.

According to the DSM-5, qualifying for a diagnosis of MDD requires five or more of the following symptoms to be present during a two-week period, and they must include either (1) depressed mood or (2) loss of interest or pleasure:

1. depressed mood most of the day, nearly every day
2. diminished interest or pleasure in all or almost all activities
3. significant weight loss (more than 5 percent of body weight in a month) or increase or decrease in appetite
4. insomnia or hypersomnia
5. psychomotor agitation or retardation
6. fatigue or loss of energy
7. feelings of worthlessness or guilt
8. diminished ability to think or concentrate, or indecisiveness
9. recurrent thoughts of death or suicide.

For a diagnosis of MDD, these symptoms should not be attributable to substance use or another medical condition, or to the recent (within two months) loss of a loved one, and they must create significant disturbance in social, occupational, or other areas of important functioning.

When experienced after a disaster, MDD symptoms may prevent survivors from engaging in necessary recovery activities, prolonging their suffering. Depression could also be induced not by the disaster experience itself but by its ripple effects: Disasters are not only life-threatening but they can create horribly depressing conditions, including economic and job loss. Consider the Deep Water Horizon oil spill in the Gulf of Mexico in 2010. Although there was some loss of life, it was also an ecological and economic catastrophe. It had a devastating effect on marine life in the Gulf; cleanup crews and fishermen got sick; there were significant economic losses in the fishing, tourism, and energy industries; and adults and children living miles from the coast reported physical and mental health symptoms (Buttke et al., 2012). Oil gushed for months and leaked for years, and the cleanup continues today, as do legal consequences. Among people with spill-related income loss, more than 83 percent experienced clinically significant depression one year after the disaster (Morris, Grattan, Mayer, & Blackburn, 2013; D'Andrea & Reddy, 2014).

In spite of the increased rates of depression following disaster, there is little evidence for increased rates of suicide. However, there is evidence that people already struggling with depression and suicidal ideation are at greater post-disaster risk (Bonanno et al., 2010). Losses from disaster, such as the economic losses that can lead to depression, can take months or years to develop, which again points to the need to monitor and screen communities long after disaster strikes. There are a number of screening tools available for major depression, including the Beck Depression Inventory II and the Center for Epidemiological Studies Depression Scale (see North & Pfefferbaum, 2013). Antidepressant medications can also provide relief from symptoms for many people with MDD, though many medications take days to weeks to begin to have an impact. If you're working with someone who reveals a history of MDD be sure to ask if they have access to needed medications and try to connect them with a healthcare provider to restore a prescription if necessary.

COMPLICATED/TRAUMATIC/PROLONGED GRIEF

Grief is an unavoidable and painful but normal reaction to loss, as we described in the previous chapter. After the death of a loved one, bereaved people often feel sorrow, anger, guilt, anxiety, and anguish. They may ruminate about the deceased person and reflect on the events that led up to the death. They can have physical reactions to their loss, such as sleeping too much or too little, and they can develop behavioral symptoms. They might not want to see friends or family or go to work. For most people, the painful feelings and thoughts gradually diminish. But, for some, the grief reaction remains and can become increasingly incapacitating. Although not listed as a disorder in DSM-5, some experts refer to this as Complicated Grief, Traumatic Grief, or Prolonged Grief (PG). People who have suddenly or violently lost loved ones in a disaster may experience Complicated Grief (Bonanno et al., 2007).

Research by Holly Prigerson and colleagues (2009) suggests that those with PG can:

* yearn for or be preoccupied with the deceased
* experience life as empty and meaningless without the deceased
* feel stunned, dazed
* feel shocked about the death
* have trouble accepting the death
* feel that a part of them died along with the deceased
* have difficulty moving on with life without the deceased
* experience a sense of numbness since the death
* find it hard to trust others since the death
* avoid reminders of the deceased
* experience survivor guilt
* feel bitterness or anger related to the death
* be on edge or jumpy since the death.

Survivors with PG sometimes want to die themselves, as there is significant emotional suffering and a desperate desire to be reunited with the deceased. Fortunately, long-term therapies for PG have been shown to be effective (Boelen, de Keijser, van den Hout, & van den Bout, 2007; Shear, Frank, Houck, & Reynolds, 2005).

OTHER HEALTH AND MENTAL HEALTH PROBLEMS

Although disaster-caused PTSD and Major Depressive Disorder receive the most attention when we consider extreme mental health reactions, there are additional serious problems that may cause suffering among individuals, families, and communities.

Disasters kill people and cause acute injuries, including permanently life-altering ones such as limb amputations and traumatic brain injuries. Even when disasters don't cause immediate physical injury they can create chronic stress that leads to physical illness over time. While 2,753 people died at the World Trade Center on 9/11, more than 9,000 were determined to be eligible for medical claims. Some were injured during the attacks, but many more were first responders or recovery workers who developed health problems only after months or years had passed. They continue to show higher rates of respiratory illness, heart disease, gastrointestinal disease, type 2 diabetes, and cancer (Centers for Disease Control and Prevention, 2014; Miller-Archie et al., 2014; Solan et al., 2013). These illnesses cause considerable stress to individuals and their families. The wear and tear on the body that grows over time as a result of exposure to repeated or chronic stress results in compromised immunity, atherosclerosis, obesity, bone decay, and atrophy of brain cells (Bonanno et al., 2010).

Clinicians and public health workers are often concerned that disasters will lead to a spike in substance abuse as survivors self-medicate their symptoms with drugs or alcohol. The good news on substance abuse is that one analysis (North, Ringwalt, Downs, Derzon, & Galvin, 2011b) of almost 700 survivors of ten disasters found that only 0.3 percent of the sample developed an acute new onset of alcohol use disorder. This is consistent with previous research that found it's rare for survivors to turn to drugs or alcohol at a problematic level for the first time post-disaster, though use of substances for occasional stress release was not uncommon. The bad news is that 83 percent of participants who had been in recovery at the time of the disaster acknowledged consuming alcohol after the event. Alcohol abuse not only harms the user's body and mind but is linked with domestic violence, sexual assault, physical and verbal abuse, and violent crime. North et al. conclude that continuing or recurring substance use disorders made up the vast majority of problematic cases, so post-disaster support should target survivors with a history of drug or alcohol use rather than focusing on assessing for new onset of substance use disorders. This underscores the importance of getting a sense of substance use patterns among those you're helping after a disaster and providing information on positive coping that steers those at risk away from relapse, such as posting information about local 12-step meetings in shelters, or encouraging those in recovery to be sure to continue whatever sobriety practices helped them in the past.

REFERRALS FOR LONG-TERM CARE

In general, helpers should be sensitive to the fact that those needing long-term treatment following exposure to disaster could be feeling reluctant, ashamed, and embarrassed about needing help, as well as fearful of the painful feelings and memories connected with the traumatic event. Keep in mind that there's a stigma to seeking any kind of mental health treatment among many groups. Making matters worse, avoidance of reminders of the traumatic event is a core symptom of PTSD, making engaging in therapy that involves talking about the experience harrowing for PTSD sufferers to even consider. Therefore, data on disaster survivors who actively pursue treatment for PTSD don't accurately reflect the number of survivors suffering from PTSD who are in need of help but resist seeking it.

Even when we're able to do screening and outreach to disaster survivors, there's a problematic gap between identifying those showing signs of psychiatric illness and getting them high-quality care. This is unfortunate, as there's substantial literature demonstrating the effectiveness of psychotherapy in the treatment of PTSD and MDD. Clients should be reassured and supported for acknowledging their problem and seeking treatment. Clinicians using evidence-based best practices are more likely to obtain positive results, so you should make referrals to clinicians you know have these practices in their toolkits. Thorough description of these treatments is beyond the scope of this book, but it is important for DMH helpers to know what forms of referrals should be made for trauma survivors. The National Center for PTSD recommends the practices listed below as the most effective current treatments (see www.ptsd.va.gov/public/treatment/therapy-med/treatment-ptsd.asp). For more detailed information, see the second edition of *Effective Treatments for PTSD: Practice Guidelines from the International Society for Traumatic Stress Studies* (Foa, Keane, Friedman, & Cohen, 2009).

Recommended Evidence-Based Long-Term Care Approaches for PTSD:

- Prolonged Exposure therapy
- Cognitive Processing Therapy
- Stress Inoculation Training
- other forms of cognitive therapy
- Eye Movement Desensitization and Reprocessing
- medication.

As this list suggests, various forms of cognitive behavioral psychotherapy are considered the treatments of choice, though there are no disaster-specific PTSD modalities, as treatments were generally developed to address PTSD in survivors of sexual assault, motor vehicle accidents, or other traumatic experiences. The efficacious, evidenced-based cognitive behavioral treatments that exist for this disorder are short-term and highly structured. Present-day state-of-the-art treatments for PTSD include Prolonged Exposure (PE) therapy (Foa, Hembree, & Rothbaum, 2007) and Cognitive Processing Therapy (CPT), among others. These treatments embrace the perspective that PTSD is treatable, and their overall philosophy is to remove "blocks" to recovery. Each treatment has a different emphasis, with PE emphasizing exposure and emotional processing. The exposure-based therapies introduce clients to reminders and memories of the traumatic material. This exposure enables clients to overcome their avoidance behaviors and to modify their emotional reactions. In CPT (Resick, Monson, & Chard, 2008), there is less exposure and increased cognitive processing—hence it is a more "frontal lobe" approach that may be appealing to those who are resistant to the idea of intense exposure to memories of the traumatic experience. CPT helps clients to learn to identify and correct distorted and unhelpful negative thoughts and maladaptive behaviors, particularly those related to the traumatic event. These are treatments of hope, with therapists serving as coaches who expect the active engagement of their clients. PTSD patients who become more hopeful during treatment are more likely to recover from depression and PTSD (Gilman, Schumm, & Chard, 2012). CPT and PE achieve a higher level of evidence for treatment effectiveness for PTSD than any other therapies.

There is a recognized undertreatment of disaster survivors with serious psychological problems (North & Pfefferbaum, 2013), and this is perhaps more true for children. Four years after Hurricane Katrina, even after living conditions had stabilized, 29 percent of pediatric patients had significant mental health problems that could have been recognized and treated earlier. As we'll discuss in the next chapter, although they are resilient, children are a large and vulnerable population. Teachers and parents can overlook children's symptoms and chastise them for being moody or acting disruptively when they are in fact suffering from a trauma-related illness. School-based screening followed by Trauma-Focused Cognitive Behavioral Therapy could help with difficulty concentrating, sleep disturbance, and academic and social adjustments. Group therapy at school and individual treatment at mental health clinics have both been shown to be successful in treating PTSD symptoms in children 15 months after Hurricane Katrina (Jaycox et al., 2010). Pediatricians and school officials can be better trained to ensure that children are evaluated and receive the post-disaster services they need (Olteanu et al., 2011).

Overall, we hope this chapter has convinced you of the need to be attentive to disaster survivors who may not fit our expected patterns of recovery and resilience, but who appear to be at risk for extreme reactions that require professional mental health support. Their suffering can be intense, but it is treatable, and even curable.

REFERENCES

APA (2013). *Diagnostic and statistical manual of mental disorders* (5th ed.). Washington, DC: American Psychiatric Association.
Boelen, P. A., de Keijser, J., van den Hout, M. A., & van den Bout, J. (2007). Treatment of complicated grief: A comparison between cognitive-behavioral therapy and supportive counseling. *Journal of Consulting Clinical Psychology*, 75(2), 277–84.

Bonanno, G. A. (2004). Loss, trauma and human resilience: Have we underestimated the human capacity to thrive after extremely aversive events? *American Psychologist*, 59(1), 20–8.

Bonanno, G. A., Rennike, C., & Dekel, S. (2005). Self-enhancement among high exposure survivors of the September 11th terrorist attack: Resilience or social maladjustment? *Journal of Personality and Social Psychology*, 88(6), 984–98.

Bonanno, G. A., Neria, Y., Mancini, A. D., Coifman, D., Litz, B. T., & Insel, B. (2007). Is there more to complicated grief than depression and PTSD? A test of incremental validity. *Journal of Abnormal Psychology*, 116(2), 342–51.

Bonanno, G. A., Brewin, C. R., Kaniasty, K., & La Greca, A. M. (2010). Weighing the costs of disaster: Consequences, risks and resilience in individuals, families, and communities. *Psychological Science in the Public Interest*, 11(1), 1–49.

Brewin, C. R., Scragg, P., Robertson, M., Thompson, M., d'Ardenne, P., & Ehlers, A. (2008). Promoting mental health following the London bombings: A screen and treat approach. *Journal of Trauma Stress*, 21(1), 3–8.

Buttke, D., Vagi, S., Bayleyegn, T., Sircar, K., Strine, T., Morrison, M., ..., & Wolkin, A. (2012). Mental health needs assessment after the Gulf Coast oil spill—Alabama and Mississippi, 2010. *Prehospital and Disaster Medicine*, 27(5), 401–8.

Calhoun, L. G., & Tedeschi, R. G. (2013). *Posttraumatic growth in clinical practice.* New York: Brunner-Routledge.

Centers for Disease Control and Prevention (2014, June). Research meeting proceedings: June 17th through 18th, 2014. Centers for Disease Control and Prevention, www.cdc.gov/wtc/proceedings.html.

Curtois, C. A., & Gold, S. N. (2009). The need for inclusion of psychological trauma in the professional curriculum: A call to action. *Psychological Trauma: Theory, Research, Practice, and Policy*, 1(1), 3–23.

D'Andrea, M. A., & Reddy, G. K. (2014). Crude oil spill exposure and human health risks, *Journal of Occupational and Environmental Medicine*, 56(10), 1029–41.

DeVoe, E. R., Klein, T. P., Bannon, W., & Miranda-Julian, C. (2011). Young children in the aftermath of the World Trade Center attacks. *Psychological Trauma: Theory, Research, Practice, and Policy*, 3(1), 1–7.

Foa, E. B., Hembree, E. A., & Rothbaum, B. O. (2007). *Prolonged exposure therapy for PTSD: Emotional processing of traumatic experiences: Therapist guide.* New York: Oxford University Press.

Foa, E. B., Keane, T. M., Friedman, M. J., & Cohen, J. A. (Eds.) (2009). *Effective treatments for PTSD: Practice guidelines from the International Society for Traumatic Stress Studies* (2nd ed.). New York: Guilford Press.

Gilman, R., Schumm, J. A., & Chard, K. M. (2012). Hope as a change mechanism in the treatment of posttraumatic stress disorder. *Psychological Trauma: Theory, Research, Practice, and Policy*, 4(3), 270–7.

Holgersen, K. H., Klöckner, C. A., Boe, H. J., Weisaeth, L., & Holen, A. (2011). Disaster survivors in their third decade: Trajectories of initial stress responses and long-term course of mental health. *Journal of Traumatic Stress*, 24(3), 334–41.

Hughes, M., Brymer, M., Chiu, W. T., Fairbank, J. A., Jones, R. T., Pynoos, R. S., ..., & Kessler, R. C. (2011). Posttraumatic stress among students after the shootings at Virginia Tech. *Psychological Trauma: Theory, Research, Practice, and Policy*, 3(4), 403–11.

Janoff-Bulman, R. (2010). *Shattered assumptions: Towards a new psychology of trauma.* New York: Simon & Schuster.

Jaycox, L. H., Cohen, J. A., Mannarino, A. P., Walker, D. W., Langley, A. K., Gegenheimer, K. L., ..., & Schonlau, M. (2010). Children's mental health care following Hurricane Katrina: A field trial of trauma-focused psychotherapies. *Journal of Traumatic Stress*, 23(2), 223–31.

Littleton, H. L., Grills-Taquechel, A. E., Axsom, D., Bye, K., & Buck, K. S. (2012). Prior sexual trauma and adjustment following the Virginia Tech campus shootings: Examination of the mediating role of schemas and social support. *Psychological Trauma: Theory, Research, Practice, and Policy*, 4(6), 578–86.

Maslow, C. B., Caramanica, K., Welch, A. E., Stellman, S. D, Brackbill, R. M., & Farfel, M. R. (2015). Trajectories of scores on a screening instrument for PTSD among World Trade Center rescue, recovery, and clean-up workers. *Journal of Traumatic Stress*, 28(3), 198–205.

Miller-Archie, S. A., Jordan, H. T., Ruff, R. R., Chamany, S., Cone, J. E., Brackbill, R. M., ..., & Stellman, S. D. (2014). Posttraumatic stress disorder and new-onset diabetes among adult survivors of the World Trade Center disaster. *Preventive Medicine*, 66, 34–8.

Morris, J. G., Grattan, L. M., Mayer, B. M., & Blackburn, J. K. (2013). Psychological responses and resilience of people and communities impacted by the Deepwater Horizon oil spill. *Transactions of the American Clinical and Climatological Association*, 124, 191–201.

Norris, F. H., Friedman, M. J., & Watson, P. J. (2002). 60,000 disaster victims speak, part II: Summary and implications of the disaster mental health research. *Psychiatry*, 65(3), 240–60.

North, C. S., & Pfefferbaum, B. (2013). Mental health response to community disasters: A systemic review. *Journal of the American Medical Association*, 310(5), 507–18.

North, C. S., Pollio, D. E., Smith, R. P., King, R. V., Pandya, A., Suris, A. M., ..., & Pfefferbaum, B. (2011a). Trauma exposure and posttraumatic stress disorder among employees of New York City companies affected by the September 11, 2001 attacks on the World Trade Center. *Disaster Medicine and Public Health Preparedness*, 5(supp. 2), S205–13.

North, C. S., Ringwalt, C. L., Downs, D., Derzon, J., & Galvin, D. (2011b). Postdisaster course of alcohol use disorders in systematically studied survivors of 10 disasters. *Archives of General Psychiatry*, 68(2), 173–80.

Olteanu, A., Arnberger, R., Grant, R., Davis, C., Abramson, D., & Asola, J. (2011). Persistence of mental health needs among children affected by Hurricane Katrina in New Orleans. *Prehospital and Disaster Medicine*, 26(1), 3–6.

Prigerson, H. G., Horowitz, M. J., Jacobs, S. C., Parkes, C. M., Aslan, M., Goodkin, K., ..., & Maciejewski, P. K. (2009). Prolonged grief disorder: Psychometric validation of criteria proposed for DSM-V and ICD-11. *PLOS Medicine*, 6(8), DOI: 10.1371/journal.pmed.1000121.

Resick, P. A., Monson, C. M., & Chard, K. M. (2008). *Cognitive processing therapy: Veteran/military version*. Washington, DC: Department of Veterans' Affairs.

Schlenger, W. E., Caddell, J. M., Ebert, L., Jordan, B. K., Rourke, K. M., Wilson, D., ..., & Kulka, R. A. (2002). Psychological reactions to terrorist attacks: Findings from the National Study of Americans' reactions to September 11. *Journal of the American Medical Association*, 288(5), 581–8.

Shear, M. K., Frank, E., Houck, P., & Reynolds, C. F. (2005). Treatment of complicated grief: A randomized controlled trial. *Journal of the American Medical Association*, 293(21), 2601–59.

Silver, R. C., Holman, E. A., McIntosh, D. N., Poulin, M., & Gil-Rivas, V. (2002). Nationwide longitudinal study of the psychological responses to September 11. *Journal of the American Medical Association*, 288(10), 1235–44.

Solan, S., Wallenstein, S., Shapiro, M., Teitelbaum, S. L., Stevenson, L., Kochman, A., ..., & Landrigan, P. J. (2013). Cancer incidence in World Trade Center rescue and recovery workers, 2001–2008. *Environmental Health Perspectives*, 121(6), 699–704.

Welch, A. E., Caramanica, K., Maslow, C. B., Brackbill, R. M., Stellman, S. D., & Farfel, M. R. (2016). Trajectories of PTSD among lower Manhattan residents and area workers following the 2001 World Trade Center disaster, 2003–2012. *Journal of Traumatic Stress*, 29(2), 158–66.

Chapter 8

Children and Families

On June 23, 2016, in less than 24 hours, up to ten inches of torrential rain fell in West Virginia. It was another of those one-in-every-1,000-year events that is occurring with frequency. There was also a brief tornado, but the flash floods throughout the state caused the major damage. In one county alone there were 15 deaths, and the victims included adults and young children who were swept away and drowned. Thousands lost homes, property, and jobs and many residents sought safety in the many shelters set up by the American Red Cross. Some residents who stayed in their homes were isolated and without power. They could not evacuate or get to shelters as dozens of roads were shut down or swept away and bridges across the state were damaged or destroyed. As the flooding receded and roads became passable, teams of Red Cross workers were deployed to assess the damage to homes, to pass out cleaning supplies, toiletries, meals, snacks, and water, and to offer mental health support.

One team sat with a family in their home that was badly damaged. The parents reported to the DMH worker that they were more worried about their son than any of the property that was lost. Their eight-year-old was complaining about stomach aches and was not eating or sleeping as he had been before the storm. The mother said: "It takes him an hour to get to sleep. He wants the light on and he wants one of us in there with him." The DMH worker suggested that the boy be examined by their pediatrician to check for any possible medical issues. She then asked a series of questions about their experience of the disaster, including: Was any family member injured? Did they know anyone who died or was seriously injured? Could they tell her what the boy saw or heard during the storm? What did he and they lose? After about an hour of conversation the boy joined them and brought his pet turtle. He said that "Scooter" was not hurt and was not afraid of the storm, as he was a good swimmer. The DMH worker then spoke with the parents alone. She explained that these were likely expected reactions to the devastating event that had just occurred and that the child's adjustment would probably coincide with home and school getting back to normal. She encouraged the parents to allow their son to talk about his feelings and that he would learn to deal with them. She also encouraged them to explain to him that he and they were safe ("All of us, even Scooter, are okay and will be okay"). She emphasized the importance for them to reestablish routines as soon as possible. If things didn't get better over the next few weeks, she suggested they contact their pediatrician to see about getting more help for his stress.

In the next few chapters we'll talk about many specific populations and cultural groups you may work with as a disaster mental health responder, but the one group you're almost guaranteed to encounter is children and families. Children and adolescents make up 24 percent of the United States population, meaning that as of the 2010 national census count there were 74.2 million people under age 18 in the country (Annie E. Casey Foundation, 2011). Despite caregivers' best efforts to protect their children, it's impossible to shield them completely from natural disasters and other complex emergencies. Horrifically, children and adolescents are targeted for violence in schools and other settings, sometimes by their own peers. When young people experience trauma the effects can be significant and long-lasting, and can be exacerbated by the ripple effects of caregivers' distress over their inability to protect their child. It's important to understand how you can support families through their experience, and equally important to understand the limits of your responsibility and competence, including when it's time to refer them to a child trauma specialist.

CHILDREN'S TRAUMA REACTIONS

In the past some people in the field liked to claim that kids are resilient and bounce back easily from negative experiences. That can be true *if* the child has a support system that can buffer him or her from the direct impact of the disaster and provide a safe recovery environment (Sprague et al., 2014), but that's a big "if." In situations in which there was not a strong family system in place to protect children during a disaster, or that system existed but was disrupted by the event, children are particularly vulnerable in a number of ways.

First, children may be unable to recognize signs of threat or to physically escape danger, so they're more susceptible to both injury and traumatic exposure. While we talk about adults having an automatic "fight or flight" reaction to threat, young children don't have the knowledge, strength, or agility to take protective action, so they often freeze and sometimes hide rather than trying to escape from a dangerous situation (Leach, 2004).

Their smaller bodies are more vulnerable than adults' to hazards such as toxic exposure or smoke inhalation, and in the case of infectious diseases or other biological threats the appropriate medication dosage or treatment for children may be unclear (see www.cdc.gov/childrenindisasters/differences.html).

Children also depend on caregivers for physical and social-emotional safety, so, if caregivers are physically or psychologically unable to care for them, they're at great risk of suffering. They're also highly perceptive and intuitive about their caregivers' emotions and can react to caregiver stress even while they're too young to understand the situation at a cognitive level. One study of mothers and 33-month-old toddlers found that mothers assessed shortly after the attacks of 9/11 demonstrated more anxiety, poorer health, and lower child acceptance than those assessed before the attacks, and their toddlers cried more and slept less (Conway, McDonough, MacKenzie, Follett, & Sameroff, 2013). While older children and adolescents demonstrated a range of negative reactions in response to their processing of the attacks, including sleep disturbance, hyperarousal, intrusive thoughts, and poor concentration (Hoven et al., 2005), it's clear that the very young children were reacting not to the event itself but to the resulting changes in maternal stress. This underlines the need to attend to children of all ages, and to remind parents to monitor their own reactions around their children if possible. On the positive side, caregivers can serve as role models for effective coping in addition to providing children with specific coping strategies to calm their distress (Pfefferbaum, Noffsinger, Wind, & Allen, 2014).

Another difference is that children don't have the life experience to provide context for an adverse occurrence (www.cdc.gov/childrenindisasters/differences.html). Adults may be able to view a disaster as one life event among many and to recognize the post-event environmental disruption as temporary, but younger children don't have that sense of time or perspective. They may feel that the current chaos is permanent. Children also tend to have very little control over their lives post-disaster, with no say in where they will live or go to school, and little power to address caregivers' distress or functioning, so their sense of general helplessness can compound their trauma reactions (Wang, Chan, & Ho, 2013).

Importantly, the impact on children and adolescents is not limited to short-term distress: Untreated stress reactions can disrupt normal development, which can lead to prolonged social-emotional difficulties. This is another major difference from adult reactions, where we refer to people returning to their baseline functioning over time. The problem is that, for children and adolescents, any trauma-related interruption in their developmental growth schedule can cause regression as well as delays in their typical growth pattern. Functioning *shouldn't* remain level for young people, since the expectation and norm are continuous growth and the acquisition of new skills and strengths across all developmental markers. These markers would include physical, academic, and emotional development as well as building social skills, independence, and all of the other normal tasks of growing up. Even assuming that a child will eventually return to pre-disaster levels in each realm, if that upward developmental trajectory gets derailed for a significant period of time, what would be seen as recovery in an adult actually means the traumatized youth will have fallen behind peers whose development continued without disruption.

This is why early interventions with children are essential, not only to address their current suffering but to prevent it from causing lasting consequences. Those consequences can be severe, especially if the child develops Posttraumatic Stress Disorder. According to the National Center for PTSD, PTSD in childhood can cause cognitive delays and impact attention, social skills, personality, self-concept, self-esteem, and impulse control. Receiving a diagnosis of PTSD before age 18 significantly increases the risk of developing other mental health disorders, including depression, anxiety, and alcohol and drug abuse.

RISK FACTORS

While all children should be viewed as vulnerable, some are at particularly high risk for negative outcomes. Specific risk factors identified by the National Child Traumatic Stress Network (see www.nctsn.org/resources/audiences/parents-caregivers) include some that are shared by adults, including proximity to the event and the amount of destruction observed, the severity of the event including physical injury or death of a loved one, and having a history of previous traumatic experiences. A risk factor that is specific to children is the effect of their caregiver's reactions, including how much they tried to protect the child and make him or her feel safe during the disaster, and how well the caregiver is currently coping.

Other risk factors relate more to the children themselves than to their experiences. One longitudinal study (Kopala-Sibley et al., 2016) found that children with a temperamental tendency towards negative emotionality, particularly anxiety or sadness, at age three displayed higher levels of depressive and anxiety symptoms respectively, according to maternal reports, after experiencing Hurricane Sandy at age ten. This suggests that a child's temperament could be a valuable tool in recognizing what type of post-disaster symptoms might be expected and, we hope, prevented. Other risk factors for more serious reactions include female gender and previous experience of trauma (Adams et al., 2014). On the positive side, family-level protective factors that have been identified as correlating with more successful recovery from disaster include the family's ability to persevere, communicate, and problem-solve during stressful times; family members' perceptions of experiencing emotional support; and perceived access to resources during times of crisis (Kopala-Sibley et al., 2016). These findings make clear why it's so important to support families and caregivers in order to support children.

It's also worth noting that rates of PTSD and clinical depression after disasters vary widely among young people. For example, among 2,000 adolescent survivors of a tornado outbreak, about one in 13 experienced a major depressive episode and one in 15 developed PTSD, with the vast majority experiencing some mental health symptoms but not at a clinical level (Adams et al., 2014). However, like adults, child distress rates tend to be higher after larger-scale events and acts of intentional violence, especially shortly after the disaster. For example, Scheeringa and Zeanah (2008) found that a shocking 62.5 percent of preschoolers who remained in New Orleans during Hurricane Katrina met diagnostic criteria for PTSD, as did 43.5 percent of those who evacuated. Rates of PTSD, anxiety, depression, and oppositional behavior were especially high among children whose caregivers displayed symptoms of PTSD, demonstrating the recognized tendency of children to mirror caregiver distress.

To determine how these negative reactions changed over time, Osofsky, Kronenberg, Bokneck, and Hansel (2015) collected data annually for four years from families of 914 children who were aged three to five at the time of Hurricane Katrina. Among their findings were the following.

- Children's posttraumatic symptoms generally decreased over time, with higher rates of improvement occurring among those who initially demonstrated higher levels of distress. This is consistent with the typical pattern of recovery among survivors of all ages after traumatic experiences.
- Children who had more direct exposure to the disaster, more disrupted relationships with the primary caregiver, and more non-human losses (pets, toys, home, or school) typically had worse long-term outcomes than those with fewer stressors, which is consistent with the idea of a dose–response relationship between exposure and negative reactions.
- Distress was higher among children whose caregivers reported experiencing trauma before or after the hurricane, again showing how sensitive young children are to their caregivers' mental states.

While none of these findings are terribly surprising, they do underscore the need to address child suffering rather than assuming that kids are resilient and will bounce back automatically. It also provides evidence for the advice we often give to caregivers as part of post-disaster psychoeducation: They truly do need to attend to their own stressors in order to buffer their children from further negative symptomology.

HELPING CHILDREN AND FAMILIES

Children's post-disaster reactions and needs must be viewed in the context of the family system: Did parents or other family members also experience the event? If so, how are they coping with their own experience? Do they feel capable of handling the child's reactions or do they feel overwhelmed? What were pre-existing strengths and weaknesses in the family, such as socio-economic status, parental conflict or unity, or other stressors? Is a family able to remain together or do post-disaster conditions require separation or relocation? Is a caregiver withdrawing emotionally or self-medicating his or her own distress with drugs or alcohol (Miller, 2012)?

All of the PFA and other early interventions we discussed in Chapters 4 and 5 describing how you could assist adults are helpful by extension to the children of caregivers. Caregivers who are calmer and better informed will do better parenting. It's often a priority for families that the kids are taken care of. You can help caregivers to problem-solve, to access their social support systems, and to find resources for themselves and their families. Make sure they take advantage of any programs that are available and help them access respite care for their children if that is appropriate or necessary. Help parents obtain needed food, water, shelter, and sanitation. They may also have specific needs for formula, cups, and bottles for feeding small children, and for diapers. Clothes and toys are often available from charitable organizations such as the Red Cross and Salvation Army. Local faith-based groups may take up collections to help disaster survivors, and they often give priority to children's needs. Confer with local clergy to advocate for families. If you're working at a disaster, there's no better feeling than seeing the smile on a small child's face after handing him or her a new stuffed animal.

Children's treatment is best framed within the family system. In particular, short-term DMH efforts are largely focused on helping caregivers help their children, both by providing psychoeducation about how children indicate distress at different developmental stages and by giving caregivers tools to support their children and themselves. Be sure to educate parents about children's common stress reactions, which vary by developmental age and by individual child.

The National Child Traumatic Stress Network (www.nctsn.org/resources/audiences/parents-caregivers) identifies the following signs of traumatic stress by age group.

Preschool children:

- feel helpless and uncertain
- fear being separated from their parent/caregiver
- cry and/or scream a lot
- eat poorly and lose weight
- return to bedwetting
- return to using baby talk
- develop new fears
- have nightmares
- recreate the trauma through play
- are not developing to the next growth stage
- have changes in behavior
- ask questions about death.

Elementary school children:

- become anxious and fearful
- worry about their own or others' safety
- become clingy with a teacher or parent
- feel guilt or shame
- tell others about the traumatic event again and again
- become upset if they get a small bump or bruise
- have a hard time concentrating
- experience numbness
- have fears that the event will happen again
- have difficulty sleeping
- show changes in school performance
- become easily startled.

Middle and high school children and adolescents:

- feel depressed and alone
- discuss the traumatic events in detail
- develop eating disorders and self-harming behaviors such as cutting
- start using or abusing alcohol or drugs
- become sexually active
- feel as if they're going crazy
- feel different from everyone else
- take too many risks
- have sleep disturbances

- don't want to go to places that remind them of the event
- say they have no feeling about the event
- show changes in behavior.

As these lists indicate, the way a particular behavior is expressed varies by age, but some common threads you can point out to parents include the following.

- Traumatized children often regress, acting younger than their age and losing developmental achievements.
- They may be needy or clingy, and refuse to be separated from the parent.
- They may "act out," having temper tantrums, kicking, or biting at younger ages or acting rebellious and taking risks in adolescence.
- Their sleep is often disturbed. Children may be unable to fall asleep or stay asleep, or they may have bad dreams or night terrors.

These reactions are common and usually temporary, but they can be upsetting for parents as well as children. Not only do these challenging behaviors make the parent concerned about the child's well-being, but they also place added strain on already stressed caregivers. Reassuring parents that these behaviors are usually short-lived may help them be tolerant of the child's needs. Encourage them to be patient and extra attentive, and to expect some level of temporary regression.

You can also encourage parents to do the following to help their children.

Reestablish routines: Sometimes after a disaster parents will think they're being kind by relaxing rules for bedtimes, homework expectations, and other habits, but the truth is that most children thrive on routine. Chances are that their world already feels disturbingly disrupted and unpredictable after a disaster, especially if they're displaced from home, so caregivers should do everything possible to maintain regular customs, if in a somewhat altered form. If the family usually has meals together, keep doing that in an emergency shelter. If they usually read to the child before bedtime, tell them a story even if their favorite book is missing. For older children, try to uphold expectations for doing homework and meeting other responsibilities. Children may complain, but most will find maintaining routine and rituals to be comforting.

Enable a return to school as soon as possible: This is closely related to the advice about routine. Not only does extended absence from school impact academic performance, but it also deprives the child of what's perceived as a kind of second home. Additionally, teachers and other school personnel sometimes have training in recognizing signs of distress among pupils, so they can provide extra monitoring and support for children who are struggling. School also allows children to get support from their peers and to engage in normal social interactions, which can be healing.

Provide opportunities for play: It's often said that play is children's natural language. Not only do they need the opportunity for physical exercise to burn off extra energy, but they need the social connectedness with peers. Of course, this can be noisy and annoying to stressed-out adults who are struggling with their disaster-related losses, so parents should try to find a safe place where kids can cut loose without upsetting those around them. This can be challenging following events with extensive property damage, such as major hurricanes. Lai, La Greca, and Llabre (2014) found a dramatic rise in children's sedentary activities, such as watching television, after Hurricane Ike in 2008, which they attributed to a combination of children's increased posttraumatic stress symptoms, parental stress, destroyed playgrounds, and unsafe or perceived unsafe environmental conditions that inhibited children's playtime. Just as we've recognized the need to get children in disaster-impacted areas back to school as quickly as possible to support their cognitive and social development, we also need to facilitate active play as a key factor in physical health and stress reduction.

Monitor the nature of that play: Children also often use play to process an unfamiliar experience, so parents shouldn't be surprised to see kids inventing disaster-themed games. This is usually a healthy way of mastering the experience, but if the play is extremely rigid and repetitive it may be a sign the child needs additional mental health support.

Control the information children are exposed to: After a disaster the adults are usually hungry for information about what happened, why, who is responsible, when they can go home again, and so on. This is completely understandable, but it often leads to a television or radio being left on constantly in the background, potentially overexposing children to material they don't really need to hear or see. Think back to the days after 9/11, when news coverage showed the plane hitting the second tower on what seemed like a constant loop. There was evidence that some children believed a new crash was happening each time. Even if children are too young to understand the facts of the coverage they may still pick up on the emotional tone of the reporters, as well as reacting to the way their parents are processing the news. For everyone's sake, parents should try to limit the media coverage children are exposed to (and to limit their own consumption along the way), and to be cautious about conversations children may overhear that could cause them further anxiety.

Provide as much reassurance and safety as possible: After any disaster there's an atmosphere of anxiety and fear, and this is truer after an act of violence such as the Boston Marathon bombing or a school shooting. Children can be afraid that they'll be the next victims or that a terrorist is hiding under their bed. Parents may have similar fears and know that they can't perfectly protect their children and themselves. However, parents should still be encouraged to provide realistic reassurance. Remind them that, although the worry is understandable, the chances that their child will be killed in a terror attack is one in 20 million, much less likely than being killed by lightning, and less likely than being killed by their own furniture. Parents can reassure children "The bad man who hurt others has been captured," or "We are safe here in our home," or "We will protect you and we'll find the bad people who did bad things." The return to routine and limiting media exposure helps to reinforce this reassurance.

Answer children's questions honestly: Parents will often ask how much they should tell their children about what happened. There's no single answer, as it depends on the event characteristics (for example, whether it was a natural disaster or a terrorist attack), the child's age and maturity, the parent's comfort level, and myriad other factors. Reassure the parents that they know their child better than anyone and can generally trust their instincts about how much to explain, but it's usually best to keep answers brief and direct and not to volunteer any additional details. If children want to know more, they'll ask again, but most will do best by absorbing information incrementally as they feel ready to learn more. Children should not be exposed to frightening or gruesome sights or sounds or stories, but at the same time it's also essential not to lie or to mislead a child, especially about a loved one's death, or to use ambiguous language that can cause confusion. Children need to trust their caregivers and feel safe and protected. Being clear, honest, and truthful while conveying information in the simplest language creates an atmosphere of trust and safety. Any distortion of the facts can lead to a sense of betrayal when the truth ultimately comes out. Clarity will limit the ambiguity that would allow children to fill in the details with the narrative they want to believe. An unclear message (for example, "Daddy's gone to be with the angels") can cause a child to hold out hope of a return, delaying the inevitable start of the mourning process. However, imparting too much information or too much truth prematurely has the potential to be detrimental. Generally, children will ask questions when they're ready to hear the answers. A child's inquisitiveness can be the most useful guide in determining how much information to provide and when to provide it.

Recognize that children will pick up on caregivers' emotional states, so they should get help for their own practical and psychological needs: This is the classic analogy to putting on your own oxygen mask on an airplane before assisting others. Parents may try to put their own mental health needs secondary to their children's, but this will have consequences for everyone. Some parents will be more willing to acknowledge their own needs if you point out that they can't take care of their family if they're not taking care of themselves. Children are extremely intuitive. They know when their parent's ability to care for them is compromised. Children will often try to care for their parents, believing that their needs can be met only if their parents are okay. This can lead to children masking their feelings and needs in order to protect their distressed parents. Helping parents understand this dynamic can help them make healthy choices regarding their own self-care.

Help parents to work together: The stress of disaster can shake a good partnership and challenge co-parenting as caregivers often have different views about what is best for the child. One parent might suggest that, for efficient cleanup and organization, their children spend a weekend or a week away with relatives, while the other parent finds this shocking and unacceptable. Other couples might be in more direct conflict. You can speak with couples, reminding them how much stress they're under and how important it is for them to compromise and be tolerant of their differences. For their children's sake, specific solutions are less important than their ability to be on the same page. Remind them that, for all concerned, they have to be a team. Ask how you can help them to keep their teamwork successful. You can model respect as you listen carefully to caregivers' views of what is best for the child. Remember that, no matter how helpful you, the school, and other professionals are, children's parents are the most important people in their lives.

TALKING WITH CHILDREN

If caregivers are present it is usually best to ask permission to speak with their child. Sit down next to them or crouch so you're at their physical level. If it's appropriate in the culture, it's okay to hold the child's hand or even put your arm around him or her, but if the child or caregivers show any discomfort you should cease the physical contact. If you hug a child be sure that it's acceptable to the child, the family, and the culture. If you're a stranger, frightened children are sometime more comfortable talking with you through a stuffed animal or toy (for example, asking "Can you tell 'Teddy' what you would like for a snack?"). Whether or not you're speaking through the toy or directly to the child, always speak slowly and calmly, listen, and be patient. You can certainly offer hope while also being truthful and realistic. To say everything will be just as before is not true. However, it would be reassuring to say something along the lines of "I know a girl just about your age who went through a very similar experience, and she was very frightened just like you are now. She was afraid for a while, but now she's just fine" (Save the Children, 2013).

MAKING REFERRALS

In many cases strengthening caregivers' understanding and self-efficacy will be sufficient to enable them to help their children, but some traumatized children and adolescents will need professional help. For those children who are demonstrating more serious distress or whose characteristics or experience suggest they're at risk for PTSD or another serious reaction some time after the disaster, your appropriate action will be to make a referral to a mental health professional with expertise in treating child trauma. One therapeutic approach that's specifically designed to treat children within a family context is Trauma-Focused Cognitive Behavioral Therapy (TF-CBT), a well-established protocol for supporting children with PTSD, depression, behavior problems, or other difficulties related to traumatic life experiences. It provides psychoeducation for children and caregivers, teaches parenting skills and relaxation techniques, and enables the child to safely confront the traumatic memory in order to master it (National Child Traumatic Stress Network, 2004). Sessions are held with the child, the caregivers, and conjointly. Randomized clinical trials have found TF-CBT to be effective in reducing symptoms of PTSD, depression, anxiety, externalizing behaviors, and feelings of shame in traumatized children (Seidler & Wagner, 2006), and in improving parenting skills and parent–child communication (Cohen, Mannarino, & Knudsen, 2005).

Beyond TF-CBT, therapists often draw on other creative evidence-supported interventions to assist traumatized children. Young children really can't communicate their feelings using language, so child therapists have developed other ways to let them express themselves, such as play therapy using dolls and puppets to act out experiences and feelings, and art therapy that uses drawing, painting, or modeling clay to allow children to depict their emotions. Older children and adolescents are very sensitive to peer perceptions, and their disaster experience may make them feel isolated or different, so they may benefit from group therapy, which allows them to connect with others who have been through a similar experience. All of these interventions must be conducted by trained and qualified professionals in order to benefit child and adolescent disaster survivors (Jordan, Perryman, & Anderson, 2013); the consequences of inappropriate interventions with this most vulnerable group are far too serious to risk trusting them to well-intentioned but unqualified helpers.

In Chapter 11 we'll review the occupational hazards of DMH work and how to best care for yourself while caring for others. Keep in mind that working with traumatized children, while very rewarding, is an established risk factor for helpers. If you spend time assisting suffering children be sure to be especially thoughtful about your own self-care.

REFERENCES

Adams, Z. W., Sumner, J. A., Danielson, C. K., McCauley, J. L., Resnick, H. S., Grös, K., ..., & Ruggiero, K. J. (2014). Prevalence and predictors of PTSD and depression among adolescent victims of the spring 2011 tornado outbreak. *Journal of Child Psychology and Psychiatry*, 55(9), 1047–55.

Annie E. Casey Foundation (2011, January 1). The changing child population of the United States: Analysis of data from the 2010 census. Annie E. Casey Foundation, www.aecf.org/resources/the-changing-child-population-of-the-united-states.

Cohen, J. A., Mannarino, A. P., & Knudsen, K. (2005). Treating sexually abused children: 1 year follow-up of a randomized controlled trial. *Child Abuse and Neglect*, 29(2), 135–45.

Conway, A., McDonough, S. C., MacKenzie, M. J., Follett, C., & Sameroff, A. (2013). Stress-related changes in toddlers and their mothers following the attack of September 11. *American Journal of Orthopsychiatry*, 83(4), 536–44.

Hoven, C. W., Duarte, C. S., Lucas, C. P., Wu, P., Mandell, D. J., Goodwin, R. D., ..., & Susser, E. (2005). Psychopathology among New York City public school children 6 months after September 11th. *Archives of General Psychiatry*, 62(5), 545–52.

Jordan, B. K., Perryman, K., & Anderson, L. (2013). A case for child-centered play therapy with natural disaster and catastrophic event survivors. *International Journal of Play Therapy*, 22(4), 219–30.

Kopala-Sibley, D. C., Danzig, A. P., Kotov, R., Bromet, E. J., Carlson, G.A., Olino, T. M., ..., & Klein, D. N. (2016). Negative emotionality and its facets moderate the effects of exposure to Hurricane Sandy on children's postdisaster depression and anxiety symptoms. *Journal of Abnormal Psychology*, 125(4), 471–81.

Lai, B. S., La Greca, A. M., & Llabre, M. M. (2014). Children's sedentary activity after hurricane exposure. *Psychological Trauma: Theory, Research, Practice, and Policy*, 6(3), 280–9.

Leach, J. (2004). Why people "freeze" in an emergency: Temporal and cognitive constraints on survival responses. *Aviation, Space, and Environmental Medicine*, 75(6), 539–42.

Miller, J. L. (2012). *Psychosocial capacity building in response to disasters*. New York: Columbia University Press.

National Child Traumatic Stress Network (2004). *How to implement Trauma-Focused Cognitive Behavioral Therapy (TF-CBT)*. Los Angeles: National Center for Child Traumatic Stress, www.nctsnet.org/nctsn_assets/pdfs/TF-CBT_Implementation_Manual.pdf.

Osofsky, J. D., Kronenberg, M., Bocknek, E., & Hansel, T. C. (2015). Longitudinal impact of attachment-related risk and exposure to trauma among young children after Hurricane Katrina. *Child Youth Care Forum*, 44(4), 493–510.

Pfefferbaum, B., Noffsinger, M. A., Wind, L. H., & Allen, J. R. (2014). Children's coping in the context of disasters and terrorism. *Journal of Loss and Trauma*, 19(1), 78–97.

Save the Children (2013). *Save the Children: Psychological first aid training manual for child practitioners*. Copenhagen: Save the Children.

Scheeringa, M. S., & Zeanah, C. H. (2008). Reconsideration of harm's way: Onsets and comorbidity patterns of disorders in preschool children and their caregivers following Hurricane Katrina. *Journal of Clinical Child and Adolescent Psychology*, 37(3), 508–18.

Seidler, G. H., & Wagner, F. E. (2006). Comparing the efficacy of EMDR and trauma-focused cognitive-behavioral therapy in the treatment of PTSD: A meta-analytic study. *Psychological Medicine*, 36(11), 1515–22.

Sprague, C. M., Kia-Keating, M., Felix, E., Afifi, T., Reyes, G., & Afifi, W. (2014). Youth psychosocial adjustment following wildfire: The role of family resilience, emotional support, and concrete support. *Child Youth Care Forum*, 44(3), 433–50.

Wang, C., Chan, C. L. W., & Ho, R. T. H. (2013). Prevalence and trajectory of psychopathology among child and adolescent survivors of disasters: A systematic review of epidemiological studies across 1987–2011. *Social Psychiatry and Psychiatric Epidemiology*, 48(11), 1697–720.

Chapter 9

Vulnerable Populations

In June 2012 intense heat covered the West Coast and began moving east. On June 25, Denver, Colorado, recorded an all-time record of 105 degrees and several counties in Kansas hit 113. It has long been known that heatwaves kill more people than other weather-related disasters, but, unlike hurricanes or wildfires, a heatwave's impact is usually not realized until much later. A Disaster Mental Health counselor met with Emma in her small apartment shortly after she was released from a hospital in the Midwest following treatment for dehydration. Emma was 85 years old and had been living alone for about 15 years since her husband died. She'd hoped that her adult children would look in on her regularly but they had busy lives and visited her less than she hoped. The grandchildren had many after-school activities and her children were busy shuffling them off to Little League and Girl Scouts. The older grandchildren were excited about their driving lessons. Emma had Parkinson's disease and was taking medication for that in addition to other medications, which contributed to her dehydration. During the heatwave, she explained, her air conditioner was not working properly and she had begun to feel weak. She thought she would be okay and did not want to trouble her grown children, but she had fainted, and a neighbor who heard her fall called an ambulance. Emma was recovering after several days in the hospital and explained that she was beginning to get her strength back. She looked uncomfortable, and through a weak smile said that, after all she had been through in life, it was strange to meet with a counselor. "Why weren't you around earlier to help me with my pain-in-the-ass sister?" she asked. The counselor explained that she was not there to diagnose her or make any changes but just to check in with her, as she had been under a lot of stress. Emma said that, a few days before she was hospitalized, she had felt dry in the mouth, sleepy, and confused, but she had felt that way many times and did not think she was dehydrated. Perhaps she was unable or unwilling to see herself as ill because she didn't want to worry her children and they didn't think it necessary to look in on her. After the development of rapport, the counselor suggested a family meeting with her two daughters and son. At the meeting, the eldest daughter noted that, when there were storms or dangers she could see, she always checked on her mom. She had had no idea the air-conditioning wasn't working properly. Solutions such as assisted living and skilled nursing home care were rejected, as Emma, like most elderly people, desperately wanted to remain in her own home. After some time, conversation, and problem-solving, the family agreed that the best solution was for Emma to stay at home with better planning around her safety. The adult children agreed to more regularly scheduled visits and phone calls. They also agreed to pay a younger, trusted neighbor to look in on Emma, shop when necessary, and make sure she was taking all of her medications. The counselor helped the family access information regarding Emma's eligibility for additional home-based services for meals and encouraged them to set up visits from her church congregants. Emma said she would try to be more responsible about reporting any discomfort or confusion. At the end of the meeting she joked: "Age doesn't make you forgetful. It's having too many stupid things to remember that makes you forgetful."

As this case study demonstrates, some people are more susceptible to negative consequences from an event to which others might be resilient and experience little lasting distress. That doesn't necessarily mean that they develop a clinically diagnosable condition, but they can still experience ongoing symptoms that cause long-term suffering. One of our goals as disaster mental health helpers should be to recognize and support these at-risk people in order to address any lingering negative effects, as well as preventing more serious psychological conditions.

What influences an individual's post-disaster reaction? We've mentioned the "dose–response" relationship and the impact of proximity to the event as strong predictors of post-disaster distress. It's also clear that certain groups of survivors merit additional attention because they may have more intense needs before, during, and after disaster. For example, members of certain populations may need more assistance evacuating due to mobility issues or special equipment requirements. They may have difficulty residing in a shelter because of physical or psychological limitations. They may have lost necessary assistive devices (glasses or hearing aids, crutches, oxygen tank) during the disaster, or lost the caregiver they relied on for support. Because members of these groups typically require extensive resources throughout the disaster cycle, they can slip between the cracks of response agencies that are already stretched thin.

In this chapter we'll discuss some of the main groups that are recognized as vulnerable populations in times of disaster, but please bear three points in mind as you read this chapter. First, this brief overview will familiarize you with some essential points about these groups' needs, but each population really merits an entire textbook of its own. We encourage you to think about the populations in your area that you're likely to work with, and to seek out further training—preferably including working collaboratively with members of these populations, as they're the experts on their own needs.

Second, be aware that an individual can be a member of more than one of these groups and therefore be subject to a combination of interrelated risk factors. On the other hand, membership in one or more vulnerable population captures only some facets of a person's identity; it doesn't define that individual. Knowing that a particular disaster survivor is a gay, undocumented immigrant with a disability provides insight into some of the recovery challenges he might face, but it's equally important to recognize that he has a loving family, a devoted partner, and good health insurance.

And, third, please remember that these populations are viewed as vulnerable not because of any intrinsic weakness or lack of autonomy, but because of certain characteristics that tend to exacerbate their suffering throughout the event.

It's likely that members of these groups will have had a more difficult experience of the event itself—a higher dose—which is itself a risk factor, *and* they may have fewer recovery resources than the general population, another risk factor. In combination with the sometimes compromised strength of their support systems, this can aggravate their reactions afterwards. However, if their practical needs are met, they face the same potential for a full recovery as members of the general population. And, while it's important to be aware of any additional challenges faced by members of these groups, it's also essential to respect their strengths and abilities, and to take a "person-first" approach to your interactions. This means viewing them as, for example, a person with a disability or a person who is older, so that the vulnerability is a characteristic but does not primarily define the individual.

FRAIL OLDER ADULTS

Older adults are a group whose needs have often been overlooked in disaster planning, but whose size is growing rapidly both in the United States and globally. According to the World Health Organization (WHO), between 2006 and 2050 the number of people age 60 and older will double to 2 billion, a rise from 11 percent of the world's population to 22 percent. By 2045, adults 60 years and older will outnumber children under age 15, and the "oldest old," those age 80 and above, are the fastest-growing group. This is good news, as it reflects the fact that people are surviving diseases and other conditions that would have been fatal in previous generations, but it does create a response challenge for disaster professionals.

Of course, older adults aren't a monolithic group with the same needs and resources, and there are different ways of assessing them. Most simply, we can categorize them by age, which can be useful because it relates to cohort effects that can shape people's values. For example, people who grew up during the Depression versus the Baby Boom typically have very different attitudes towards money and towards accepting assistance and mental health care. However, in terms of disaster reactions, it's more useful to think in terms of functional categories.

While healthy older adults' needs may be no different from those of younger adults, frail elderly people who are already coping with limitations in one or more functional realms that impact their activities of daily living may be more susceptible to a cascade of negative effects from disasters. They may have mobility problems that impair their ability to take protective action or to cope with conditions in a shelter. Pre-existing medical conditions may be exacerbated, especially if access to medications or assistive devices is disrupted. Even mild cognitive limitations are likely to worsen under stressful or chaotic post-disaster conditions such as emergency shelters, so older adults are often particularly resistant to evacuation, especially if it means separation from a beloved pet.

Specific risk factors that contribute to vulnerability in older adults include the following. As you'll see, these common areas of functional limitations tend to intersect with the physical and logistical demands produced by disasters, increasing this population's risk of harm and complicating their recovery.

Physical Factors

Decreased physical mobility and agility: Many older adults experience a progressive loss of bone density and muscle mass, impeding their balance and increasing their risk of injury from falls and other events and preventing them from moving quickly to evade danger. It can also make physical conditions in a shelter, such as sleeping on a cot or standing in line for food, exhausting or painful.

Sensory limitations: Aging often involves decreased acuity of vision, hearing, smell, and touch, which may reduce perceptions of danger and prevent the person from receiving a warning. Related assistive devices such as glasses and hearing aids may be lost in a disaster, limiting communications and increasing dependence on others.

Chronic medical conditions: Many older adults develop one or more (and sometimes multiple) health problems that require treatment and monitoring, such as arthritis, hypertension, heart disease, type 2 diabetes, and respiratory disorders. These can be intensified by post-disaster conditions, especially if access to needed medications or treatments is disrupted.

Cognitive decline: This may include age-related dementias, such as Alzheimer's disease, or a simple slowing of one's thought process and decision-making abilities. While under normal conditions this general decline in acuity can be seen as being offset by a deeper wisdom gained from a lifetime of experience, it does risk leaving the older adult less equipped to make rapid decisions in a fast-moving disaster situation or less able to adapt to unfamiliar conditions in a shelter or other new environment.

Psychosocial Factors

Depression: This is not uncommon in older adults, especially those with chronic health conditions, but it's often overlooked or minimized as a normal part of aging. Depression is also associated with suicide among older adults, who have the highest suicide rates of any age group, especially among men (American Psychological Association, 2009).

Grief: As we've discussed, grief is a natural response to the multiple losses that can occur in disasters, including loss of family members and members of the community, and of cherished possessions. Older adults can be particularly sensitive to the loss of a beloved pet, which may have been their main source of companionship. They also may mourn the loss of independence if a disaster permanently displaces them from home. Perhaps the most significant factor to be aware of regarding older people's grief is that, when they do experience losses, they may have a foreshortened sense of future, a belief that they won't live long enough to create the "new normal" that younger adults hold out hope for. Middle-aged adults typically learn to live with loss, while older adults really might not have the time to recover and can lose hope—a significant risk factor for prolonged suffering.

Self-esteem: American culture tends not to value our older generations, too often infantilizing them or disrespecting their accomplishments and strengths. As a result, many older adults describe feeling like a burden on others. These experiences of marginalization and stigmatization can lead older adults to downplay their own needs and redirect resources to others.

Anxiety: Some older adults are able to function adequately when they're in a familiar and predictable environment, but they struggle to adapt to new settings. As a result they may become very anxious when faced with the possibility of evacuating and may resist leaving home—even if that means possibly dying. They also can experience ongoing anxiety related to the disruption to routine and prolonged uncertainty involved in coping with displacement or other changes.

Socioeconomic Factors

Poverty: As more older adults survive long beyond the traditional retirement age, many live on limited fixed incomes or have to rely on family members or government assistance for financial support. This means they may have little expendable income for disaster supplies or to fund an evacuation, or to repair damage after a disaster.

Vulnerability to elder abuse: Sadly, older adults are often the targets of abuse, including physical maltreatment and financial exploitation. These crimes can be committed by family members, paid caregivers, or con artists who pursue what are often seen as easy targets; this includes scammers who pose as contractors offering to fix up a house after a disaster, but who disappear with a deposit before doing any work.

Helping Frail Older Adults

First, it's absolutely key to recognize the assets older adults bring to any experience, not just their vulnerabilities. Many older adults exemplify strength, resilience, and inspiration. They can be a vital source of knowledge, experience, skills, and wisdom in all phases of emergency and disaster response (Deeny, Vitale, Spelman, & Duggan, 2010). Many have lived through various tragedies on a personal scale as well as disasters on a larger scale, so they may have direct experience with the types of situations that younger adults can feel unprepared to address. This is, essentially, the opposite of children's lack of perspective about disasters, discussed in the last chapter. People who reach an advanced age generally have plenty of experience with loss and change, so they may have a breadth and depth of coping resources that they can use to help themselves and others.

In addition to recognizing older people's strengths and resilience, other ways to help this group include the following.

- See to practical and physical needs first, including restoring access to medications and assistive devices.
- Reestablish a sense of routine as quickly as possible.
- Adapt shelter or other post-disaster setting conditions to accommodate older adults' needs as much as possible. For example, you could help set up a (relatively) quiet corner for their cots, or organize volunteers to bring them meals so they don't have to stand in line.
- Connect them with a positive support network of family members, peers, or whoever is likely to treat them with respect.
- Involve them in assisting others if possible.

- Do outreach to find people in need, including (if appropriate) going door to door to find residents who didn't evacuate.
- Probe gently for signs of distress, while accepting that many older adults may be reluctant to seek mental health services. They may see such services as not helpful for them, or perceive the need for external help as signifying a personal or spiritual failure.

As you see from this list, the most important interventions for helping older adults are practical in nature rather than psychological, and almost all are directed at restoring stability as quickly as possible. If that can be accomplished, many of their emotional reactions are likely to resolve on their own, or with the same basic support we know to provide to all survivors. Depending on their pre-existing level of health and general functioning, and the degree of support they are receiving, older adults may be no more or less susceptible to extreme negative reactions to stress than the general public, and their emotional resilience should not be underestimated.

PEOPLE WITH PHYSICAL DISABILITIES

In many ways, the needs of our next vulnerable group, people with physical disabilities, overlap with those of older adults, particularly in terms of mobility and sensory impairments (plus, many people with disabilities are also older, and vice versa). This is another enormous and growing population: According to the World Health Organization (2011), about 15 percent of the world's population—more than a billion people—have some form of disability, and for between 110 million and 190 million people that causes significant difficulties in functioning. Like being elderly and frail, in many cases these disabilities can increase the risk of exposure to disaster, and they create additional challenges in the recovery process.

In considering this group's needs, remember that the impact of a specific disability results from the interaction between an individual's impairment and his or her environment, including physical barriers and availability of services and assistive technologies. The same condition may be completely manageable in one setting or with access to certain aids, but highly debilitating in another. How many of us would instantly become disabled if we merely lost our eyeglasses in a disaster? As this example suggests, the primary goal in assisting people with physical disabilities is to restore needed services or equipment, or to remove barriers that worsen mobility or sensory impairments.

Physical disabilities can be broadly categorized by the type of functional impairment they cause, or by their timing: chronic (long-term or permanent), acute (currently present but perhaps temporary), or intermittent (sometimes present, sometimes not). While those with chronic disabilities might be expected to face the biggest difficulties, they may actually have adapted effectively to their conditions and be better able to function than someone with a more acute disability. For example, someone who has used crutches all his or her life may be able to get out of harm's way more quickly than someone with a broken ankle who has not mastered moving on crutches. However, the person with the chronic disability might be more dependent for daily living on a support system that is disrupted by a disaster, so chronic conditions are certainly not to be minimized.

Mobility impairments may limit a person's ability to walk or run, drive, stand or sit, feed him- or herself, or otherwise perform typical activities of daily life. They may be caused by spinal injury, an injured limb or muscle, a condition such as arthritis that causes severe pain, a congenital condition such as cerebral palsy, or myriad other problems. Many people with mobility impairments rely on assistive devices such as wheelchairs, walkers, canes, or crutches, which may be lost or broken during a disaster, and those whose impairment causes pain may be dependent on prescription painkillers to improve functioning.

While people with mobility impairments may be able to receive warnings aimed at the general public, it can be difficult for them to take protective action before or during a disaster. For example, they may need transportation assistance to evacuate from an area that a storm or flood is approaching. They may take additional time to reach a safe spot to shelter in place during a tornado or earthquake. They may be stranded in tall buildings if electrical power for elevators is lost and they're unable to walk down stairs or use a fire escape. All of these limits to mobility increase the risk of additional injuries and distress.

Mobility impairments also may make post-disaster sheltering and recovering difficult: Is a shelter accessible to someone who uses a wheelchair or who can't climb stairs? Does the person rely on medical equipment that's been lost or damaged, or that requires electrical power that's not functioning? Does he or she need assistance with personal care, such as bathing or toileting? Does pain or limited range of motion make sleeping on a cot impossible? Does the loss of needed medications increase pain or other symptoms, or cause withdrawal symptoms?

Post-disaster environmental conditions also may exacerbate mobility issues. For example, extensive debris on the ground, as is typically seen after earthquakes and major storms, makes neighborhoods impassable to people using wheelchairs and creates great challenges for those who walk with difficulty. This may prevent people from being able to return home or limit access to temporary housing, and it may prevent them from reaching work, essentially worsening the functional impairment and increasing dependence on others for aid.

Sensory impairments primarily affect vision and hearing. They may reduce a person's capacity to receive a warning, or to react to it. For example, a warning in the form of a siren or radio bulletin will be of little use to a person who is deaf, while televised weather reports that rely on text captions or maps to show threatened areas will be inaccessible to people who are blind. As a result, people with sensory impairments may be reliant on family members or neighbors to alert them about disaster warnings, and to assist them with evacuating or taking other protective actions.

Like mobility impairments, vision and hearing limitations can make life in shelters difficult, and people with sensory disabilities may require additional help, such as a sign language interpreter or a scribe, to navigate an unfamiliar setting, understand briefings and announcements, complete paperwork, etc. If people with visual impairments are able to return home they may need help cleaning up and returning the home to a navigable state in order to restore their independence.

Illness is not necessarily categorized as a physical disability, but it clearly can create related difficulties during and after disasters. If someone is sick—either from a chronic condition such as cancer or an acute one such as flu—do they have the energy or strength to take protective action? Does a disaster prevent essential treatments, such as chemotherapy or dialysis, or access to needed medications, such as insulin? If a person has a contagious condition such as flu or cholera, how can he or she be sheltered without exposing others? Even if a condition is not communicable, there is often stigma around visible illness, with irrational but very real fears about contagion or contamination that may make other survivors hostile towards the ill person.

Environmental conditions post-disaster can also intensify many illnesses. Dust from collapsed buildings and smoke from wildfires, burned buildings, or the intentional burning of debris during cleanup can cause respiratory problems, as can the mold growth in homes that often follows floods. Of course, these conditions can make previously healthy people sick as well, but they may present a particular threat to those with pre-existing illnesses—who also may be less able to participate in cleaning up their homes to get rid of the source.

Like older adults, people with physical disabilities are a far from a homogeneous group, yet they're often treated that way in disaster planning and response, leading to inappropriate communications or services that fail to help large segments of those in need (National Council on Disability, 2009). Their vulnerability is compounded by the fact that people with serious disabilities often have limited employment options and may be living at the lower end of the economic spectrum of their community. This means they may lack the discretionary funds to pay for transportation or to stockpile food, water, and other supplies, and they may live in less sturdy housing that can't withstand extreme weather conditions. The National Council on Disability also points out that members of these populations may face so many challenges with activities of daily living that disaster preparedness is likely to be a low priority, leaving them unready for catastrophic events.

Helping People with Physical Disabilities

Virtually all of the advice given above for assisting older adults also applies to this group, including the essential need to respect their strengths and autonomy. There are a few other specific suggestions for helping people with physical disabilities.

- Prioritize replacing needed assistive devices, such as crutches or hearing aids. This may essentially cancel out the disability, restoring the person's ability to function independently.
- Try to restore or replace needed caregiving services, such as an aide for personal hygiene or a sign language interpreter, but be aware that this may be challenging, as there's rarely an adequate supply of these services under normal conditions, let alone after a disaster.
- Research what local services and organizations are available to assist the person with his or her disability-related needs. There's no need to reinvent the wheel if local resources and expertise are available.

Again, the disaster-related needs that differentiate people with physical disabilities from the general population are primarily logistical rather than emotional, so addressing those needs as quickly as possible is the best way to foster their recovery. With this population it is especially important to "work the Maslow hierarchy," along with the other elements of PFA and other supportive interventions.

PEOPLE WITH MENTAL DISABILITIES

The term "mental disability" comprises a wide range of different diagnoses, and within each diagnosis individuals may experience symptoms on a spectrum of severity. This spectrum is due in part to natural variations in the disease process, and in part to the effectiveness and availability of treatment. Like physical disabilities, psychiatric disabilities are widely prevalent. About one in five American adults has experienced some type of mental illness, primarily anxiety disorders and major depression (see www.nami. org/Learn-More/Mental-Health-By-the-Numbers). Here again, remember the emphasis on context: If a pre-existing condition does not impair a person's ability to function in his or her environment, it shouldn't be viewed as a disability in that context. However, a condition that was well controlled before a disaster may become a disability after it if treatment is unavailable or the distress of the event causes a spike in symptoms.

The broad term "mental disability" comprises a number of types of conditions.

Intellectual disabilities involve a condition of arrested or incomplete development of the mind that can limit cognitive, language, motor, and/or social abilities. These disabilities can be caused by genetic conditions, such as Down syndrome, by problems during pregnancy or birth, by severe malnutrition or certain illnesses in childhood that impact brain development, or by childhood exposure to environmental toxins such as lead.

The severity of intellectual disabilities can vary widely, and can impede an individual in areas such as social skills and the ability to care for oneself, communicate, and learn. Because their effects typically begin early in life, children with intellectual disabilities may experience delays in typical development of skills, and they may require additional time and support to learn to speak, walk, read, and achieve other developmental milestones. Depending on the severity and the available support, they may eventually catch up to peers, or they may remain dependent on caregivers for assistance with some or all activities of daily living into adulthood. If that support is not available due to the disaster, people with intellectual disabilities may be particularly vulnerable to negative psychosocial reactions.

While intellectual disabilities begin early in life and delay or prevent the development of important skills, other **cognitive disorders** usually occur later in life and cause a sudden or progressive loss of skills. Traumatic brain injuries (TBIs) can occur at any age. Their effects can be transient or permanent depending on the extent and type of injury. The losses due to Alzheimer's disease and other types of dementia tend to progress gradually and do not begin until later in life, when a person's responsibilities may be less taxing. There is no cure or effective way to slow these diseases, though the use of certain psychotropic medications such as antidepressants or anti-anxiety drugs can help reduce some symptoms.

With both TBIs and dementias a family must adapt to the changing role of the person with the condition, so there is emotional distress as well as the practical need to provide care. This can create a significant economic burden as well, due to the likely loss or reduction of income (of the person with the condition, and/or of another family member who stops work to become a caregiver) or the need to pay for care. As with people with intellectual disabilities, those with serious cognitive disabilities are at risk if needed support systems are disrupted by disaster.

While there are dozens of diagnoses that could be included in the category of **psychiatric disabilities**, those that are most likely to affect people's functioning during and after disasters include depression, PTSD, schizophrenia, and anxiety disorders. People with any of these conditions may benefit from taking appropriate medications, so you should be sure to inquire whether they have been taking medications and, if so, if they currently have access to them. This is yet another example of the potential impact of context: A condition that was well controlled before a disaster may become a disability after it if treatment is unavailable or the distress of the event causes a spike in symptoms.

Like members of the general population, a major predictor of post-disaster functioning for people with mental disabilities is their pre-disaster functioning: Those who were able to cope with life successfully before the disaster typically will continue to do so after the disaster. However, the nature of serious mental disorders means that sufferers may not have been coping particularly well previously, so they may have had a worse experience during the disaster as well as facing additional barriers to recovery. These include the following challenges.

Functional deficits in life skills: People with cognitive or intellectual disabilities and those with severe symptoms, such as psychosis, may have a difficult time meeting the demands of daily life. Predictability leads to a sense of controllability, so some people with these conditions may be able to live independently under calm conditions when their coping skills aren't challenged by unexpected changes, but they may lose that capacity when conditions are disrupted by disasters. Others may live with family members, or in institutional settings such as hospitals or group homes, so their functioning is tied to whether that support system remains intact.

Need for continuity of care: Related to the point about disrupted support networks, people with mental disabilities may depend on a variety of services, such as visits from a social worker or aide, regular sessions with a counsellor or psychiatrist, and/or medication, to keep symptoms in check. Disruption of these services results in a loss of continuity of care, which can worsen already fragile mental and emotional states, intensifying post-trauma reactions.

Socioeconomic status: Unfortunately, some people with mental disabilities live on the margins of society, especially if the condition limited their education or impedes their ability to work. As a result, they may live in housing that increases their exposure to disasters, and they may have few financial resources to recover from losses.

Isolation from family and friends: While many people with mental disabilities receive care and support from friends and families, others may have little contact with them—either by their own choice or because their past actions have alienated those around them. This deprives them of both the instrumental and emotional support we know are key factors in positive adjustment to trauma.

Previous history of trauma: People with mental disabilities often experience more interpersonal trauma than the general population. They're often the targets of abuse by caregivers or predators, and their symptoms may lead to homelessness or other marginalized lifestyles, exposing them to crime and violence. This cumulative experience may make recovering from a new traumatic experience such as a disaster more difficult, especially if previous negative experiences with authorities make them resistant to seeking help.

Stigma: If a mentally ill person's behaviors are alarming or offputting to loved ones, they can be even more troubling to community members, who may fear or shun them. This is especially problematic if a psychologically unstable individual is housed with the general population in a shelter: Even though very few mentally ill people ever commit acts of violence, when those events do occur they tend to receive extensive media coverage, so members of the public often have a vastly inflated perception of the risk of exposure to this group (www.nami.org/Learn-More/Mental-Health-By-the-Numbers). As a result, people with mental disorders may be the target of hostility, or have needed services such as sheltering denied.

As a result of this combination of potential issues, people with mental disabilities may have difficulty adjusting to new situations, and their symptoms may be triggered by unplanned environmental changes. They may experience greater distress or confusion than others during a disaster or in a shelter. They also may have few of the self-advocacy or organizational skills that would be useful in identifying resources and making contact with agencies that could help them. The availability of medication is another critical issue, as disruption of regular medication schedules can result in a return of previously managed symptoms, or in unpleasant withdrawal symptoms.

Helping People with Mental Disabilities

The following are primary ways you can assist this population after a disaster. Of course, what is needed from you will vary greatly depending on the situation and the nature of the person's disability, so flexibility is essential.

Address the person, not the diagnosis: Even for those with some training and experience working with people with mental disorders, it can be easy to let the diagnostic label overshadow the individual as a person. It's important to allow people to tell their own stories and to be validated for their experiences, and not to assume that a pre-existing disability makes their disaster experience any less personally significant.

Communicate clearly: Certain mental disabilities can cause symptoms and behaviors that impair a person's ability to interact or connect with others, especially if he or she is particularly agitated or upset, as is likely post-disaster. You may need to slow down your speech and pause to make sure you're being understood. Avoid complex statements or multiple commands; ask or state one thing at a time, so you don't confuse the person further. If people are delusional, don't argue with them or try to talk them out of their belief. Just let them know you are there to help them. And don't talk down or patronize but treat the person with genuineness and respect, using a calm demeanor.

Restore access to medication: Sudden withdrawal from many psychotropic medications can cause symptoms of the disorder to return, such as psychosis or depression, as well as potentially causing physically and emotionally distressing withdrawal symptoms. Therefore, connecting the survivor with access to needed medications should be a priority. Of course, this may not be easy. If a disaster impairs infrastructure and hospitals and clinics are closed, needed drugs may be in limited supply. Even if medications are available, a survivor may not be able to recall or communicate what type and dosage he or she needs, which is especially problematic when medical records are destroyed or inaccessible. If it's impossible to determine precisely what medication regime a survivor had been on, you can at least connect him or her with a psychiatrist or other healthcare professional who can attempt to recreate an appropriate treatment.

Restore a calm environment: This may be easier said than done, but decreasing environmental stimulation may reduce some of the anxiety and situational reactions the survivor is experiencing. Try to bring the person to a quiet area, away from anyone who might be staring or making him or her feel uncomfortable.

Restore past support sources: Again, this may be difficult or impossible if infrastructure is seriously disrupted, but using local, trusted resources such as peer helpers or other community members for outreach and delivery of services is likely to be more effective than unfamiliar providers, who survivors may be reluctant to trust. It's important to encourage the survivor to participate in his or her own recovery by communicating the need for services and reinforcing his or her right to receive assistance like other community members.

Beyond that, because the needs of members of this population can vary so widely, the only way to know how to help most effectively is to ask. These questions will help you understand the survivor's past and current situation.

- What is the person's level of "adaptive behavior," meaning skills of daily living, communication, and social interaction? Are those skills stable, improving, or declining?
- Where did he or she live prior to the disaster—with family, independently, in a group home or care facility? Is that setting intact? If not, can the person cope with conditions in available temporary housing, such as a shelter? Do special arrangements need to be made?

- How can the survivor's support network be restored to return a sense of stability?
- Does he or she need medications? If so, does he or she know the names and dosages?
- How can the survivor be included in the recovery effort?

DMH helpers can also reduce concerns among other shelter residents by providing some psychoeducation about mental illness in general in order to reduce stigmatization, but this must be done in a way that respects the privacy of the individual with the disability.

People with mental disabilities clearly may face additional psychosocial demands during and after disasters relative to the general population, and your primary focus in assisting them should be on stabilization—of their living environment, of their medication regime, and of whatever remains of their support network. You can't expect to prevent them from experiencing post-disaster reactions just like the rest of the affected community, but you may be able to limit the degree that these posttrauma symptoms interact with pre-existing symptoms by helping them access needed care.

OTHER VULNERABLE POPULATIONS

We'll briefly describe a few other groups you're likely to encounter who may be at risk for more negative outcomes after disasters.

People Living in Poverty

You might hear the cliché "Disasters don't discriminate." That's true to some degree, as wealth or status aren't a magical shield against harm, but in reality people at the lower end of the socioeconomic spectrum (SES) are often disproportionately impacted by disasters. They may experience greater exposure to natural disasters because of the location of neighborhoods in high-risk areas, particularly in flood plains. (It's no accident that the wealthy settlers of New Orleans claimed the high ground for themselves and left low-lying areas to poorer communities.) This geographic threat is often accompanied by lower-quality construction of housing stock, so more damage is suffered due to flooding, strong winds, earthquakes, and other destructive natural forces than in sturdier buildings.

Lower-SES survivors may not be able to afford to evacuate before a predicted event, and if they do they may have no other option than to go to the stressful setting of an emergency shelter, while people with more disposable income might be able go to a motel, where at least they have some privacy and control.

Once they're displaced, it can be difficult to get back home again if the disaster causes extensive damage. Homeowners may have minimal or no insurance to repair property damage. Renters are often even less protected: Only about one-third of American renters have insurance to cover lost or damaged property (Leamy, 2013), and whether to repair or rebuild is the landlord's decision, not their own. After disasters that cause widespread damage to housing stock, landlords often increase rents on intact properties, which may make it impossible for lower-SES families to remain in the area. This raises difficult decisions about where to live, and whether families can stay together or they need to be separated so that children can attend school and parents can work. Family separation is highly stressful, not surprisingly, but the loss of a familiar neighborhood and associated social support network is also a secondary trauma (Sultan, Norris, Avendano, Roberts, & Davis, 2014), especially for relocated adolescents, who feel the loss of school and peers acutely (Hansel, Osofsky, Osofsky, & Friedrich, 2013).

Finally, people living in poverty have higher-than-average rates of some health problems, including asthma, type 2 diabetes, and hypertension, which may be worsened by stress and by post-disaster conditions such as mold or smoke exposure, or by limited access to healthy foods, especially if the supply of medications is also lost. In general, lower-SES people may have limited access to physical and psychological care, making them vulnerable to longer lasting post-disaster effects than necessary.

Recent and Undocumented Immigrants

The United States is a nation of immigrants and their descendants. Recent immigrants who are in the country legally can face the general challenges of adjusting to a new environment, including overcoming language barriers and learning to navigate a different system. While some immigrants are motivated to relocate because of economic opportunities or other positive factors, it's important to be aware that many have felt obligated to leave their homeland because of war, chronic violence, government corruption, or other distressing experiences, so they may have a personal trauma history that precedes any new disaster exposure. They also tend to be living at the lower end of the socioeconomic spectrum as they establish their new lives, so they may face the poverty-related challenges described above—but perhaps without the strong social ties that can somewhat offset a lack of material resources (Sultan et al., 2014).

Undocumented immigrants who are in the country illegally face even more stressors. This population of 11.3 million makes up 3.5 percent of the nation's population but 5.1 percent of the US labor force (Krogstad, Passel,

& Cohn, 2016), demonstrating their importance to the economy. While this group isn't eligible for FEMA funding or some other types of state or federal assistance, they do have full access to post-disaster services from the American Red Cross and other non-governmental groups.

However, fears about arrest or deportation can cause undocumented immigrants to avoid engaging with the system in any way, depriving them of much-needed assistance. It may be necessary to do outreach to this group through spiritual care providers, community advocates, or other trusted leaders. We'll return to this point in the next chapter.

Regardless of legal status, immigrants may experience a degree of mistrust of government authorities based on their prior experience, which undermines a potential source of support, according to Rhodes and Tran (2012), who examined the impact of perceived quality of the governmental response to a disaster on posttraumatic stress and posttraumatic growth among survivors. They found that, among their 980 participants, more positive views of the governmental response were associated with greater posttraumatic growth while more negative views of the response correlated with greater posttraumatic stress symptomology. They describe this as the impact of perceiving a "healing community" that supports positive adaptation—a resource that may be unavailable to those with a history of abuse by government officials.

LGBTQ Individuals

We hesitate somewhat to identify members of the LGBTQ population as vulnerable in times of disaster because, unlike the other groups we've discussed in this chapter, there's really nothing that distinguishes them from other survivors while disasters are unfolding. However, their treatment both before and after the event may influence their recovery.

Members of this population, especially transgender and gender-variant people whose identity varies from the biological sex they were assigned at birth, often have past experiences of rejection or abuse by parents and peers that may influence the way they process new traumatic experiences (Mascis, 2011). They also may face homophobia or transphobia among responders and other survivors post-disaster, increasing distress, whether it's expressed as overt hostility or more subtle microaggressions (Robinson & Rubin, 2016).

Some questions to consider while supporting LGBTQ survivors include the following.

- Experiencing a disaster may lead to identity disclosure and discrimination. How will this affect their relationships? How will it affect their employment? Will they be safe after this disclosure? Don't assume that people are open about their identity just because they come out to you. Reasons for disclosing/not disclosing identities vary, and can be related to safety concerns. Do not "out" them to anyone. Respect their confidentiality.

- When assisting someone with contacting family members, respect their decision about who they would like to contact. Don't assume that biological relatives make up an individual's family. Instead, close friends or extended family may be identified as their family of choice.
- Pay attention to how previously existing stressors may affect current experiences. Do they have access to adequate healthcare and medications? What are their support networks like? How do people in their area generally view LGBTQ individuals? Neighborhoods, communities, and regions vary tremendously in their comfort with and acceptance of the LGBTQ community.
- Laws and policies related to protection against violence and discrimination vary by state, so be aware of what relevant laws apply where you're responding.
- An individual's name may not match his or her legal name on his or her ID. How can this affect access to resources?
- If people need to stay in a shelter, will they be safe? Will they be permitted to use the bathroom that they're comfortable in? Will they have access to hormones or any necessary medications? If the shelter is separated by gender, will they be placed where they prefer and feel safe?

We also must note the potential for this group to be targeted for violence because of their sexual orientation or identity. Historically, crimes against the LGBTQ population have consisted primarily of individual assaults, including murders, but the terrorist attack on the Pulse gay nightclub in Orlando in June 2016 all too vividly demonstrates the group's vulnerability to mass terrorism as well as individual hate crimes.

First Responders

A final population to consider is professional first responders, including police officers, firefighters, 911 call takers, and emergency medical technicians. Each of these groups has a very distinct culture that includes an emphasis on strength and toughness. Even though they may receive substantial doses of exposure to trauma, members of these groups are typically not viewed as vulnerable, for several reasons:

- They're self-selected, meaning they chose to enter a challenging field because they believed they had the capacity to handle the work.

- They receive extensive training, which tends to have a protective effect.
- They often receive post-event support within their group, rather than turning to outside assistance.

While these factors are generally positive in helping first responders cope with the stress of routine emergencies, they can become liabilities in times of disaster. That's particularly true when the disaster occurs in the responder's own community, so he or she must juggle professional demands with personal losses and stressors. At that point the professional distancing that allows responders to focus on their work can break down, causing distress. Exposure to human remains is also a clear risk factor for worse reactions among professional responders (Cetin et al., 2005).

Benedek, Fullerton, and Ursano (2007) point out that disaster-related distress may be expressed in particular ways among these groups: While most will experience the usual pattern of transient distress followed by recovery, and a minority will develop psychiatric illnesses such as PTSD, a portion are likely to experience moderate symptoms that wouldn't qualify for an official diagnosis but that can impact functioning at work and in relationships. These include anxiety, persistent insomnia, and changes in travel patterns or workplace behavior. Responders with these symptoms could benefit from psychological intervention, but many are reluctant to accept support from disaster mental health responders. This is easy to understand if DMH assistance is being offered in the middle of or soon after an operation, while first responders are immersed in their jobs and need to stay focused on protecting their communities. However, this reluctance is often compounded by the fact that DMH helpers generally have little familiarity with the values and culture of these groups, and because some working-class firefighters and police can be concerned that DMH professionals have negative stereotypes of them. In large cities first responder organizations frequently have their own mental health supports, but in small communities or those with volunteer firefighters there can be very little mental health support available. To bridge this gap, DMH helpers could spend some time developing a relationship before disaster strikes, and listening and learning about these cultures.

This chapter has barely skimmed the surface of this important topic, but we hope it will encourage you to consider how you'll address the special needs of these and other vulnerable populations throughout the disaster cycle. We've focused on groups that are likely to be present in any community, but you should also consider your own region and how you'll prepare for other groups with specific needs. For example, do you have a large population of immigrants or members of a particular faith who you'll need to adapt post-disaster services for? Is there a large elderly population in the area, or a residential program for people with autism spectrum disorders or other developmental disorders? Planning in advance for reaching and supporting these populations is essential but often overlooked—and this process should directly involve members of each group, as they're the best advocates for their needs. Be sure to focus on what you can do *with* them to support their recovery, not what you should do *for* them.

REFERENCES

American Psychological Association (2009, September). Depression and suicide in older adults resource guide. American Psychological Association, www.apa.org/pi/aging/resources/guides/depression.aspx.

Benedek, D. M., Fullerton, C. S., & Ursano, R. J. (2007). First responders: Mental health consequences of natural and human-made disasters for public health and public safety workers. *Annual Review of Public Health*, 28, 55–68.

Cetin, M., Kose, S., Ebrinc, S., Yigit, S., Elhai, J. &, Basoglu, C. (2005). Identification and posttraumatic stress disorder symptoms in rescue workers in the Marmara, Turkey, earthquake. *Journal of Traumatic Stress*, 18(5), 485–9.

Deeny, P., Vitale, C. T., Spelman, R., & Duggan, S. (2010). Addressing the imbalance: Empowering older people in disaster response and preparedness. *International Journal of Older People Nursing*, 5(1), 77–80.

Hansel, T. C., Osofsky, J. D., Osofsky, H. J., & Friedrich, P. (2013). The effect of long-term relocation on child and adolescent survivors of Hurricane Katrina. *Journal of Traumatic Stress*, 26(5), 613–20.

Krogstad, J. M., Passel, J. S., & Cohn, D. (2016, November 3). Five facts about illegal immigration in the US. Pew Research Center, www.pewresearch.org/fact-tank/2016/11/03/5-facts-about-illegal-immigration-in-the-u-s.

Leamy, E. (2013, March 11). Survey shows only a third of renters have insurance. ABC News, http://abcnews.go.com/Business/survey-shows-renters-insurance/story?id=18685618.

Mascis, A. N. (2011). Working with transgender survivors. *Journal of Gay and Lesbian Mental Health*, 15(2), 200–10.

Miller, J. L. (2012). *Psychosocial capacity building in response to disasters*. New York: Columbia University Press.

National Council on Disability (2009). *The current state of health care for people with disabilities*. Washington, DC: National Council on Disability.

Rhodes, A. M., & Tran, T. V. (2012). Predictors of posttraumatic stress and growth among black and white survivors of Hurricane Katrina: Does perceived quality of governmental response matter? *Race and Social Problems*, 4(3/4), 144–57.

Robinson, J. L., & Rubin, L. J. (2016). Homonegative microaggressions and posttraumatic stress symptoms. *Journal of Gay and Lesbian Mental Health*, 20(1), 57–69.

Sultan, D. H., Norris, C. M., Avendano, M., Roberts, M., & Davis, B. (2014). An examination of class differences in network capital, social support and psychological distress in Orleans Parish prior to Hurricane Katrina. *Health Sociology Review*, 23(3), 178–89.

WHO (2011). *World report on disability*. Geneva: World Health Organization, http://whqlibdoc.who.int/publications/2011/9789240685215_eng.pdf.

Chapter 10

Cultural Competence

A category three hurricane struck the Gulf Coast of Texas late in a relatively quiet hurricane season. Warnings about the expected intensity and path had been widely disseminated in English and Spanish, but, because there had been several recent false alarms about storms that never materialized, many residents ignored the warnings and did not evacuate or board up windows. Several communities along the coast where the storm made landfall were severely damaged, with the worst impact largely destroying several mobile home parks that had housed low-income residents. Many of them were Mexican migrant workers employed by local farms; some had documentation but many were living in the United States illegally. A number of people who had tried to ride out the storm at home were killed, and many others had much more frightening experiences during the event than they would have if they had followed the warnings.

Two weeks after the storm, close to 200 people were still living in an American Red Cross shelter because there was no affordable housing left intact in the region. The shelter manager learned that some undocumented immigrants were sleeping in their vehicles because they'd heard rumors that, if they came to the shelter, the Red Cross would report them to the Immigration and Naturalization Service and they'd be deported. Those rumors were false, but they meant that some families had been separated from a parent and experienced additional anxiety. Most adults in the shelter had no transportation, so they were unable to return to work. The pressures of life in a crowded shelter, with an uncertain future, were taking a psychological toll on residents of all ages.

A disaster mental health helper who had been deployed to the shelter for several days was struggling to connect with the residents, but felt equally hampered by her lack of Spanish language skills and by the residents' apparent mistrust of the shelter staff and volunteers. She decided to start to build rapport by playing with the many children. They were bored and restless from being out of school, so the DMH worker created a "school game," in which she pretended to be the pupil while the children gave her Spanish lessons. This then led to exchanging smiles and brief words with the parents, who were amused by her terrible accent. She also spoke to the shelter manager about including some traditional Mexican dishes in the daily menu options to provide a sense of comfort.

There were several bilingual volunteers working in the shelter who had been assisting with translation of announcements and helping with paperwork, but it was clear to the DMH worker that the shelter residents were still wary about pursuing financial aid and resources they were entitled to if that meant interacting with government agencies. After asking around about what churches in the area were most popular with the Mexican community, the DMH worker invited clergy members to visit the shelter and talk to their parishioners there, both to provide spiritual support and to help explain the assistance system. The clergy members also agreed to do some outreach in the community to clear up the rumors about the Red Cross being a government agency. Hearing that information from a trusted source helped increase the residents' comfort level and self-advocacy.

While the DMH helper never conducted a traditional mental health intervention with any of the Mexican families during her time at the shelter, she felt she had been able to reduce at least some of their stress and support their recovery despite the cultural differences. She returned home vowing to learn basic Spanish before her next deployment.

Like the effects of membership in a vulnerable population, the impact of disaster survivors' culture on their reactions and recovery is complex, individual, and significant. And, like developing expertise in working with vulnerable populations, acquiring competence in working with members of other cultures is a never-ending process. It's also an essential element of effective disaster mental health response: **A helper's failure to understand and respect a survivor's cultural perspectives is likely to create a barrier between them that limits the kind of trust we know is essential to any helping relationship.**

In addition to striving to become familiar with important aspects of a survivor's culture, it's also important that helpers recognize our own cultural values and beliefs and acknowledge how these can shape our response to others. This is particularly true given the power imbalance that's inherent in the helper–survivor relationship. Miller (2012) points out that the field of disaster mental health was created in the developed, Western world and most practitioners are highly educated and trained in Western principles of psychology or counseling. This, he says, shapes their expectations of survivor reactions and recovery trajectories in four specific ways.

1. Western helpers tend to view change as a linear process, exemplified by the series of post-disaster phases they expect people to move through. However, some cultures, such as Buddhists and Hindus,

have a more cyclical understanding of time, including cycles of creation and destruction. This shapes the way they process events such as disasters and loss.

2. Most disaster mental health response models emphasize the need for professional training and position these professionals as the primary sources of assistance. But some cultures don't privilege professionalization in this way, instead turning to community members or spiritual care providers for support in times of crisis. Implying that only trained mental health professionals can really help risks undermining the local support system—which, after all, will be what's left in place when external helpers leave.

3. Western-trained mental health interventions tend to focus on the individual rather than the community, but this may not be appropriate in more collectively oriented cultures, which might emphasize the well-being of the group over individual suffering.

4. Professional helpers tend to emphasize an internal locus of control for change, suggesting that each survivor has the power to determine his or her own recovery. However, people who believe in karma or fate, or that gods or spirits determine their destinies, may have a different perception of how much control they have over their lives.

All of these assumptions, Miller (2012) notes, can make Western interventions ineffective and potentially even harmful if they're applied without thought for their appropriateness for a particular survivor or community. So, please be conscious of your own cultural background and biases as you learn to work with people whose values and recovery needs may differ from yours.

HOW CULTURE SHAPES REACTIONS TO DISASTER

The National Child Traumatic Stress Network (see www.nctsn.org/resources/topics/culture-and-trauma) defines culture as "a common heritage or set of beliefs, norms, and values; the shared, and largely learned, attributes of a group of people; a system of shared meanings." This includes, but isn't limited to:

- language
- race
- ethnic identity
- religion
- socioeconomic status
- gender identity
- sexual orientation
- physical ability level.

This means that all of us have multiple intersecting cultural identities that can be of greater or lesser salience at any given time. For example, you may not pay particular attention to your cultural characteristic of being an English speaker until you travel to a community in which another language is spoken and communication becomes challenging. Relevance of a cultural factor can also shift over time, as, for example, people become more or less devout in their faith during different periods of their life, or identify more or less closely with their ethnic heritage depending on the setting. There will also be variation in inter-individual levels of acculturation across members of a particular group, with some members of the community relying primarily on traditional beliefs and practices while others may prefer those of the dominant culture, or they may try to integrate both systems (Boyd, Quevillon, & Engdahl, 2010).

When it comes to mental health interventions, the National Institute of Mental Health defines cross-cultural issues as "variations in the meaning or expression of thoughts, feelings, or behaviors related to ethnic or religious identity or place of origin. Such differences may influence the validity of assessment, response to treatment, and appropriate ways of interacting with survivor population." When considering working with members of other groups, many of us tend to think of cross-cultural sensitivity in terms of behaviors: Is it appropriate to make eye contact with someone, or for an unrelated male and female to be alone together? How formally should a survivor be addressed? Is it acceptable to touch someone? These are certainly important issues to be aware of when working with a survivor from another background so you don't inadvertently cause offense or give someone reason to reject your assistance.

But the broader point is that culture deeply shapes survivors' reactions to disaster, including their **appraisal** of a traumatic event, how they **express** their distress, and how they **cope** with it. Aspects such as religion, language, beliefs, and traditions influence how people understand and respond to their experiences, and these influences tend to become especially powerful in times of great stress. In particular, expressions of mourning and grief are strongly tied to cultural beliefs and customs. For example, the intense expressiveness of some cultures in response to sudden death might lead a mental health provider to overestimate the gravity of the client's reaction, while a culture that teaches quiet grief might lead a provider to underestimate its intensity. An inability to follow sacred traditions in the disrupted post-disaster environment may compound the loss, adding a sense of guilt or failure to honor the dead to the grief about the death itself. This is especially true in groups that believe certain rituals must be followed in order to release the dead person's soul from the body or allow it to achieve a peaceful afterlife; survivors who can't complete these rites may experience great distress from the belief that the deceased person can't rest or move on.

Cultural beliefs may shape survivors' perceptions of responsibility for an event, and expectations about punishment (Lord, Hook, & English, 2003). Do they view a natural disaster as God's will, as fate or karma brought about by the victims' actions, or as a random act of nature? Clearly, those different attributions will influence how one makes meaning of the event, which is an important step in accepting its impact. For a human-caused disaster, do those impacted want vengeance against the perpetrator, believe the legal system should hand down justice, or believe that punishment is solely God's responsibility? We've already discussed how the inability to achieve justice through the legal system can be a secondary trauma for survivors, but we also need to consider what happens if there's a mismatch between an individual's preferences and the process imposed by the society he or she is living in. For example, if a survivor's religion dictates that only God has the right to punish wrongdoers, being required to testify in criminal proceedings against a perpetrator can cause distress and concern about displeasing God (Lord et al., 2003).

Carr (2010) also points out differences in the acceptance of negative events, which then influences reactions to them. Some religious groups, such as Buddhists, believe that suffering is an unavoidable part of life, so they may not view disasters as shocking or unfair. Members of groups that have experienced chronic political conflict and violence may have a more resigned attitude towards further stressors caused by a disaster. In a sense, the experience of past losses has given these individuals coping skills they can draw on the face of trauma, while people who have led a more privileged life may be blindsided by a disaster that is far outside the scope of their past experiences. However, Carr (2010) also notes that some of the practices that allow these survivors to remain stoical in the face of grief, such as suppressing their emotions or not discussing their experiences, may actually impede their long-term recovery. (And, of course, we don't want to imply that the costs of long-term suffering outweigh the transient benefits of absorbing new trauma more readily.)

Another important cultural factor to be sensitive to is survivors' trust in and comfort with authority figures. Immigrants may have come from countries with corrupt or abusive rulers, creating suspicion about government representatives (Miller, 2012). Undocumented immigrants are likely to avoid any contact with the system out of fear of deportation. Members of some racial groups may have a deeply entrenched mistrust of police and other authority figures due to a history of mistreatment, and they may perceive any failures in the response operation as being racially motivated (Boyd-Franklin, 2010). This mistrust can lead residents to reject evacuation notices or other warnings before a disaster (Boyd et al., 2010), and it may make some survivors hesitant to seek or accept needed assistance after a disaster—including assistance from you as a DMH helper if they perceive you as a representative of the system they fear or mistrust. Building connections through a trusted representative of the group, such as a clergy member or respected elder, can help to overcome this suspicion among group members, and it can help you be more confident that you're interacting with the population in an appropriate manner (Lord et al., 2003). Forging those bonds can be difficult to manage in the post-disaster environment, so consider establishing connections in advance with appropriate members of cultural groups in your area.

You also may encounter resistance to accepting mental health care out of culturally based traditions of shame or stigma around acknowledging psychological problems (www.nctsn.org/resources/topics/culture-and-trauma), or out of mistrust of mental health providers. For example, Boyd-Franklin (2010) describes how the history of mistreatment by authority figures across generations has created a tradition of "cultural mistrust" among many African Americans that can impede the establishment of a therapeutic alliance with a helper of another race. She also notes the importance of addressing black clients' experience of, and anger about, racism and classism as a part of any intervention. Many studies after Hurricane Katrina found very different perceptions of the role of race in the failed rescue efforts between black and white residents of the region, with black residents seeing discrimination as a much bigger factor in the government's lackadaisical response. Those perceptions of racism and injustice are an important part of the survivor's experience, and denying or downplaying them disrespects the client and will undermine your ability to help.

Despite the many ways in which cultural differences can complicate reactions to disasters, related practices and traditions can also be a vital source of support and comfort to survivors. Every group has established methods for surviving difficult times, and these rituals can provide a sense of stability and hope for recovery (Miller, 2012). Also, as we've discussed repeatedly, social connectedness is one of the most important aids to recovery after disasters, and some cultural groups (for example, a cluster of immigrants from the same region, or a city's LGBTQ community) may have a pre-existing bond they can draw on for support—provided that community is not badly disrupted or displaced after the event. This unfortunately was the case among both Vietnamese immigrants and African American residents of New Orleans after Hurricane Katrina (Dass-Brailsford, 2010; Miller, 2012). Both groups were displaced, sometimes with no control over where they were relocated. They lost their livelihoods as well as the social capital and instrumental support they'd been able to share within their neighborhoods. Instead of living in a cohesive neighborhood with similar others they could rely on for instrumental and emotional support, many were sent to majority white communities where the reception by the racial and ethnic majority residents was not always warm or understanding, exposing some to racism (Boyd-Franklin, 2010) and many to the struggles of adapting to a new and unfamiliar environment with barriers to finding work or establishing a new sense of community (Miller, 2012). Compounding the stress of relocation, for both groups the displacement also carried traumatic historic echoes—of fleeing the war for the Vietnamese families (Miller, 2012) and of their ancestors being captured and transported into slavery for the African Americans (Boyd-Franklin, 2010). For these groups the loss of community was a true secondary disaster that extended suffering and complicated recovery.

However, when community members are able to stay together and help each other out, they can build on the collective efficacy Hobfoll et al. (2007) list as a key element of recovery, in part by mourning together and drawing on culturally shared ways of making meaning of the event. As an outsider you may not be familiar with their specific practices, but you can always encourage survivors to call on their heritage and traditions as a source of pride and strength.

CROSS-CULTURAL ISSUES IN SHELTERS

As we discussed in the previous chapter, disasters don't discriminate, though they do tend to disproportionately impact people at the lower end of the socioeconomic scale. This means that, when people are displaced from home, emergency shelter clients are likely to include a cross-section of the impacted community, including members of whatever ethnic, religious, and racial groups reside there.

Most people find living in a shelter to be highly stressful, and this means that any existing concerns or sources of friction can be heightened. This can result in an increase in distress for an individual, and/or conflict between residents. As a disaster mental health helper deployed to a shelter, you might be able help reduce resident stress related to these potential intra- and inter-individual cultural issues.

Language barriers: For people with limited English-language skills, being unable to understand announcements, complete paperwork, and generally participate in necessary activities can be very isolating and disorienting, and in addition to causing emotional suffering it may lead to them not receiving services they're entitled to. Even non-native speakers with fairly good English proficiency often lose some linguistic competence in times of stress.

One dilemma that often arises is whether it's appropriate to use children as translators as they may be more fluent than their immigrant parents. This should be avoided if at all possible, since it may expose children to information about the family situation or parental emotions they should ideally be shielded from. It also may embarrass or shame parents to be reliant in this way on the child. Using an adult community member to translate is preferable, though this also risks breaching family confidentiality. The ideal is to bring in a professional translator, though of course that's often not feasible post-disaster. Technology may also be helpful: There are commercial operations that provide translation services by telephone, as well as translation apps you can download to your phone or tablet. It's not easy to hold a conversation this way, but it may be necessary.

Dietary needs: Some shelter residents will have health-based diet restrictions while others may follow religious laws that prevent them from consuming certain foods. Shelter managers should be encouraged to accommodate these needs as sensitively as possible. Even more relevant to mental health, remember that food is a source of comfort in times of stress, especially the kinds of meals one grew up eating. If you have a number of residents from a particular ethnic background, suggest providing meal options that will seem familiar and appealing.

Differences in expectations of children's behavior and parents' treatment of children: This is a common source of conflict in shelters. As we discussed in Chapter 8, children often regress and act out after traumatic experiences, so they may be perceived by other adults as misbehaving, and parents are often overwhelmed and less able to comfort or control children than usual. As a result, they may be judged by other shelter residents and possibly staff as bad parents who can't control their children, or considered abusive if they shout at a child or use any kind of physical punishment (Boyd et al., 2010). DMH helpers can best help by providing psychoeducation and stress management techniques to help parents, and perhaps by offering to take children to a supervised play area so they can burn off energy and the parent can take a break.

Prayer/ritual habits: Followers of some religions, including Muslims and Orthodox Jews, gather at specific times to pray several times per day. If possible, see if a private area can be created in the shelter where they can do so without an audience of curious gawkers.

Exacerbation of pre-existing racial/ethnic/religious tensions: While diverse community members often come together immediately after disasters to support each other, that cohesion doesn't necessarily last much beyond the honeymoon phase. Any existing friction or mistrust between groups is likely to surface and perhaps worsen, as living in close quarters amid the stressful shelter environment activates the human tendency towards in-group/out-group biases. There may be concerns about theft of whatever possessions residents managed to bring with them, fears of sexual assault, reluctance about sharing bathrooms with a disliked group, and so on. DMH helpers should be attuned to any pre-existing or newly developing tensions and step in quickly to de-escalate conflicts before they become problematic.

IMPROVING YOUR ABILITY TO HELP ACROSS CULTURES

No one can be an expert on all cultural subtleties, but you can work on pursuing appropriate ways of interacting with survivor populations—while always remembering that any particular survivor may not fully share the values or beliefs of their group. Here are some guiding principles.

Develop your religious literacy: The United States is arguably the most religiously diverse country in the world (Eck, 2001). Islamic centers, mosques, and Buddhist and Hindu temples can be found in small towns and large cities throughout the country. Some large cities in America can have as many as 200 different religious groups. The National Disaster Interfaiths Network and the University of Southern California Center for Religion and Civic Culture, working with the California Emergency Management Agency, have published the *Religious Literacy Primer for Crises, Disasters, and Public Health Emergencies: A Field Guide Companion for Religious Literacy and Competency* and its companion, *Working with US Faith Communities during Crises, Disasters and Public Health Emergencies: A Field Guide for Engagement, Partnerships and Religious Competency*. We strongly recommend that you read this material to improve your literacy, or as a "just in time training" if you know in advance that you'll be working with a particular faith group. Materials include user-friendly "Tip sheets for interfaith partners" that will enable you to be more competent when sheltering and delivering mass care to different religious groups from A to Z—or Anabaptists to Zoroastrians. These tip sheets cover greetings and physical interaction, shelter settings, prayer and prayer space, feeding, dress, core religious beliefs, and medical, emotional, and spiritual care. The latest versions of the documents can be found at www.n-din.org or crcc.usc.edu.

Involve the local community in each stage of assessment and development of interventions: This is probably the most important goal to strive for. There has been a problematic tradition, in both disaster mental health and humanitarian aid response, of outsiders "parachuting in" to devastated communities to deliver pre-established interventions, with no regard for what the survivors actually need or want, or as cover for evangelizing a religion. For example, after the 2004 Indian Ocean tsunami, a flood of international aid groups and faith-based organizations (including Scientologists) descended on Sri Lanka and other impacted areas, delivering a variety of dubious and culturally insensitive psychosocial interventions, when what community members really wanted help with was rebuilding homes and schools (Wickramage, 2006). To avoid this, all planning and delivery of services should try to include a multicultural team that incorporates members of the impacted group, who can advocate for their community's real needs.

Don't instill a sense of helplessness or powerlessness: This is closely related to the previous point. While the arrival of outside aid may (or may not) be welcomed by a disaster-impacted community, the very fact that this

assistance is needed risks implying that community members are simply victims who can't take care of themselves, or that their leaders are incapable of
caring for them—a message that may remain in place once the external aid
has been withdrawn, leaving people with no trust in indigenous resources
(Miller, 2012). Instead of this approach, which positions the mental health
helper as rescuer, the focus should be on "capacity building." This means
working with local helpers, ideally including spiritual care providers, community leaders, respected elders, and whoever else is involved in caring for
the well-being of the group, to capitalize on their knowledge and strengths
in rebuilding their own community.

Don't break cultural taboos: You may need to do some research into
what a particular group considers appropriate. Is it socially acceptable to
acknowledge one's emotional distress, or to talk about a deceased person?
Is assistance from an outsider—particularly a mental health professional—
welcome or would it be viewed as shameful? Do what you can to learn the
appropriate customs in advance, don't be afraid to ask questions, and don't
hesitate to apologize if you realize you've made a mistake. Most people are
forgiving of cultural faux pas, provided they believe your intentions are
good and your respect for their values is genuine.

Pay attention to your language: Language is particularly important
regarding people's names and forms of address. Regardless of survivors' cultural background, you should always ask what they would like to be called.
Some people, especially older adults, find it disrespectful to be called by
their first name, preferring "Mr." or "Mrs." or an honorific such as "Sir"
or "Ma'am." Some people don't mind endearments such as "Hon," while
others find them grating or patronizing. If you're working with a transgender person, ask what pronoun they prefer to be referred to by. While these
seem like small matters, they demonstrate respect and reinforce that you
recognize the person as an individual, not just a part of a crowd of survivors.

As this chapter has shown, culture is an essential part of people's identities (including ours as helpers), and it becomes especially salient in times
of distress such as disasters. In general, we advise you to become familiar
with values and customs for the various religious and ethnic groups you may
encounter in disaster response in your community, and whenever possible
to enlist appropriate community leaders or spiritual care providers in your
response plans to ensure they're sensitive and appropriate.

REFERENCES

Boyd, B., Quevillon, R. P., & Engdahl, R. M. (2010). Working with rural and diverse
    communities after disasters. In P. Dass-Brailsford (Ed.), *Crisis and disaster coun-
    seling: Lessons learned from Hurricane Katrina and other disasters*. Los Angeles: Sage,
    pp. 149–63.

Boyd-Franklin, N. (2010). Families affected by Hurricane Katrina and other disasters: Learning from the experiences of African American survivors. In P. Dass-Brailsford (Ed.), *Crisis and disaster counseling: Lessons learned from Hurricane Katrina and other disasters*. Los Angeles: Sage, pp. 67–82.

Carr, K. F. (2010). A community-based approach to coping with crises in Africa. In P. Dass-Brailsford (Ed.), *Crisis and disaster counseling: Lessons learned from Hurricane Katrina and other disasters*. Los Angeles: Sage, pp. 197–211.

Dass-Brailsford, P. (Ed.) (2010). *Crisis and disaster counseling: Lessons learned from Hurricane Katrina and other disasters*. Los Angeles: Sage.

Eck, D. L. (2001). *A new religious America: How a "Christian country" has become the world's most religiously diverse nation*. San Francisco: Harper.

Hobfoll, S. E., Watson, P. J., Bell, C. C., Bryant, R. A., Brymer, M. J., Friedman, M. J., …, & Ursano, R. J. (2007). Five essential elements of immediate and mid-term mass trauma intervention: Empirical evidence. *Psychiatry: Interpersonal and Biological Processes*, 70(4), 283–315.

Lord, J. H., Hook, M., & English, S. (2003). Different faiths, different perceptions of public tragedy. In M. Lattanzi-Licht & K. J. Doka (Eds.), *Living with grief: Coping with public tragedy*. New York: Brunner-Routledge, pp. 91–107.

Miller, J. L. (2012). *Psychosocial capacity building in response to disasters*. New York: Columbia University Press.

Wickramage, K. (2006). Sri Lanka's post-tsunami psychosocial playground: Lessons for future psychosocial programming and interventions. *Intervention*, 4(2), 167–72.

Chapter 11

Maintaining Helper Wellness and Competence

Residents of a Harlem neighborhood in New York City smelled gas and called the local utility company. The next morning more residents reported that they smelled gas. Then, at 9:31 a.m. on March 12, 2014, two buildings containing 15 apartments with a church and piano store on the ground floors exploded. The force of the blast was so great that, blocks away, people thought they were in the middle of an earthquake as buildings shook and windows were blown out. Eight died in the blast, at least 70 were injured, and five were missing. Within minutes first responders arrived at the site of the explosion and witnessed the devastation. That night the Red Cross provided shelter for the displaced. Soon a Disaster Recovery Center was established in a nearby school. Residents of the destroyed buildings were permanently displaced, along with inhabitants of buildings close by who could not immediately return to their homes. Some lost everything, as the blast had turned belongings to dust. Those who lost loved ones understood the excruciating truth about material things being replaceable, unlike people. Their grief was immense. The DRC provided a wide range of services for all survivors. Providing assistance after a disaster can be very meaningful but also difficult and hazardous. My mistakes responding to this disaster are intended as a cautionary tale. Before traveling to the DRC I was told that, based on the latest information, grieving families were no longer coming to the DRC, where the focus was now on providing logistical resources. I juggled work responsibilities that morning and rushed to the scene, anticipating that I would be speaking with survivors with practical needs. I also anticipated speaking with staff and volunteers about what they had seen and heard and I knew that I would thank them for their contribution to the community and to the lives and souls touched by disaster. When I arrived I saw dozens of survivors looking for a range of practical services. Who would pay for their temporary lodging? What could be done about long-term lodging? What legal resources were available? If they stayed somewhere out of the neighborhood, how would children get to local schools? Then I was told that, as an experienced DMH worker,

I would be meeting with a family who had lost a loved one and who would soon be arriving at the DRC. I sat with a chaplain, a Red Cross family assistance worker and the two brothers, a sister, and the aunt of a young woman who had died in the explosion. Family members talked about their sister, and how her teenage son and daughter would manage. We spent an hour talking about how they would break the news to their aging mother. I believed that we had helped the family when we all said goodbye, and I went off to a social engagement. At my gathering that evening I knew people did not want to hear about building explosions or grieving families, so I engaged in small talk. It was only after feeling depressed for several days that I realized my self-care in response to the disaster was deeply flawed. It was careless, and I paid the price. Working at disasters necessitates attention, forethought, and a self-care plan.

—James Halpern

Mental health professionals are typically well trained to support and assist others, but we can neglect our own well-being during and after a response as we focus on those we're trying to help. For trauma and disaster workers this can have substantial negative consequences. However, practicing self-care appropriately can not only protect our own mental health but also help us to experience great satisfaction from being able to support survivors. In this chapter, we'll outline the unique stressors inherent in disaster service, discuss how to prevent them, and provide guidance on transitioning back to normal life once your part in the response operation concludes. As you review the logistics of deployment, helper reactions, and self-care, think about how you would avoid the mistakes described in the case study.

LOGISTICS OF DEPLOYMENT

First, we'll discuss some of the practical factors that can influence your experience as a DMH worker. These details may seem less relevant than higher-level concerns such as the pursuit of compassion satisfaction from helping those in need, but Maslow's hierarchy reminds us of their importance: If your feet are killing you because you packed the wrong footwear, or you're distracted by knowing your family is furious at you for accepting an assignment that means you're missing a child's birthday, you won't be an engaged and effective helper. We encourage you to take these logistical factors seriously as you begin work in this field.

Challenges at Home or Away

In this chapter we refer to "deployment," which typically means travelling to a distant location to participate in the response when local resources can't meet post-disaster demands, but most of the same points apply when you respond in your own community. There are advantages and disadvantages to deployment in your community. If you're close to home you can sleep in your own bed, have access to many of the comforts of home, have fewer concerns about issues such as who is looking after your family in your absence, and experience less stress from trying to help in an unfamiliar environment. However, factors such as these are likely to be offset by the fact that you may have close friends or family impacted by the disaster—or that you were impacted directly and may essentially be working a double shift, juggling your professional responsibilities with your own recovery needs. If the disaster impacted your community, you don't get the opportunity to create physical and psychological distance from the event, leaving you vulnerable to sadness and distress long after the event. In contrast, if you're deployed away from home, you can focus on your work at the disaster without the additional responsibilities and chores of home life. However, you might find yourself in an unfamiliar setting, not knowing the culture, climate, or how to navigate from place to place. You'll also have to make decisions about what to pack, which can be stressful if you're going on vacation, let alone anticipating working at a catastrophe.

One of the defining characteristics of disaster mental health work is that every event is different, making it difficult to predict exactly what conditions you'll be heading into. That means that even very experienced responders need to remain flexible and adaptable. Still, there are some general preparation lessons you can learn from veterans in the DMH field.

Is it the Right Time for You?

Assuming that you have some choice in whether to get involved in a response (which may not be the case if the event occurs in your community and your agency has an obligation to respond), the most basic preparation begins with evaluating your personal readiness to participate, and acting now to address any barriers to deployment that are within your control. Otherwise, it's far too easy to overlook a need or responsibility that will later impede your ability to work safely and productively. It's difficult to be fully engaged in helping survivors if you're distracted by concerns about home.

To this end, Rosser (2008) has identified three primary considerations to address prior to disaster deployment.

- **Ethical considerations to family**: Could my family manage well in my absence from home?
- **Professional obligations**: Is there anything so important in my work that I could not respond immediately?

- **Ethical consideration to self**: Will I be useful and am I volunteering for the right reasons?

To be certain that your circumstances will permit you to be an effective helper, you should not only engage in self-reflection but also have conversations with friends, family, and work associates well before you go on an assignment. Can you leave work or your family if there's a community emergency? How much time can you commit to being available or on-call in the event of a disaster without overextending yourself? These conversations should be attended to in advance of accepting an assignment, since desperate calls from work or an overburdened spouse can interfere with or undermine your effectiveness while on the job. You'll be a more effective disaster mental health worker if you feel supported by colleagues, family, and friends while on assignment.

Sometimes disaster work isn't a good fit for someone at a particular point in his or her life. Perhaps you have young children or an elderly parent who needs care, or a particularly demanding work schedule, or a patient in crisis. Perhaps you've recently experienced a personal loss. Perhaps you don't feel seasoned enough as a clinician. It's entirely permissible—and advisable—to postpone doing this work to a time better suited to your capacity to respond. If there's one thing we can guarantee it's that there will always be ample opportunities to get involved at a later time. Also, you may feel prepared to respond only to some types of events, such as floods or fires that caused property damage, but not to a mass casualty incident such as a plane crash, or to work with certain survivor populations but not others, such as a school bus accident that caused deaths or injuries to children. As a beginning DMH helper you should not feel required to respond to such difficult or "hardship" assignments. It would be a shame if you overburdened yourself at your first disaster assignment and then did not want to accept the next one. As disasters become more frequent and more intense, responders need to stay fit and engaged, and to remain within their competence level.

What to Bring

If you're deployed to a distant location, you'll want to balance packing as efficiently as possible with making sure you have everything you need to keep functioning, including any items you'll want for self-care and stress relief. You may not know the settings you'll be working in (for example, remaining inside a shelter or walking around a neighborhood doing outreach), so try to be prepared for whatever the season and climate may present. Basic recommendations include the following.

Attire:

- comfortable clothing, preferably items that can be washed in a sink and hung dry if necessary
- footwear that's sturdy, comfortable for hours of standing or walking, and—ideally—waterproof (deployment is not the time to break in new boots!)
- seasonal accessories: warm hat, scarf, and gloves for winter events; sunglasses, hat, sunscreen, and insect repellant for warm-weather events
- an extra pair of eyeglasses.

Comfort/stress-relieving items—to be tailored to your personal preferences:

- books or other reading materials
- smartphone/other device with games, music, other pastimes (don't forget the charger)
- photos of loved ones or other reminders of home
- Bible/Koran/other spiritual care materials.

Other:

- evidence of relevant credentials (badge, proof of licensure/certification)
- driver's license and healthcare insurance information
- personal hygiene items
- medications (prescriptions, aspirin, vitamins)
- breath mints or chewing gum
- hand sanitizer
- granola bars/other healthy transportable snacks
- small flashlight (preferably hand- or solar-chargeable)
- small notebook and writing implements.

Also consider useful apps to load on your phone or tablet, such as:

- GPS/mapping
- language translation tools
- flashlight
- PFA reminders
- first aid guide
- weather tracker
- Skype or Facetime to stay connected with home.

If you get a notification—by phone call, text, or e-mail—that you're needed at a complex emergency or disaster, it's understandable that you can feel stressed and a bit discombobulated. If you need to pack in a hurry it can be easy to forget essential items, so even if you don't go so far as having a pre-packed "go bag" on hand (which is ideal but not always practical) it can be very useful to write up a checklist of everything you'd like to bring. That way, when an event occurs you're simply following the list rather than having to make a lot of decisions.

HELPER REACTIONS

Next, we'll examine the range of responses DMH helpers can experience from doing this work. As when we describe survivor reactions, there's often a tendency to dwell on the negative. It is very important to attend to the risks described below, but please keep those occupational hazards framed within the tremendous rewards many responders experience.

The Compassion Continuum

Helpers can experience a range of reactions, from feeling good about the assistance they've provided to feeling distressed about witnessing another's suffering. These reactions span the "**compassion satisfaction to compassion fatigue continuum**." Compassion fatigue, defined as "the cost of caring for those in emotional pain," is the emotional duress experienced by those in close contact with trauma survivors. Compassion satisfaction, on the other hand, refers to the rewards that stem from helping those who are suffering and the "pleasure you derive from doing your work" (see www.proqol.org).

Serving others during times of extreme crisis shapes helpers, most often in positive and satisfying ways. Mental health workers who have responded to catastrophic events have reported many rewards, including immediate and gratifying personal satisfaction from helping others, feelings of empowerment during times of potentially debilitating crisis, relief from routine mental health work, emotional bonding with responder teams and community, and a sense of privilege resulting from providing mental health services in unique circumstances when they're sorely needed (Stamm, 2010).

An often unanticipated reward that many disaster and emergency responders identify is how the professional "lessons learned" can positively impact their personal lives. Although much has been written about the dangers of work life spilling over into personal/family life, this effect has potentially positive benefits as well. Responders report feeling greater empathy and compassion for and with family members and friends, a greater awareness of what is important in life, appreciation for the value of human connection, tolerance for difference, and profound gratitude for the opportunities and relationships they have in their lives. Responders report that they're grateful for the opportunity to provide comfort to those who are suffering; this benefit is viewed as well worth the cost of the effort (Cohen & Collens, 2012). Compassion satisfaction can include a sense of accomplishment, a sense of purpose, and a sense of competence in being able to help others. Although having a sense of humility about our skills is appropriate, it's important that we also have the ability to acknowledge our competence and accomplishments. Compassion satisfaction can be experienced only if we don't downplay the impact of our work.

However, without the proper overall preparation and mindset, helpers can also suffer negative consequences from this work. Vicarious forms of trauma and burnout are well documented among responders, but self-care can play a significant role in coping with and preventing problems resulting from disaster experiences. If self-care is ignored, unmanaged distress may adversely affect not only your personal well-being but also, potentially, that of your clients and the response effort as a whole. This can raise professional concerns regarding your effectiveness and competence. As a result, practicing good self-care to maintain your personal welfare is not a luxury but an ethical responsibility.

The occupational hazards and rewards of the work can occur simultaneously. A summary of 20 published studies (Cohen & Collens, 2012) shows that trauma work often increases short- and long-term levels of distress but the negative impact can be managed through personal and organizational coping strategies. The research also shows that the distress of the work does not preclude growth and, in fact, is often conducive to growth. Trauma and disaster work changes the way we think—both positively and negatively. Our experiential world becomes more complex and richer, leading to **vicarious posttraumatic growth**. This is most likely to occur if we're exposed to the growth of those we're assisting—an experience that happens frequently when we assist disaster survivors in their time of need.

Occupational Hazards of Disaster Work

Factors frequently associated with humanitarian or trauma work, such as interpersonal conflicts, communication difficulties, workload, lack of control over one's work life and work conditions, and organizational bureaucracy, present considerable psychosocial risk to helpers over time (Kramen-Kahn & Downing Hansen, 1998). The unique factors associated with disaster/emergency work impose an additional burden. The World Health Organization summarized the major concerns of relief workers (not only mental health professionals) who provided services during the 2004 tsunami (WHO, 2005) as the following.

- You are repeatedly exposed to grim experiences, such as handling bodies, dealing with multiple casualties, powerful emotions, and tormenting stories of people affected by death and loss.
- You frequently carry out physically difficult, exhausting, or dangerous tasks.
- You are exposed to unusual personal demands to help meet the needs of survivors.
- Frequently, you put your own physical and emotional needs at a low priority to ensure maximum service to disaster-affected people.
- You neglect your sleep, food, and even personal hygiene in your excessive concern for survivors.
- At times you perceive that you are not able to do enough for people and therefore you feel frustrated and helpless.
- At times you feel guilty that you have better access to food, shelter, and other resources than the survivors.
- Frequently, you face moral and ethical dilemmas.
- You are exposed to the anger and apparent lack of gratitude of some affected people.
- You may be away from your home and family, a separation that deprives you of a very effective psychosocial support system.
- You may feel frustrated by the policies and decisions of your superiors.

Just as disaster survivors may have a variety of emotional reactions to their experiences, mental health helpers can be impacted by their work in a number of recognized ways. And, just as it's helpful for disaster survivors to be able to label their suffering, it's helpful for helpers to have accurate labels for their distress. **Compassion fatigue**, **vicarious trauma**, **secondary traumatic stress**, and **burnout** are all terms that are used to try to capture the effect of clients' suffering on the mental health of helpers. These terms have sometimes been used interchangeably, but there are important differences between them (Trippany, White Kress, & Wilcoxon, 2004).

Compassion fatigue (CF) is defined as the emotional duress experienced by those in close contact with those in pain. Compassion fatigue is caused by overextending one's capacity for selflessness, resulting in a variety of symptoms including feelings of numbness or helplessness, apathy, decreased self-esteem, impatience, sleep changes, withdrawal from relationships, loss of purpose, and decreased morale and motivation (Figley, 1995). Mathieu (2012) describes compassion fatigue as "[t]he profound exhaustion that helping professionals and caregivers can develop over the course of their career as helpers. It is a gradual erosion of all the things that keep us connected to others in our caregiver role: our empathy, our hope, and of course our compassion—not only for others but also for ourselves." The cumulative result of these symptoms is a general disengagement from the desire to help others, which can be deeply distressing for mental health professionals, whose identity is largely based on our perceptions of ourselves as helpers. Fortunately, CF is a "treatable" reaction and one that can be mitigated through self-care.

Vicarious trauma (VT) occurs when a helper experiences a trauma reaction due to exposure to a client's traumatic experiences. Vicarious trauma is rooted in mental health professionals' empathy for their clients: By listening to the intimate or explicit details of a client's story, helpers can come to feel as though they witnessed these events personally. Vicarious trauma is specific to those assisting trauma victims (such as trauma therapists, rescue workers, and hospital and emergency medical staff), and it can lead to "profound changes in the core aspects of the therapist's self" (Pearlman & Saakvitne, 1995) that may require professional treatment. Signs can include spiritual disconnection (Charney & Pearlman, 1998), disrupted schemas about self and others and resulting relationship difficulties, and affect dysregulation (Huggard, Stamm, & Pearlman, 2013). If all of those symptoms weren't difficult enough, we now know that VT is also linked to a decrease in sexual desire (Branson, Weigand, & Keller, 2014). Here it is described by van Dernoot Lipsky (2009): "I finally came to understand that my exposure to other people's trauma had changed me on a fundamental level. There had been an osmosis: I had absorbed and accumulated trauma to the point that it had become part of me, and my view of the world had changed."

Secondary traumatic stress (STS) is described by Hudnall Stamm (1999) as resulting from work-related, secondary exposure to extremely stressful events. Many professionals in the field see secondary traumatic stress as a more pernicious form of vicarious trauma or compassion fatigue, with a direct relationship to Posttraumatic Stress Disorder. For the purpose of this chapter, we can understand STS as a consequence of unaddressed compassion fatigue. If we do not address the warning signs of compassion fatigue, this fatigue can develop into STS, with disruptive symptoms that mimic PTSD. STS symptoms can be rapid in onset and are usually associated with a particular event. The primary symptoms of STS include:

- re-experiencing the crisis/trauma (e.g., images, nightmares)
- avoiding reminders of the disturbing experiences
- demonstrating persistent hyperarousal, characterized by rapid heart rate and respiration, elevated blood pressure, or a feeling of being on edge.

(Figley, 1995; Stamm, 1999)

Burnout is the gradual exhaustion and depletion of emotional energy that comes from being overworked, without sufficient rest, reward, or recovery. It's characterized by chronic exhaustion, cynicism, and a lack of personal accomplishment. This concept was first used in the occupational stress literature to describe emotional consequences resulting from an impossible work situation specific to "people work" for human service workers and mental health professionals who work intensely with other people's problems (Maslach, Jackson, & Leiter, 1996). Mental health workers with higher initial levels of burnout report more physical health complaints, including sleep disturbances, headaches, respiratory infections, and gastrointestinal infections, and a faster rate of deterioration in physical health (Kim, Ji, & Kao, 2011). The work environment is known to be a significant cause of burnout, particularly if there are high job demands and low job resources (Alarcon, 2011; Demerouti & Bakker, 2011; Lee & Ashforth, 1996). But it is not just difficult work conditions that lead to burnout. Perfectionism plays a significant role in the development of the syndrome, because it predisposes workers to cope ineffectively with their high job demands (Swider & Zimmerman, 2010).

In addition to these more psychological hazards, you should also be aware of potential **physical health concerns** of deployment. Mental health workers should not knowingly be sent into an area with environmental hazards. However, you should always be aware that there are risks that may be unknown at the time of deployment, and that things can change rapidly at disaster sites. Issues such as air quality and safe water are two examples. Smoke from fires, floodwaters, very low temperatures, and downed power lines are dangerous! After the attacks on the World Trade Center, some mental health workers assisted first responders and grieving family members at the site. Although the Environmental Protection Agency declared the air to be safe, it wasn't, and these helpers were exposed to toxins, resulting in serious health problems for some. After Hurricanes Katrina and Sandy, many homes were infected with dangerous mold, and, although they were warned, some helpers entered those homes to talk with survivors when they should have encouraged survivors to come outside to talk. Please don't put yourself at risk. Take necessary precautions to protect your physical health and safety, and be sure to review the Centers for Disease Control and Prevention guidance at www.cdc.gov/travel about specific immunizations or cautions about hazards in the affected area.

Risk Factors for Occupational Hazards

How common are these occupational hazards for trauma workers? According to Mathieu (2012), between 40 and 85 percent of helping professionals develop some aspect of CF, VT, or STS. The International Society of Traumatic Stress Studies acknowledges that "anyone who encounters trauma survivors empathically and is committed to helping them" may be vulnerable to the array of occupational hazards discussed above. Compassion fatigue is an aspect of being human, and reflects our ability to care for others, empathize with their suffering, and genuinely seek to help them. As Figley (1995) describes, "[S]ometimes ... we become emotionally drained by [caring so much]; we are adversely affected by our efforts." When we find ourselves caring for others in highly stressful situations, such as in crises and disasters, and we feel obligated to help as many people as possible, we are vulnerable to these hazards.

Figley identifies four reasons why helpers may be vulnerable to compassion fatigue:

1. Empathy is a major resource for helpers to help the traumatized and suffering.
2. Most helpers have experienced some traumatic event in their lives.
3. Unresolved trauma on the part of helpers can be activated by reports of similar trauma or suffering in those they seek to help.
4. Children's trauma is particularly provocative for helpers, and helpers in disaster situations cannot escape seeing the suffering of children.

Unlike burnout, CF, STS, and VT are precipitated not by workload or institutional stress but by exposure to the trauma and suffering of others. These hazards have a similar disruptive effect on the helper to that which they have on the person directly affected by the crisis or traumatic event. There can be profoundly detrimental effects on the professional or volunteer helper. If left unaddressed, they can disrupt the helpers' feelings, personal relationships, physical well-being, work performance, and overall view of the world.

Contributing factors to all of these occupation hazards include:

- unique aspects of the helping relationship
- exposure to multiple traumatic and grief experiences
- concern for distress of colleagues
- chronic stressors that exacerbate reactions
- individual past/present traumatic and unresolved grief experiences
- feelings of helplessness to assist others, or, in some instances, to save lives
- need to maintain confidentiality, which prohibits discussion of cases with family and/or friends, precluding valuable sources of social support
- need to tolerate a great deal of ambiguity and uncertainty—in many cases not knowing the outcome of contact with those we help.

(Halpern & Tramontin, 2007)

Another risk factor for developing these occupational hazards is lack of experience and training. Volunteer responders to disasters show a higher vulnerability than professionals (Avieli, Ben-David, & Levy, 2016). An aware-ness of ethical codes, professional values, and rules of conduct can be a protective factor. Experienced professionals, while striving to be empathi-cally engaged, are trained to maintain appropriate emotional boundaries between themselves and clients. They may also have more realistic expec-tations about what they can accomplish. Perhaps volunteers and those with less experience are more confused about the closeness they should feel and express towards survivors and their sense of obligation to them. Training and adherence to ethical codes concerning boundaries, competence, and multiple relationships contribute to self-care.

SELF-CARE

Finally, we'll discuss practices you can develop to minimize your suscep-tibility to these occupational hazards. This is an ongoing process, not a box you can check off as a part of your training that you've completed. Your own needs will evolve as your personal life changes over time, and you'll need to adapt your self-care practices to each specific response. The following guidelines are based on both research and personal experience.

Effective Stress Management

Stress management requires continuous, ongoing attention to self-care. It is not something that is practiced once in a while, or just when you really need it. In order to be effective, stress management strategies must be a regular part of one's daily activities.

People often ask stress management experts: "What is the best stress management strategy?" The answer to that question is simple, and similar to another often question of health experts: "What is the best diet?" *It's the strategy that you'll actually do, every day.* It's less important which strat-egy you practice than that you practice it daily. Stress management is some-thing that you *do*, not something that you know about or plan to do. Good stress management strategies can improve the way we feel and allow us to function more effectively.

Many people engage in short-term (and short-sighted) stress manage-ment strategies that help them feel better temporarily. An example is hav-ing too much alcohol at the end of a long, stressful day. Does the drinking help us feel better in the moment? For many the answer is "Yes." How-ever, for most of us, the alcohol probably will not help us function better. It's tempting to go for short-term relief, and we shouldn't discount this temptation. But short-term relief is not enough; we have to combine relief with longer-term benefit.

We should also note that some people focus on strategies that they believe will help them function, but not feel, better. A typical example here is working more hours when we're under time pressure to complete a deadline. In the short term, working many hours may help us function better (at least at work, albeit with questionable effects upon our personal lives) in terms of meeting that deadline. However, in the longer term, working chronically long hours will likely reduce our effectiveness and efficiency. Thus, *we need to balance doing what helps us function better with what helps us feel better over the longer term.* Ironically, overworking and overindulging can go together, as people can justify their excessive eating and drinking because they have overextended themselves.

Comprehensive Approach to Self-Care Practices

Maintaining self-care practices during disaster assignments presents particular challenges. Helpers are out of their usual habitats, away from comforting routines and resources that they regularly use to manage stress, including separation from supportive family and friends. Because of these unique challenges, disaster workers need to plan how they will maintain self-care practices before, during, and after assignments.

A basic principle to remember is this: Maintaining self-care takes effort and discipline on deployment. The suggestions here might sound like platitudes, the kind of advice we heard from parents and teachers. We all know that we should eat plenty of fruits and vegetables, drink plenty of water, and get enough sleep. However, the demands of working in complex emergencies make it necessary for us to take these suggestions more seriously than we would in normal circumstances. The only way we can maintain these practices while deployed is to plan and prepare.

Preparing Mentally for Deployment: Stress Inoculation

Earlier we discussed logistical preparations for deployment, such as making sure work and family needs are covered and making a list of what to pack. It's equally important that you prepare mentally for your role in a disaster response, particularly if you're new to the field and have limited experience to draw on, or you're being assigned to a very intense event where you may be exposed to a great deal of survivor distress.

The principles of stress inoculation (Meichenbaum, 2007) can be very useful in this regard. Stress inoculation begins with the assumption that an upcoming experience *will* expose you to some unavoidable level of stress. Rather than trying to eliminate that stress, which would be impossible, the goal is to manage it. This involves several steps that, ideally, should be undertaken before the exposure actually occurs. It's a kind of mental dress rehearsal for what you might experience and how you'll successfully cope with it.

First, **identify potential stressors**, including environmental stimuli (troubling sights, sounds, and smells you may be exposed to at the site), likely organizational hassles (inter-agency chaos, inadequate resources, frustrated or hostile clients), and personal concerns (such as worries about family while you're deployed).

Second, **appraise those stressors**. How likely is each to occur? Most importantly, do you perceive it as a threat or a challenge? Perceiving a particular issue as a threat is likely to overwhelm your coping mechanisms and lead to negative self-talk that further undermines your ability to address the issue. In contrast, reframing it as a challenge or problem to be solved can help to activate your resources and coping skills. It's the difference between entering a situation thinking "I can't handle this" and "This will be difficult but I know I'll do my best."

Third, **identify potential coping strategies**. These should be both personal and professional. How will you break down seemingly overwhelming problems into manageable pieces? Who can you turn to for professional back-up and supervision? How will you remain in touch with family to make sure they're safe? How will you release your stress at the end of each day? Before you leave for the disaster think about the calls you may need to make—or to screen, if they're likely to increase rather than decrease your stress. Who will you assign to reassure a worried family member? Identify whom you will call for effective supervision, advice, and support and how you will calm yourself if you encounter insufficient resources or an incompetent site manager.

You certainly won't be able to foresee every possible issue that you'll encounter, but making the effort to have at least a basic mental game plan in place before you deploy can go far towards keeping your stress manageable while you're engaged in the response.

Managing Stress during a Response

No doubt we've all seen those lists of good self-care practices: Eat well, meditate or pray, exercise, and so on—all of the things that we know we should do but that are often difficult to maintain in daily life, let alone during periods of intense demands. Acknowledging that some healthy habits just won't be possible at certain times underscores the importance of having multiple self-care strategies in your personal toolkit so that, when one isn't available, you have other options to fall back on.

Best-practice self-care strategies used by mental health professionals to minimize disaster distress include the following:

- social support and countering isolation professionally and personally, including staying in touch with family and friends, sharing with "disaster buddies" (for example, another volunteer you agree to have coffee with every day so you can talk to someone who understands what you're experiencing), and seeking supervision as needed
- physical self-care through taking breaks, exercising (perhaps taking a short walk during a break), and eating as healthy a diet as possible
- mindful awareness and self-reflection, including journaling and meditation
- spiritual activities, including praying, speaking with a chaplain, cultivating meaning in the experience, appreciating nature, and empathetic engagement with clients
- relaxation exercises, such as stretching, guided imagery, or deep breathing.

Of course, not all of these activities will appeal to or provide comfort for every helper, so, just as you should encourage clients to use coping mechanisms that have worked for them in the past, you should think about what helps you deal with stress and plan for how you can practice that during and after a disaster response. You're far more likely to implement activities you've mapped out in advance than to develop positive habits on the fly in the midst of the response, so we encourage you to take some time to develop your own self-care plan now. The bottom line: Identify what works for you, and be sure to do it. And don't forget to include props for relaxation when packing.

Disengaging and Transitioning back to Normal Life

New DMH helpers are often surprised that one of the most challenging parts of the experience isn't the intense period of deployment but the return to ordinary life afterwards. Whether you were away on a disaster assignment for weeks or spent one day immersed in an extreme crisis, you'll have been functioning at a heightened tempo in stimulating, meaningful, and extraordinary circumstances, and this new rhythm doesn't just come to a halt when you leave the operation and return to more mundane activities.

We don't mean to suggest that co-workers, friends, and family won't be understanding of the challenges you faced when deployed or supportive of the work you did—but they might not be. When you return home your excitement and adrenaline level may be at odds with those around you. You may wish to share your stories, but those closest to you may not be able to relate or process these with you. They have undoubtedly missed you and have their own stories they've been waiting to share. They may even be resentful about the additional work they had to do to cover for your absence. Co-workers may tell you that, now that you've returned from your heroic adventure, you have to make up for the on-call responsibilities you missed. Your spouse might make clear that you have to compensate for the chores you avoided while away. Or you may feel your experiences are a private matter but find that others are curious and ask lots of invasive-feeling questions. Be prepared for this kind of discrepancy between your post-deployment functioning and that of those around you who didn't share your powerful experience.

Specific suggestions for effective post-deployment adjustment include the following.

- If possible, take some time off before returning to your normal duties. This might not be easy if you've been away for some time, but it is a good idea to get back a bit early before you have to resume normal activities.
- Take time to decompress physically and emotionally by engaging in activities that are both enjoyable and feel restorative.
- Use positive coping mechanisms.
- Talk with someone before leaving the assignment (e.g., staff/stress counselor, peer support helper, etc.) or soon upon returning home.

As this list suggests, you may need to give yourself time to get used to a very different intensity and pace, including returning to work issues that can seem banal or tedious relative to the rush of disaster mental health work. You may also need to expand your normal sources of social support and identify someone you can speak with who really understands what you've just been through, if that's your wish or need. Just as military veterans sometimes find each other to be the most understanding of their experiences, you may find you're most comfortable talking to another DMH helper or supervisor.

Barriers to Self-Care

Let's face it, self-care is never easy, and it's particularly difficult during a disaster. Our identity and priority as mental health professionals is to focus on helping others, not ourselves, and it's very easy not to push back against perhaps surmountable impediments to practicing what we preach. Let's look at common barriers to self-care to see if, by acknowledging what we're up against, we might be better able to over-come these obstacles.

Situational barriers: There might be a very difficult, noisy uncomfortable **work setting** and not enough **time** to do what needs to be done. You might have **colleagues** or **supervisors** who are inexperienced or ineffective. Don't assume that all disaster workers are thoughtful, experienced humanitarians. Most are, but some can be untried, incompetent, and irritating. You might also not get the support you would like from the home front—where you are being inundated with **demands from family members** who, when you have time off, want to let you know that the car broke down or your child got a bad report card. At the disaster you'll undoubtedly be affected by a general **lack of resources**. Survivors will need more than what is available. You may want to make copies of a handout to give to survivors, but the copy machine is broken and no one knows how to fix it or there's no paper. You might also experience your own **financial stress** as you take time to volunteer on the disaster or hear from home that the babysitter quit. For some, disaster work can make us aware of **physical limitations**. You may not be sleeping in your own bed, with your own routine, or you might feel the need to lift a box of supplies that's just too heavy. The demands of the situation may be so severe that it would take extraordinary discipline to maintain a balance of care for self while caring for others.

Personal and belief-based barriers: Even if we are fortunate enough to find ourselves with effective colleagues and resources (and, if we're away from home, bunking with a quiet roommate who doesn't snore), there can be many personal and cognitive factors that keep us from effective self-care. We might **lack basic knowledge** about the risks and hazards of the work and the importance of self-care. We might **lack self-awareness** of our own needs and limits. We might suffer from a **hero complex** and not be able to accept our limits. Sometimes a personal barrier to self-care could be as simple as being **resistant to making any changes** or as complex as a general **lack of self-esteem** or a sense of worthlessness. Some helpers can suffer from "**privilege guilt**," whereby they see others' suffering as so much more compelling than their own needs. As helpers, we can also suffer from any taint of being seen as or thinking of ourselves as **selfish** or **needy**. Many helpers have an aversion to accepting care from others or reaching out and advocating on their own behalf. There could also be a barrier of "**all or nothing thinking**," that, if we don't exercise or get to the gym every day, we might as well not do anything.

That's a long list of obstacles, but these are expectable challenges that can be overcome. Part of your self-care planning should be to consider which of these barriers you might be most susceptible to personally, and how you can overcome them. Maybe you won't be able to get to a gym for a traditional workout, but you can pack your sneakers and carve out time to run around the neighborhood, or up and down the motel staircase if conditions outside are unsafe. Prone to privilege guilt that makes you disregard your own well-being? Ask your "disaster buddy" to point out when you've stretched yourself too thin and need to take a break—and then actually take it. Frustrated by an overly demanding and micromanaging supervisor? Remind yourself that the working relationship is temporary and you can set limits without worrying about your long-term career prospects.

Above all, do not underestimate the psychological impact of your experience. If you find that you're struggling during or after a response, you don't have to be alone. Reach out to friends, family, colleagues, and faith-based resources, and remember that professional help is available if you need it. Just as we support clients who realize they need the help of a professional counsellor to process their disaster experience, we need to extend the same openness to our own needs.

Self-care is not optional. Many physical and psychosocial stress-related problems can be prevented through regular self-care practices. However, maintaining wellness requires daily practice. We need to commit ourselves to integrating self-care into our daily practices; think about how we can flourish rather than survive as disaster mental health helpers, and always consider the reciprocal relationship between care of self and care of others (Wise, Hersh, & Gibson, 2012). Rabbi Hillel understood well over 2,000 years ago that care for others is intertwined with care for the self: "If I am not for myself, who will be for me? If I am only for myself, what am I? And, if not now, when?"

REFERENCES

Alarcon, G. M. (2011). A meta-analysis of burnout with job demands, resources, and attitudes. *Journal of Vocational Behavior*, 79(2), 549–62.

Avieli, H., Ben-David, S., & Levy, I. (2016). Predicting professional quality of life among professional and volunteer caregivers. *Psychological Trauma: Theory, Research, Practice, and Policy*, 8(1), 80–7.

Branson, D. C., Weigand, D. A., & Keller, J. E. (2014). Vicarious trauma and decreased sexual desire: A hidden hazard of helping others. *Psychological Trauma: Theory, Research, Practice, and Policy*, 6(4), 398–403.

Charney, A. E., & Pearlman, L. A. (1998). The ecstasy and the agony: The impact of disaster and trauma work on the self of the clinician. In P. M. Kleespies (Ed.), *Emergencies in mental health practice: Evaluation and management*. New York: Guilford Press, pp. 418–35.

Cohen, K., & Collens, P. (2012). The impact of trauma work on trauma workers: A metasynthesis on vicarious trauma and vicarious posttraumatic growth. *Psychological Trauma: Theory, Research, Practice, and Policy*, 5(6), 570–80.

Demerouti, E., & Bakker, A. B. (2011). The job demands–resources model: Challenges for future research. *South African Journal of Industrial Psychology*, 37(2), 1–9.

Figley, C. R. (Ed.) (1995). *Compassion fatigue: Coping with secondary traumatic stress disorder in those who treat the traumatized.* New York: Routledge.

Halpern, J., & Tramontin, M. (2007). *Disaster mental health: Theory and practice.* Belmont, CA: Brooks/Cole.

Huggard, P., Stamm, B. H., & Pearlman, L. A. (2013). Physician stress: Compassion satisfaction, compassion fatigue and vicarious traumatization. In C. R. Figley, P. Huggard, & C. Rees (Eds.), *First do no self-harm: Understanding and promoting physician stress resilience.* New York: Oxford University Press, pp. 127–45.

Kim, H., Ji, J., & Kao, D. (2011). Burnout and physical health among social workers: A three-year longitudinal study. *Social Work,* 56(3), 258–68.

Kramen-Kahn, B., & Downing Hansen, N. (1998). Rafting the rapids: Occupational hazards, rewards, and coping strategies of psychotherapists. *Professional Psychology: Research and Practice,* 29(2), 130–4.

Lee, R. T., & Ashford, B. E. (1996). A meta-analytic examination of the correlates of the three dimensions of job burnout. *Journal of Applied Psychology,* 81(2), 123–33.

Maslach, C., Jackson, S. E., & Leiter, M. P. (1996). *The Maslach burnout inventory,* (3rd ed.). Palo Alto, CA: Consulting Psychologists Press.

Mathieu, F. (2012). *The compassion fatigue workbook: Creative tools for transforming compassion fatigue and vicarious traumatization.* New York: Routledge.

Meichenbaum, D. (2007). Stress inoculation training: A preventative and treatment approach. In P. M. Lehrer, R. L. Woolfolk, & W. E. Sime (Eds.), *Principles and practice of stress management* (3rd ed.). New York: Guilford Press, pp. 497–516.

Pearlman, L. A., & Saakvitne, K. W. (1995). Treating therapists with vicarious traumatization and secondary traumatic stress disorders. In C. R. Figley (Ed.), *Compassion fatigue: Coping with secondary traumatic stress disorder in those who treat the traumatized.* New York: Routledge, pp. 150–77.

Rosser, B. R. S. (2008). Working as a psychologist in the Medical Reserve Corps: Providing emergency mental health relief services in Hurricanes Katrina and Rita. *Professional Psychology: Research and Practice,* 39(1), 37–44.

Stamm, B. H. (Ed.) (1999). *Secondary traumatic stress: Self-care issues for clinicians, researchers, and educators* (3rd ed.). Baltimore: Sidran Press.

Stamm, B. H. (2010). *The Concise ProQOL manual: The concise manual for the professional quality of life scale* (2nd ed.). Pocatello, ID: ProQOL.org, www.proqol.org/uploads/ProQOL_Concise_2ndEd_12-2010.pdf.

Swider, B. W., & Zimmerman, R. D. (2010). Born to burnout: A meta-analytic path model of personality, job burnout, and work outcomes. *Journal of Vocational Behavior,* 76(3), 487–506.

Trippany, R. L., White Kress, V. E., & Wilcoxon, S. A. (2004). Preventing vicarious trauma: What counselors should know when working with trauma survivors. *Journal of Counseling and Development,* 82(1), 31–7.

Van Dernoot Lipsky, L. (2009). *Trauma stewardship: An everyday guide to caring for self while caring for others.* Oakland, CA: Berrett-Koehler.

WHO (2005). Psychosocial care of tsunami-affected populations: Caring for your own emotional well-being: Guidelines for relief workers. New Delhi: World Health Organization, Regional Office for South-East Asia, www.searo.who.int/entity/emergencies/documents/caring_for_your_own_emotional_well_being.pdf?ua=1.

Wise, E. H., Hersh, M. A., & Gibson, C. M. (2012). Ethics, self-care and well-being for psychologists: Reenvisioning the stress–distress continuum. *Professional Psychology: Research and Practice,* 43(5), 487–94.

Chapter 12

Conclusions and New Directions

For those of us who are immersed in the constantly evolving field of disaster mental health, it's always startling to stop and think about how young this field really is. As we described in Chapter 1, it started to coalesce as a distinct practice in the 1970s, and really began to expand in the 1990s after the American Red Cross created a dedicated DMH function. Since then it has become an established element of disaster response, and we hope by this point in the book you understand why that's appropriate. With today's increase in disaster frequency and intensity, as well as other sources of trauma worldwide, it's hard to imagine that the field will do anything but continue to grow and gain respect. In this final chapter we'll discuss some of the directions we expect that growth to take.

ADAPTING THE RESPONSE TO CHRONIC THREATS

Just as DMH evolved out of efforts to address other forms of trauma, including hysteria, war, and sexual and domestic abuse (Herman, 1992), the practices and interventions that have been developed to treat disaster survivors will need to be adapted in turn to treat victims of the other types of collective trauma that plague humanity today.

Forced Migration

As we wrote this book, the world was experiencing an unprecedented crisis of people who have been forced from their homes due to war or political conflict—even more than during the Second World War, according to the Office of the United Nations High Commissioner on Refugees (UNHCR), the lead international agency that addresses this issue. As of summer 2016 the UNHCR estimated there were 65.3 million forcibly displaced people worldwide, including 21.3 million refugees—more than half of them under age 18. The crisis shows no sign of slowing: Close to 34,000 more people are forced to flee their homes every day due to conflict and persecution (see www.unhcr.org/pages/49c3646c146.html). Victims include two broad groups.

Refugees are people who have been forced out of their home country into another nation, often with very little warning and sometimes literally bringing nothing but the clothes on their backs. While escaping their home nation generally means that they've relocated to a safer area, it also means they're now living in an unfamiliar culture that may have very different values and customs. They may need to learn a new language, often struggle to find work, and must deal with all of the other challenges of immigration. In some circumstances refugees are able to integrate into their new home, gaining asylum so they can't be sent back to their country of origin against their will. However, given the massive influx of millions of desperate people into some nations, particularly those adjacent to troubled countries such as Syria and Somalia, refugees are often unwelcome, and are treated as an economic burden and a cultural threat whose values are inconsistent with the host country's. They may be isolated in refugee camps, where they're forced to remain dependent on governmental and humanitarian aid groups, and they often lead a marginal existence—sometimes for years or even generations.

Internally displaced people (IDPs) also have had to leave their homes, but they remain within the borders of their own nation. While that might seem preferable to emigrating unwillingly, IDPs are often more vulnerable than refugees because they are not subject to protection by the United Nations. Instead they're at the mercy of the same rulers who forced them from home or targeted them in a civil war (www.unhcr.org/pages/49c3646c146.html). These rulers often deprive their citizens of access to support from humanitarian aid groups and non-governmental organizations (NGOs). IDPs suffer and die of starvation, from lack of access to medical care, and in extreme cases, such as the Assad regime in Syria, from intentional bombing and chemical attacks ordered by their own government (Shaheen, 2015).

Recognition of the need to address mental health issues among refugees has been growing—and the need is intense indeed. Not only are these people dealing with the resettlement stressors described above, but they also carry the trauma history of whatever forced them to leave their homes. That may include civil war, with exposure to bombings and shootings in their neighborhoods; religious or ethnic persecution; sexual assault; inadequate access to food, water, and medical care; imprisonment; and torture (see www.ptsd.va.gov/professional/trauma/other/ptsd-refugees. asp). Some have been physically injured or are suffering from untreated illnesses. Children are often malnourished—and some of these children have never known a life without violence and fear, making emotionally healthy future development doubtful. Not surprisingly, the prevalence of psychological distress is high; one study found rates of depression as high as 31 percent and of PTSD at a shocking 81 percent among some refugee groups (Hollifield et al., 2002). It's as if these families are trapped in the disillusionment stage of disaster response, with few resources available to instill hope for eventual recovery.

While the need for mental health support for these groups is clear, there are many barriers to providing it. Generally, IDPs are inaccessible to aid organizations that might try to support their mental health needs, leaving them victimized by their rulers emotionally as well as physically. This means the people who are most in need are the least likely to receive help (www. unhcr.org/pages/49c3646c146.html). Refugees may be more accessible, but given the sheer scope of the current crisis there simply are not enough resources available—and, not surprisingly, when providing basic survival essentials such as food, water, and shelter is a struggle, emotional needs tend to be viewed as a low priority by aid providers.

There are usually very limited local mental health resources or response infrastructure in developing nations or conflict-ridden areas, so a reliance on outside helpers may be necessary, though it's not clear that Western counseling practices are appropriate for these cultures (Nitza, 2011). Some host governments, and NGOs such as Doctors Without Borders/Médecins Sans Frontières, do try to incorporate what they usually refer to as "psychosocial" support into their response efforts, and so does the United Nations. But even those with good intentions face extreme versions of the cross-cultural challenges discussed in Chapter 10, including helpers' lack of familiarity with local beliefs and values and survivors' stigma about seeking mental health care.

Miller (2012) proposes that, rather than being offered traditional Western one-on-one counseling, refugees and survivors of humanitarian crises may benefit more from group-based interventions that incorporate traditional cultural practices, especially when working with members of collectivist cultures. Not only is this an efficient use of limited resources, but it can help to reduce feelings of isolation and restore bonds that have been broken by the traumatic betrayal by malevolent rulers. Groups can focus on providing psychoeducation and mutual support, accomplishing specific tasks, and/or completing activities that are both enjoyable and therapeutic, such as sports, dancing, singing, and theater. Importantly, local paraprofessionals such as teachers and undergraduate students can be trained to facilitate groups, increasing regional capacity and decreasing reliance on outside mental health professionals (Nitza, 2011).

Chronic Political Conflict

Throughout the world there are ongoing conflicts that put civilians' health and mental health at risk. Whole populations suffer not only from PTSD but also from debilitating fear resulting from the real danger they're living in. Of course, settling these conflicts is the best way to heal the traumas, but perhaps addressing the traumatic reactions can help to mitigate conflict. One project (Findley, Halpern, Rodriguez, & Vermeulen, 2016) that attempted to manage and mitigate conflict by addressing trauma, funded by the United States Agency for International Development, brought together Americans from the Institute for Disaster Mental Health at SUNY New Paltz with Russian-, Arab-, and Hebrew-speaking Israelis and Palestinians from Gaza and the West Bank. The chronic stressors in the region result in high rates of depression, PTSD, physical symptoms, and conflict (Besser & Neria, 2012; Dickstein et al., 2012; Hobfoll, Mancini, Hall, Canetti, & Bonanno, 2011). Children are particularly vulnerable, with students performing poorly in school (Pat-Horenczyk et al., 2009) and in many cases developing hostile perceptions that persist into adulthood. Adults also suffer when they feel unable to protect their children, though supportive parenting practices can mitigate distress in children (Thabet & Vostanis, 2011).

To address these needs, the American, Palestinian, and Israeli partners worked together to develop psychoeducational materials and Psychological First Aid trainings. Workshop participants then brought these trainings back to their communities in order to reduce stress, suffering, and conflict in the region. Data from the workshop confirmed that the *people-to-people* activities changed participant attitudes significantly. Israelis and Palestinians alike reported that as a result of the workshop they understood and felt more understood by the other. Participants also learned the principles and practices of PFA and expressed confidence that they could assist members of their community in times of crisis. Perhaps most significantly, by the end of the workshop they agreed that the training in PFA could help to reduce blame or conflict in their community. This is a region that has been severely traumatized with considerable stress, conflict, and loss. Even if this approach does not further the peace process, at least those trained will be better able to assist their friends and neighbors in distress. As one Palestinian doctor from Gaza noted: "If one mother does not punish her child for wetting the bed because she understands that it's due to stress and not because he's a bad boy, we have succeeded."

Helpers working in refugee camps, with IDPs, or in conflict zones face exceptional challenges. They are subject not only to the occupational hazards of working with trauma survivors, such as vicarious trauma and secondary traumatic stress, but also to the same traumatic conditions as the populations they're trying to help. This has been described as "shared traumatic or shared war reality" (Pruginin, Segal-Engelchin, Isralowitz, & Resnik, 2016). These conditions create such enormous stress on the entire population that the support seeking we usually recommend is not an effective coping mechanism (Halpern, 2016). Survivors looking for external support are disappointed to discover that friends and family are in the same situation and are less capable of offering support. Survivors and DMH helpers may need to find coping and self-care strategies that are uniquely appropriate to "shared traumatic reality" conditions.

Climate Change

While forced migration and wars tend to be focused in particular political hotspots around the globe, no one on earth is immune to the growing effects of climate change. Obviously, climate change is directly increasing the frequency and size of many weather-related disasters, particularly hurricanes, floods, and wildfires. It also contributes to emerging public health concerns, such as the drastic increase in Lyme disease that has sickened and disabled so many people in recent years as it spreads through the Northeast and Midwest regions of the United States (see www.cdc.gov/lyme/stats/index.html).

We've discussed the "dose–response" relationship, which means that people with exposure to these serious events are likely to experience strong negative emotional responses. But what about stress resulting from climate change itself? The traditional goal of disaster mental health has been to help people return to pre-event functioning. However, current shifts in weather patterns mean that this process now involves not only coping with the trauma of a particular incident but also adapting to our changing environment. It's less a question of "getting back to normal" and more a matter of learning to cope with the ever-evolving "new normal." Unfortunately, meeting this demand runs counter to the way humans evolved to cope with threats. As a species, we're remarkably good at mobilizing our physical and mental resources to deal with an urgent hazard. We flee or fight, and when the danger is over we return to our baseline and rebuild our internal resources to cope with the next peril to come along. But what can we do in the face of a threat that we know is increasing over time rather than diminishing?

In one sense, responding to more powerful disasters is, while certainly not the easy part, at least the part we know how to do. Of course, meeting greater need requires more trained professional responders and other resources, but that's primarily a matter of scaling up existing knowledge and preparation and adapting them to a lengthier response cycle. In contrast, climate change's ripple effects are creating unfamiliar challenges that we must now figure out how to address. According to the US Department of Defense (2014), some of these needs involve issues of security—both concerns about food and water insecurity, related to droughts and temperature increases that will impact crop production, and challenges for national security, as climate change serves as a "threat multiplier" with the potential to exacerbate problems globally, including infectious disease outbreaks, forced migration, political instability, and terrorism. These varied challenges are expected to stretch military resources worryingly thin.

Looking specifically at mental health effects of climate change, the National Wildlife Foundation (2012) predicts that, in response to the related physical and economic destruction, "the incidences of mental and social disorders will rise steeply. These will include depressive and anxiety disorders, posttraumatic stress disorders, substance abuse, suicides, and widespread outbreaks of violence. Children, the poor, the elderly, and those with existing mental health disorders are especially vulnerable and will be hardest hit." Children in particular are at risk of psychological distress, the foundation suggests, as they confront existential worry about their futures as well as dealing with current effects. Additionally, responders will risk becoming overwhelmed as they attempt to cope with constant demands for help.

Healthcare providers are also bracing for an increase in various infectious diseases and other threats to health as climate change interacts with other societal factors such as increasing population density and global travel. The World Health Organization (WHO, 2016) predicts that climate change will cause approximately 250,000 additional deaths per year worldwide between 2030 and 2050, including 38,000 due to heat exposure in elderly people, 48,000 due to diarrhea, 60,000 due to malaria, and 95,000 due to childhood under-nutrition. The WHO also cites water quality and quantity, food security, and protection from disasters (including both coastal flooding and extreme drought) as mechanisms through which climate change is expected to compromise health worldwide.

At this point it's really not clear what can be done to address the psychological impact of climate change, though researchers are beginning to explore the topic. One of the most difficult aspects of climate change for many adults is how uncontrollable it seems. This is even truer for young people, who have little power to influence public policies or other mitigation efforts, yet who understand that they will have to live with the long-term consequences of current global energy use practices. One study by a Swedish researcher (Ojala, 2012) examined how children, adolescents, and young adults dealt with their worries about climate change's impact on their futures. Participants were asked, "When you feel the most worried, do you do anything to not worry so much? If yes, describe what you do." These responses were grouped into the following coping style themes and sub-themes.

Emotion-focused coping: This style of coping is often used in an attempt to control or reduce negative thoughts or feelings that are evoked by a stressor, which was clearly the case here. Sub-themes included de-emphasizing the seriousness of climate change, by arguing that the issue is exaggerated or of no personal consequence; distancing oneself from the problem, by avoiding reminders and distracting oneself when cues are encountered; and seeking social support from friends and relatives, to regulate worry and gain comfort. Some of the older participants also reported hyperactivation, or an elevated awareness of the issue, involving rumination, helplessness, fatalism, or venting of anger.

Problem-focused coping: Responses in this group involved actions the young people were taking to try to mitigate climate change themselves. Sub-themes included preparatory actions, such as thinking about the issue, researching information, and making plans about what to do; and direct actions, including saving energy, avoiding driving, and buying environmentally friendly products, as well as persuading others to take similar actions. Another strategy that acknowledged the limitation of individual activities was encouraging collective problem-focused actions, such as working together to combat climate change.

Meaning-focused coping: The final group of responses reflected efforts to balance some degree of optimism with an acknowledgment of the seriousness of the problem. Sub-themes here included positive reappraisal, such as focusing on growing public awareness of climate change's consequences; positive thinking/existential hope that the problem will eventually be solved; trust that scientists, environmental groups, or politicians will develop innovative solutions to counter the effects of climate change; and faith that God will provide protection.

Overall, the emotion- and problem-focused strategies were mostly commonly used to combat worry, while the meaning-focused strategies were more commonly used to promote hope (Ojala, 2012). This is a lesson that could be implemented while trying to help clients cope with stress related to climate change: If an individual is ruminating about the threat, emotion-focused actions such as seeking social support might help reduce distress. If one is feeling helpless, encouraging individual or collective activities to address the problem directly could restore some sense of control.

And, if someone is feeling hopeless about climate change's consequences, meaning-focused activities such as reframing the issue to focus on global efforts to contain those effects could instill some optimism about the future. Of course, none of these strategies actually solve the underlying problem of climate change, but they might help individuals at least manage their emotional reactions while bigger solutions are pursued.

INCORPORATING TECHNOLOGY

The disaster response field has embraced technology as a tool for streamlining logistics, managing resources, collecting and disseminating information, and so on. While the mental health side has been somewhat slower to incorporate technology into our interventions, there are a growing number of apps and other tools for both survivors and DMH responders. The National Center for PTSD is a leader in developing free apps for both groups.

Apps for providers:
www.ptsd.va.gov/professional/materials/apps

Apps for patients and families:
www.ptsd.va.gov/public/materials/apps/index.asp

The National Center for PTSD's PFA Mobile app, which was created in partnership with the National Child Traumatic Stress Network, the Department of Defense's National Center for Telehealth and Technology, and the Veterans Administration's Patient Care Services, is especially handy as a refresher on Psychological First Aid actions you can carry with you on deployment.

Another very useful source for free apps is the Substance Abuse and Services Administration (SAMHSA), whose Disaster App can help behavioral health responders prepare before deployment, provide on-the-ground assistance, and find post-deployment resources and self-care support. You can find and provide tip sheets and guides for teachers and caregivers as well as a directory of mental health providers in the impacted area. Resources can be pre-downloaded if you anticipate limited internet connectivity in the area.

www.store.samhsa.gov/apps/disaster

The American Red Cross also has developed a number of free apps, including first aid guides for humans and pets, and a series of disaster-specific guides with notifications and tips on surviving hurricanes, tornadoes, wildfires, and other events.

www.redcross.org/get-help/prepare-for-emergencies/mobile-apps

Chapter 11 suggested some other useful apps to bring with you on deployment, such as GPS, language translation tools, and weather apps. There are also many self-care apps available, including mindfulness and breathing exercises, and soothing sounds, such as rainfall and white noise, to help you unwind at the end the day. And, if you're deploying to an unfamiliar area, it can be useful to ask local volunteers or staff members if there are any region-specific apps they find helpful, either for disaster-related information or more general local intelligence. For example, an app that provided subway route guidance became a valuable navigation tool for Hurricane Sandy response volunteers who were unfamiliar with the New York City public transportation system.

We do have two caveats about relying on technological tools. First, using these resources at all assumes access to a smartphone or a computer or tablet with an internet connection—expensive luxuries for people living in poverty, and unfamiliar technologies for some older adults, so members of certain vulnerable groups may not benefit from them. Second, if cell tower service is disrupted by a disaster or electrical power is lost for an extended period, access may be missing just when it's needed most. We have some concern about over-reliance on fallible technologies, but these tools certainly can be a valuable supplement to other types of response efforts, and we expect their use to grow.

THE CONTINUING NEED FOR RESEARCH

Finally, we'll address a problem that has plagued the disaster mental health field since its inception: a lack of high-quality research on the effectiveness of our interventions (Reifels et al., 2013). Empirical research on mental health interventions is never easy, but it's even more complex in DMH response, for a number of reasons.

First, disasters are usually unpredictable, with perhaps a few days' warning for some events and no advance notice for others. This makes it extremely hard to organize studies in advance, so researchers often react rather than anticipate, and they miss collecting critical early data. This also means that we rarely have baseline data on how people were functioning before the disaster, undermining our ability to assess their recovery accurately.

Second, there are some serious ethical difficulties in pursuing the so-called "gold standard" of research, the randomized experiment in which people with similar characteristics are assigned to different experiences or treatments in order to isolate the impact of the intervention. Even if a potential research target could be identified in advance, such as a group of residents of a tornado-prone area, and baseline data was collected, ethics forbid randomly assigning some unlucky participants to a "no warning" control group, as individuals certainly can't be exposed to unnecessary harm simply for the purposes of research; nor should we ever withhold PFA from a group just to see what happens. It is possible to assign groups to different forms of treatment afterwards to compare effectiveness (for example, using Prolonged Exposure Therapy versus Cognitive Processing Therapy), or to compare a treatment group with a waitlisted group who will receive the intervention later, but those clinical interventions are long-term therapies offered weeks or months after the disaster. Another ethical concern is whether it's appropriate to spend any resources on research rather than on directly assisting people in need, though we would argue that the longer-term benefits of improving our interventions more than justify the short-term investment. Some also question whether one can obtain valid informed consent from people in the immediate aftermath of a disaster, and normal standards of confidentiality are also very difficult to maintain in a chaotic post-disaster situation.

Third, the whole point of Psychological First Aid is that it's not standardized but is customized to each survivor's needs at that particular point in time. This flexibility is its main strength, but it makes it virtually impossible to compare results across recipients, since every PFA interaction is unique. That's why we generally describe PFA as "evidence-informed" rather than "evidence-based."

This absence of solid research results in two key issues. First, we would like to know that we're delivering services in the most effective way possible, and to change our procedures if we're not. The second is more of a public relations problem: Because we can't generally describe our efforts as evidence-based or demonstrate their impact empirically, it leaves the field open to attack by those who don't value the inclusion of mental health in disaster response and think those resources are better used in other ways. We hope that the next stage in the DMH field's development will include more innovative approaches to research that will allow us to demonstrate its importance and maximize its efficacy.

A FINAL NOTE

This concludes our overview of the field of disaster mental health. Whether you're an experienced practitioner looking to expand your expertise or a student considering a career path, we hope you'll feel motivated to incorporate disaster response into your professional or volunteer repertoire. The work is challenging, to be sure, and attention to self-care is essential. But being able to support survivors on what may feel like the worst days of their lives provides a satisfaction that's hard to achieve in ordinary life.

REFERENCES

Besser, A., & Neria, Y. (2012). When home isn't a safe haven: insecure attachment orientations, perceived social support, and PTSD symptoms among Israeli evacuees under missile threat. *Psychological Trauma: Theory, Research, Practice, and Policy,* 4(1), 34–46.

Department of Defense (2014). 2014 climate change adaptation roadmap. Alexandria, VA: Department of Defense, ppec.asme.org/wp-content/uploads/2014/10/CCARprint.pdf.

Dickstein, B. D., Schorr, Y., Stein, N., Krantz, L. H., Solomon, Z., & Litz, B. T. (2012). Coping and the mental health outcomes among Israelis living with the chronic threat of terrorism. *Psychological Trauma: Theory, Research, Practice, and Policy,* 4(4), 392–9.

Findley, P. A., Halpern, J., Rodriguez, R., & Vermeulen, K. (2016). Psychological first aid: a tool for mitigating conflict in the Middle East. In R. Isralowitz & P. A. Findley (Eds.), *Mental health and addiction care in the Middle East.* Cham, Switzerland: Springer, pp. 155–70.

Halpern, J. (2016). Maintaining helper wellness and competence in a shared trauma reality. *Israel Journal of Health Policy Research,* 5, DOI: 10.1186/s13584-016-0102-7.

Herman, J. L. (1992). *Trauma and recovery: The aftermath of violence—from domestic abuse to political terror.* New York: Basic Books.

Hobfoll, S. E., Mancini, A. D., Hall, B. J., Canetti, D., & Bonanno, G. A. (2011). The limits of resilience: distress following chronic political violence among Palestinians. *Social Science and Medicine,* 72(8), 1400–8.

Hollifield, M., Warner, T. D., Lian, N., Krakow, B., Jenkins, J. H., Kesler, J., ..., & Westermeyer, J. (2002). Measuring trauma and health status in refugees: a critical review. *Journal of the American Medical Association,* 288(5), 611–21.

Miller, J. L. (2012). *Psychosocial capacity building in response to disasters.* New York: Columbia University Press.

National Wildlife Foundation (2012). *The psychological effects of global warming on the United States: And why the US mental health care system is not adequately prepared.* Merrifield, VA: National Wildlife Foundation, www.nwf.org/~/media/PDFs/Global-Warming/Reports/Psych_Effects_Climate_Change_Full_3_23.ashx.

Nitza, A. (2011). Group processes in experiential training groups in Botswana. *Journal for Specialists in Group Work,* 36(3), 222–42.

Ojala, M. (2012). Regulating worry, promoting hope: how do children, adolescents, and young adults cope with climate change? *International Journal of Environmental and Science Education,* 3(3), 537–61.

Pat-Horenczyk, R., Qasrawi, R., Lesack, R., Haj-Yahia, M., Peled, O., Shaheen, M., ..., & Abdeen, Z. (2009). Posttraumatic symptoms, functional impairment, and coping among adolescents on both sides of the Israeli-Palestinian conflict: a cross-cultural approach. *Applied Psychology,* 58(4), 688–708.

Pruginin, I., Segal-Engelchin, D., Isralowitz, R., & Reznik, A. (2016). Shared war reality effects on the professional quality of life of mental health professionals. *Israel Journal of Health Policy Research,* 5, DOI: 10.1186/s13584-016-0075-6.

Reifels, L., Pietrantoni, L., Prati, G., Kim, Y., Kilpatrick, D. G., Dyb, G., ..., & O'Donnell, M. (2013). Lessons learned about psychosocial responses to disaster and mass trauma: an international perspective. *European Journal of Psychotraumatology,* 4, DOI: 10.3402/ejpt.v4i0.22897.

Shaheen, K. (2015, May 24). Assad regime accused of 35 chlorine attacks since mid-March. *Guardian,* www.theguardian.com/world/2015/may/24/syria-regime-accused-of-using-chlorine-bombs-on-civilians.

Thabet, A. A., & Vostanis, P. (2011). Impact of political violence and trauma in Gaza on children's mental health and types of interventions: a review of research evidence in a historical context. *International Journal of Peace and Development Studies,* 2(8), 214–18.

World Health Organization (2016, June). Climate change and health fact sheet. World Health Organization, www.who.int/mediacentre/factsheets/fs266/en.

Index

Note: **bold** page numbers refer to tables

9/11 World Trade Center attacks 6, 46, 51, 82, 92, 93, 108, 176; children and 106, 124, 130; first responders 35, 47, 90, 108, 115–16;PTSD and 47, 102–3, 104–5, 108; survivor (self)-blame 54, 71

acknowledgment 58, 60–1
Acute Stress Disorder 37, 76
adaptability 7–8, 79, 81, 89, 106
affective reaction to loss 86
African Americans 161–2
afterlife 86, 93, 160
Allison, Tropical Storm 3–4
American Psychiatric Association (APA) 5, 6
American Psychological Association 6, 10
American Red Cross 10, 45, 53, 57, 62, 63, 80, 82, 127, 152, 193; disaster mental health and 6, 9, 78, 186; shelters 12, 13, 19, 122, 156–7, 167–8
The Anatomy of Bereavement 92
anger 27–8, 29, 37, 38, 59, **76**, 87, 89–90, 95, 110, 111, 112, 114, 115, 174
anhedonia 87, 112, 113
anniversaries 45, 95, 99–100; *see also* memorials
anxiety 1, 27, 37, 38, 42, 55, 58, 87, 145, 147, 191; of caregivers 124, 126; in

children 125, 126, 128, 130, 133; in helpers 154; information and 62, 64; in older adults 140; reducing 55, 60, 62, 149; separation from children 33, 43, 156; *see also* calming
arousal levels 14, 37, 41, 43, 44, 55, 58, 78, 110–11; hyperarousal 77, 175
Asian cultures 39
assessment 2, 16, 26, 36, 39, 45, 73–7, 103, 111–13, 139
assistive devices 137, 139, 142, 143, 145

Beck Depression Inventory II 114
behavioral reactions to disaster 38–9
behavioral reactions to loss 87–8
behavior-based assessment 75–6
belongingness and love needs 57
bereavement 85–101; characteristics of deaths 88–91; multiple losses 24–5, 89; posttraumatic growth 51; private rituals 91–3; public rituals 94–5; reactions to loss 87–8; supporting the bereaved 65–6, 75, 95–9; *see also* grief
bioterrorism 20, 27, 29
blame 18, 27–8, 29, 32, 37, 38, 43, 68, 72, 89, 110, 112; self-blame 32, 38, 43, 48, 54, 71, 89
Bonanno, George 49, 107
Boston 6, 82, 130

Brewin, Chris 76–7
Buddhism 158, 160, 164
building practices 26, 107, 150
burnout 174, 175–6, 177

Calhoun, Lawrence 50, 51
California Emergency Management
    Agency 164
calming 55, 58, 60
Catholic Charities 10
cause of disaster **23**, 26–31, 104–5
Centers for Disease Control and
    Prevention 176
Center for Epidemiological Studies
    Depression Scale 114
characteristics of disasters 1, 18–19,
    22–34
characteristics of families 105, 106–7
characteristics of individuals 23, **23**,
    35–6, 41; *see also* vulnerable groups
children: 9/11 World Trade Center
    attacks 106, 124, 130; anxiety in 125,
    126, 128, 130, 133; depression in 125,
    126, 128, 133, 189, 191; empowering
    65; and extreme reactions 105, 106;
    and helper trauma 133, 177; helping
    127–32; as internally displaced
    people 188; play 130, 133; PTSD
    and 118, 125, 126, 133; recovery
    and 123, 125–6; referrals 133; risk
    factors 125–7; safety and 123, 124,
    125, 128, 130–1; in shelters 12, 163;
    sleep disruption in 128, 129; stress
    reactions of 64, 124–5, 127–9, 163;
    talking with 132; as translators 162–3;
    see also families; schools
Chile 24, 26
"chronic" group of survivors 107–8
Churchill, Winston 1
climate change 18, 21, 26, 41
Clinician-Administered PTSD Scale
    (CAPS-5) 108
cognitive disorders 140, 146
Cognitive Processing Therapy (CPT) 7,
    117, 118
cognitive reactions to disaster 6, 33,
    38, 39, 41, 48, 49, 61, 63, 76, 109,
    110; *see also* concentration problems;
    memory problems
cognitive reactions to loss 88
collective efficacy 81–2

Columbia space shuttle 90
Columbia University Journalism
    School 90
communities: community spirit 44–5,
    162; impacted by disasters 19–20, **23**,
    24, 104; involving 164–5; resilience
    and 50, 69, 79, 83
compassion fatigue (CF) 2, 172, 174–5,
    176, 177
compassion satisfaction 172
Complicated Grief 114–15
concentration problems 38, 39, 64, **76**,
    88, 111, 112, 113, 128
conflict mitigation 2, 73, 163
connectedness 55
Connor–Davidson Resilience Scale 79
construction practices 26, 107, 150
coping mechanisms 28, 41, 46, 50, 64,
    64, 69, 73, 160, 173, 180, 182
Council for Accreditation of
    Counseling and Related Educational
    Programs (CACREP) 6
Crisis Counseling Assistance and
    Training Program (CCP) 9, 103
Critical Incident Stress Debriefing 8, 78
Critical Incident Stress Management 78
crying 39, 65, 87, 128
cultural issues 132, 156–66, 188;
    appropriate assistance 66, 74, 86;
    definition of culture 158–9; diet 74,
    157, 163; reactions and 2, 27, 39,
    88; resilience 50; rituals 91; shelters
    and 12, 74, 162–3; Western bias of
    disaster mental health 188;
    see also immigrants

Danieli, Yael 15
Dart Center 90
deaths, disaster-caused 88–91
debriefing *see* Psychological Debriefing
Deep Water Horizon oil spill 114
denial 5, 42, 43, 51
Department of Health 10
Department of Homeland Security 80
Department of Labor 10
Department of Mental Health 10
deployment logistics 15, 168–72, 179–80
depression 1, 11, 15, 37, 38, 76, 87,
    95, 106, 118, 145, 147, 189, 191; in
    children 125, 126, 128, 133, 189, 191;
    of first responders/helpers 16, 168;

Major Depressive Disorder (MDD) 113–14, 115; in older adults 140; refugees and 188
diagnoses 16, 73
Diagnostic and Statistical Manual 5; *see also* DSM-5
dietary issues 38, **64**, 74, 157, 163, 181
disaster, definition 19–20
Disaster Distress Helpline 6
disaster life cycles 41–6
disaster plans 79–80, 138, 144; *see also* preparedness
Disaster Relief Act (1974) 6
Disaster Response Centers (DRCs) 4, 7, 8, 10, 12–13, 14, 167–8; *see also* shelters
disasters: characteristics of 1, 18–19, 22–34; and emergencies 19, 21–2; examples 20–1; during impact 43–4; post-impact 44–6; pre-impact 41–3, 55
diseases 21, 29–30, 88, 124, 191
disillusionment phase 44–5
dissociation 5, 36, 76, 110
DMH (disaster mental health): definition 3–17; history of 4–6, 186
Doctors Without Borders 188
domestic abuse 5, 116, 186
dose-response relationship 26, 46–7, 105, 126, 137, 138
DSM-5 (*Diagnostic and Statistical Manual, fifth edition*) 46, 109, 112, 113, 164–5
dual process model 96
duration of disaster 24, 25–6, 44, 75, 111

early interventions 53–67, 68–84; assessment 73–7; conflict mitigation 2, 73, 163; correcting self-cognitions 70–2; evidence-based principles 55–6; importance 54–5; problem-solving 69–70; Psychological Debriefing 77–8; referrals 77; resilience building 79–83; rumor control 72–3; *see also* Psychological First Aid (PFA)
early responders *see* first responders
earthquakes 7, 20, 24, 25, 31; Chile 24, 26; Haiti 24, 26, 34, 92, 107; Japan 26, 92–3; Pakistan 33–4

Effective Treatments for PTSD: Practice Guidelines 117
EgyptAir flight 990 53
elderly people *see* older adults
emergencies versus disasters 19, 21–2
emotional reactions *see* reactions to disaster
empathy 56, 57, 58, 59, 61; helpers and 172, 174, 175, 176–7, 178; reciprocal 73; *see also* vicarious trauma (VT)
Environmental Protection Agency 176
esteem needs 57
ethnic minorities 105
evacuations 14, 18, 31, 75, 107, 113, 126, 160–1; vulnerable groups and 137, 139, 140, 141, 143, 144, 150, 160–1; warnings and 18, 31, 32, 42–3, 54, 156, 160–1
evidence-based treatments 2, 55–6, 77, 103, 117–18
expected disasters 23, 31–2; *see also* warnings of disasters
experience-based assessment 74–5
Eye Movement Desensitization and Reprocessing 7, 117

false alarms 18, 32, 43, 156
Family Assistance Centers (FACs) 4, 10, 12, 13–14; *see also* shelters
families 33, 36, 43, 105, 106–7, 122–35, 151; of helpers 169–70, 180, 181–2, 183; *see also* children
Family Service Centers *see* Family Assistance Centers (FACs)
FBI victim services 10
Federal Emergency Management Agency (FEMA) 9, 12–13, 62, 80, 152
females: abuse and 5, 106; mental health issues and 105, 106, 125
fight, flight or freeze response 37, 43, 44, 111, 123
Figley, Charles 177
fire codes 26
fires 6, 18, 26, 35, 43, 79, 176, 190
first responders 2, 8, 16–17, 21, 46–7, 153–5; 9/11 World Trade Center attacks 35, 47, 90, 108, 115–16; depression 16, 168; PFA and 56, 66; Psychological Debriefing and 69, 78; PTSD and 16, 47, 78, 108, 154
First World War 5

Flood Control Act (1928) 68–9
floods 3–4, 25, 26, 32, 59, 60, 68, 72, 91, 104, 122, 144, 150, 190; *see also* New Orleans
Freud, Sigmund 5
Friedman, Matthew 104
functioning realms: in older adults 139; reactions to disaster and 37–41, 107–8; reactions to loss 87–8
funerals 65, 91, 92; *see also* rituals

general public: Psychological Debriefing and 2, 8, 69, 78; public rituals 94–5; *see also* preparedness
genuineness, showing 56, 57, 58, 59
God 4, 11, 27, 28, 39, 48, 55, 87, 97, 160, 192; *see also* spiritual care
grief 85–101, 114–15, 143, 159, 160; assisting with 58, 65–6, 93, 95–9; *see also* bereavement
Grief, Complicated/Prolonged/Traumatic 114–15
group-based interventions 188–9
guilt 38, 48–9, 87, 93, 96, 110, 112, 113; children and 128; helpers and 174, 183, 184; performance 48; privilege 183, 184; relief and 87, 96; rituals and 93, 159; survivor 48, 115; warnings and 31–2, 33, 43, 48, 89–90
Gustav, Hurricane 43

H1N1 pandemic 30
Haiti 24, 26, 34, 92, 107
heatwaves 20, 136–7
helpers: compassion fatigue in 177; empathy and 172, 174, 175, 176–7, 178; families of 169–70, 180, 181–2, 183; guilt and 174, 183, 184; helplessness of 174, 177; mental health needs 46–7; psychosocial factors and 173, 174, 184; PTSD and 47, 103; *see also* first responders
helplessness 27, 88, 128, 164–5; of helpers 174, 177
Herman, Judith 4–5, 49
hero complex 183
heroes 35, 48, 90
heroic phase 44
hierarchy of needs (Maslow) 57, 145, 168
Hillel, Rabbi 184

Hinduism 158, 164
Hobfoll, Stevan 55, 162
Holocaust 15
honeymoon period 44, 45
hopefulness 55, 79
hopelessness 37, 38, 88, 107, 140
Hudson River plane accident 22, 34
human-caused disasters **23**, 26, 27–9, 160
hurricanes 20, 21, 24, 25, 26, 43, 130, 156–7; Katrina 24, 26, 35, 43, 54, 68–9, 72, 82, 118, 126, 161, 176; Sandy 24, 82, 125, 176, 194
Husband, Evelyn 90
hyperarousal 77, 175, 224
hypervigilance 6, 38, 42, 43, 111, 112
hysteria 5, 76

Ike, Hurricane 130
immigrants 151–2, 156–7, 160, 161, 187; *see also* migrants
Indian Ocean tsunami 92, 164, 173–4
individual characteristics 23, **23**, 35–6, 41; *see also* vulnerable groups
industrial accidents 27, 33, 104
influenza 29, 30, 92
information gathering 69–70
information provision 12–13, 15, 30–1, 40, 41–2, 58, 61, 62–3, 72–3, 74; children and 130, 131
Institute for Disaster Mental Health 6
instrumental support 61
insurance 4, 10, 13, 45, 62, 75, 89, 107, 151, 171
intellectual disabilities 146
intensity of disaster 24–5, 27, 44
inter-individual reaction differences 36
internally displaced people (IDPs) 187–9
Internal Revenue Service 10
The International Society of Traumatic Stress Studies 176–7
intra-individual reaction differences 36, 41
introducing yourself 8–9
Islam 91, 163, 164
isolation of sick people 30

Japan 26, 92–3
Judaism 91, 163

Katrina, Hurricane 24, 26, 35, 43, 54, 68–9, 72, 82, 118, 126, 161, 176
Kübler-Ross, Elisabeth 95

language barriers 162–3
Lanza, Adam 85; see also Sandy Hook
legal proceedings 29, 89, 114, 160
LGBTQ individuals 25, 152–3, 165
life cycle of disaster 41–6
Lindemann, Eric 6
location, reactions by 46–7
logistical issues of disasters 19, 23, 25–6, 33, 34, 59, 139, 145
logistics of deployment 15, 168–72, 179–80
London bombings 2005 77, 112
long-term difficulties 2, 21, 44, 45, 54, 55, 71, 77, 106, 160
long-term treatment 2, 55, 57, 77, 103, 115, 116–18, 195
loss, disaster-related 2, 31–2, 85–101; characteristics of deaths 88–91; private rituals 91–3; public rituals 94–5; reactions to 14, 28, 40, 87–8, 140; supporting the bereaved 65, 95–100; see also grief

Major Depressive Disorder (MDD) 113–14, 117
males, mental health issues and 105, 140
Maslow, Abraham 56, 57, 145, 168
Médecins Sans Frontières 188
media 44, 45–6, 50, 60–1, 71, 85, 90, 94, 100, 148; influence of 46, 90, 100, 110, 130, 131
medically unexplained physical symptoms ("MUPS") 30
medication: access to 60, 75, 114, 139, 140, 141, 144, 147, 148, 149, 150, 153; antidepressants 114, 117, 146
memorials 11, 45, 66, 93, 94–5, 99–100
memory problems 38, 39, 76, 88
mental disabilities 145–50
migrants 186–9
Miller, Joshua 157–8, 188
"Miracle on the Hudson" 22
Mitchell, Jeffrey 78
mobility impairments 137, 139, 142, 143

mourning 55, 86, 88, 89, 90, 91, 92, 93, 95, 96, 131, 159, 162; see also funerals; memorials
Muslims 91, 163, 164

na-tech events 26
National Association of Social Workers 6, 10
National Center for PTSD 57, 69, 117, 125
National Child Traumatic Stress Network 57, 69, 125, 127, 158
National Council on Disability 145
National Disaster Interfaiths Network 164
National Guard 10
National Institute of Mental Health (NIMH) 56, 57, 63, 74, 78, 159
National Transportation Safety Board 10
natural disasters 21, 23, 27, 31, 150, 160; see also weather events
New Jersey 82
New Orleans 26, 43, 54, 68–9, 82, 126, 150, 161–2; see also Katrina, Hurricane
New York 80, 82, 167–8; see also 9/11 World Trade Center attacks
The New York Times 90
nightclub disasters 6, 20, 21, 25
non-governmental organizations (NGOs) 187, 188
normality, returning to 20, 44, 45, 107, 140, 168, 181–2, 190
Norris, Fran 104, 105, 106, 107

occupational hazards 2, 57, 133, 172, 173–8; see also self-care; vicarious trauma (VT)
Office for Victims of Crime 10
Office of Children and Family Services 10
Office of Temporary and Disability Assistance 10
Office of the United Nations High Commissioner on Refugees (UNHCR) 187
Oklahoma City bombing 6
older adults 105–6, 136–7, 138–42
Orlando, Florida 25, 153
Oso, Washington 47

Page, Herbert 5–6
Pakistan 33–4
pandemics 20, 26, 30, 92
panic 38, 43, 76
PCL-5 20-item questionnaire 109, 112–13
performance guilt 48
personality factors 106
pets 12, 18, 42, 75, 80, 86, 88, 103, 122, 126, 139, 140
physical disabilities 142–5
physical health of helpers 176
physical reactions 37, 38, 39
physical risk factors of older adults 137, 139–40
physiological needs, addressing 59, 60
physiological reactions 30, 37, 44, 55, 57, 88, 110
place attachment 82
plane accidents 22, 28–9, 34, 53–4, 91, 98
play 130, 133
Points of Dispensing (PODs) 30
post-impact of disaster 44–6
posttraumatic growth (PTG) 40, 50–1, 152, 173
Posttraumatic Stress Disorder (PTSD) 1, 5–6, 29, 37, 46, 62, 71, 103, 147, 193; assessment for 76–7, **76**; children and 118, 125, 126, 133; diagnosing 108–13; first responders and 16, 47, 78, 108, 154; helpers and 103; longer-term treatment 2, 116–18; Psychological Debriefing and 78; refugees and 188; risk factors 104–7; and secondary traumatic stress (STS) 175
poverty 141, 150–1, 194; see also socioeconomic status
pre-impact of disaster 41–3, 55
preparedness 1, 11, 15, 55, 69, 77, 79–80, 81, 82–3, 89, 145, 154–5, 161
prevention 26, 28, 79–83
privacy issues 11, 12, 13, 90, 156
private rituals 91–3, 100
privilege guilt 183, 184
problem-solving 69–70
Prolonged Exposure (PE) therapy 7, 117–18
Prolonged Grief (PG) 114
psychiatric illnesses 103, 145–50

psychoeducation 12, 40, 45, 58, 63–4, **64**, 85, 99, 127, 133, 150, 188
Psychological Debriefing 69, 77–8
Psychological First Aid (PFA) 2, 6, 12, 34, 40, 53–67, 74, 127, 145; see also early interventions
psychological reactions see reactions to disaster
psychosocial factors 140, 146, 150, 164, 188; helpers and 173, 174, 184
public health disasters 20, 27, 29–31, 92
public rituals 94–5, 99–100
Pulse nightclub, Orlando 25, 153

quarantine 30, 92

racism 161, 162
railway accidents 5–6
"railway spine" 5–6
Raphael, Beverly 92
reactions to disaster 1, 22–33, **23**, 35–52; behavioral 37, 38–9; children 122–35; cognitive 37, 38, 39; disaster causes and 23, **23**, 26–31; disaster life cycle 41–6; expectedness 23, 31–2; of helpers 2, 172–8; individual characteristics 22–3, **23**, 35–6, 41; by location 46–7; and realms of functioning 37–41; size of disaster 23, **23**, 24–6; stage of disaster 31; and timing 23, 33–4; Western expectations 157–8; see also individual reactions
reactions to disaster, extreme 102–21; disordered grief 114–15; health problems 115–16; Major Depressive Disorder (MDD) 113–14; PTSD 108–9; referrals 116–18; risk factors 104–7
reactions to loss 87–8
reactivity, altered 110–11
reconstruction phase 44
recovery: beginning 24, 25, 36–7, 59; children and 123, 125–6; cultural issues 157–8, 160, 161, 162; environment for 19, 23, **23**, 26, 33–4, 40, 55, 62, 73–4, 79; long-term **23**, 45–6, 55, 99, 108, 160; vulnerable groups and 138, 139, 142, 145, 147, 149, 150, 152, 154, 155
Red Cross see American Red Cross

referrals 2, 11, 12, 14, 66, 74, 75, 76, 77, 107, 116–18; for children 123, 133
refugees 187; *see also* immigrants
relief 87, 96–7
Religious Literacy Primer for Crises, Disasters, and Public Health Emergencies 164
remains: absent 93; identifying 63, 65, 90, 91, 92; viewing 85–6, 92
resilience 23, 40, 49–50, 51, 69, 107, 108; building 55, 79–83; older adults and 141, 142
response characteristics **23**, 36, 41; *see also* reactions to disaster
restoration-orientation 96
revenge 27, 28, 70, 89
risk factors 2, 74–5; children 125–7; frail older adults 137, 139–41; for occupational hazards 176–8; for PTSD 104–5
rituals 55, 88, 90–1, 159–60, 163; private 91–3, 100; public 94–5, 99–100
Rogers, Carl 56
routines, importance of 24, 60, 85, 123, 129, 131, 141
rumor control 2, 30, 68, 72–3

safety 7, 25, 43, 55, 56, 57, 58, 59–60, 74, 85, 152–3; children and 123, 124, 125, 128, 130–1; helpers and 11–12, 13, 44, 108, 174
Salvation Army 10, 82, 127
Sandy Hook 85–6, 90; *see also* Lanza, Adam
Sandy, Hurricane 24, 82, 125, 176, 194
schools: disasters in 21, 26, 85–6, 90, 123, 130; loss of 24, 126, 151; poor performance in 128, 189; return to 55, 60, 123, 129–30; screening and support in 106, 111, 118; as shelters 12, 167
scope of disaster 24, 25, 27, 44
screening 2, 73–7, **76**, 108, 109, 111–13, 114, 117, 118
seasonal factors 34–5
secondary traumatic stress (STS) 174, 175, 176, 177
self-actualization 57
self-blame 32, 38, 43, 48, 54, 71, 89; and PTSD 110, 112; reaction to loss 87

self-care 14, 133, 168, 170, 173, 175, 178–84; of parents 131–2; planning 2, 168, 181, 183
self-efficacy 50, 55, 106, 133
self-esteem 87, 88, 109, 125, 140, 174, 183
self-identity 86, 87
self-injuring 87–8
self-talk 54, 55
sensory impairments 139, 142, 144
service centers *see* Family Assistance Centers (FACs)
settings 11–15
sexual abuse 5, 19, 106, 109–10, 116, 117, 163, 186, 187
shame 31, 38, 43, 48–9, 71, 89, 110, 112; in children 128, 133
"shell shock" 5
shelters 4, 8, 11, 12, 16–17, 63, 82; children in 12, 163; conflict mitigation 73, 163; cultural issues 12, 162–3; diet 74, 157, 163; immigrants 156–7; LGBTQ individuals 153; and low socioeconomic status 150; mental disabilities and 148, 149, 150; older adults and 137, 139, 140, 141; physical disabilities and 143, 144; *see also* Disaster Response Centers (DRCs); Family Assistance Centers (FACs)
shooter incidents 21, 25, 27, 85–6, 90, 98, 104, 105, 106, 130
size of disaster 23, 24–6
Skills for Psychological Recovery (SPR) 69
sleep disruption 5, 37, 38, 56, **64**, 88; in children 128, 129; first responders and 154; and grief 114; and MMD 113; and PTSD 103, 111, 112
Small Business Administration 10
social media 72, 94
social support 50, 55, 56, 61–2, 93, 96, 107–8, 127, 151, 192; of helpers 174, 177, 181, 182; negative 58, 62
social trust 82
socioeconomic status 24, 106, 107, 127, 141, 144–5, 147, 150–1, 156, 162
Somalia 187
somatic complaints 38, 39, 88
spiritual care 10–11, 27, 66, 92, 93, 158, 163, 164, 165
spiritual reactions 39

Sri Lanka, tsunami 164
stage of disaster 31
startle responses 6, 37, 38, 64, 69, 103, 111, 112, 128
state agencies 10, 12–13
storms 3–4, 31, 34, 42, 80, 143, 156; *see also* hurricanes
Stress Inoculation Training 117, 179–80
stress management for self-care 73, 178–81
stress reactions 7, 30, 63, 64, 105; children's 124–5, 127–9; and physical illness 115–16; during recovery 36, 37
substance abuse 116, 127, 128
suffering, in disaster-related deaths 98–9
suicide 11, 113, 114, 140, 191
Sullivan, Harry Stack 58
survivor characteristics, and extreme reactions 105–6
survivor guilt 48, 115
survivors, terminology of 15
symptom-based assessment 76–7, **76**
Syria 187

Tedeschi, Richard 50, 51
television 85, 90, 104, 111, 130
terrorism 21, 25, 27, 29, 32, 54, 130–1, 191; bioterrorism 27, 29; *see also individual incidents*
time stages, reactions by 41–6
timing of disasters 23, 33–4
transportation disasters 5–6, 20, 27, 28, 77, 104; *see also* plane accidents
trauma 4–6, 15, 19, 54–5, 109–10, 186; children and 123–33, 163; definition 109; and the media 90; pre-existing 106, 125, 148, 151; reactions to 107–8; as risk factor 105
Trauma-Focused Cognitive Behavioral Therapy (TF-CBT) 118, 133
Trauma-Screening Questionnaire **76**
traumatic grief 65–6, 85, 114–15
triage 2, 4, 73–7
tsunamis 21, 26, 92–3, 164, 173–4

unexpected disasters 32–3
United Nations 187, 188

United Way 10
University of Southern California Center for Religion and Civic Culture 164

Van Dernoot Lipsky, Laura 175
veterans 5, 182, 193
vicarious posttraumatic growth 173
vicarious trauma (VT) 46, 78; of helpers 2, 57, 133, 173, 174, 175, 176, 177; of journalists 90
Vietnamese immigrants in New Orleans 161, 162
Vietnam War 5
Virginia Tech shooting 105, 106
Voluntary Organizations Active in Disaster (VOAD) 10
vulnerable groups 2, 105–6, 136–55; first responders 153–5; frail older adults 34, 138–42; immigrants 151–2; LGBTQ individuals 152–3; low socioeconomic status 150–1; mentally disabled 145–50; physically disabled 142–5; *see also* children

warmth, providing 56, 58–9
warnings of disasters **23**, 25, 31, 33, 41–3, 105, 156, 194–5; disregarded 31–2, 33, 43, 48, 54, 89–90; false 18, 32, 43, 156; vulnerable groups and 139, 143, 144, 160–1
Watson, Patricia 104
weather events 20, 21, 27, 31, 34, 39, 41, 136, 144–5, 190; *see also* floods; hurricanes; storms
Western bias of disaster mental health field 157–8, 188
West Virginia 2016 floods 122–3
wildfires 18, 19, 20, 21, 32; *see also* fires
women *see* females
working the line 3–4, 14
Working with US Faith Communities during Crises, Disasters and Public Health Emergencies 164
World Health Organization (WHO) 138, 142, 173

 Taylor & Francis eBooks

Helping you to choose the right eBooks for your Library

Add Routledge titles to your library's digital collection today. Taylor and Francis ebooks contains over 50,000 titles in the Humanities, Social Sciences, Behavioural Sciences, Built Environment and Law.

Choose from a range of subject packages or create your own!

Benefits for you

>> Free MARC records
>> COUNTER-compliant usage statistics
>> Flexible purchase and pricing options
>> All titles DRM-free.

Benefits for your user

>> Off-site, anytime access via Athens or referring URL
>> Print or copy pages or chapters
>> Full content search
>> Bookmark, highlight and annotate text
>> Access to thousands of pages of quality research at the click of a button.

REQUEST YOUR **FREE** INSTITUTIONAL TRIAL TODAY

Free Trials Available
We offer free trials to qualifying academic, corporate and government customers.

eCollections – Choose from over 30 subject eCollections, including:

Archaeology	Language Learning
Architecture	Law
Asian Studies	Literature
Business & Management	Media & Communication
Classical Studies	Middle East Studies
Construction	Music
Creative & Media Arts	Philosophy
Criminology & Criminal Justice	Planning
Economics	Politics
Education	Psychology & Mental Health
Energy	Religion
Engineering	Security
English Language & Linguistics	Social Work
Environment & Sustainability	Sociology
Geography	Sport
Health Studies	Theatre & Performance
History	Tourism, Hospitality & Events

For more information, pricing enquiries or to order a free trial, please contact your local sales team: **www.tandfebooks.com/page/sales**

 Routledge
Taylor & Francis Group

The home of Routledge books

www.tandfebooks.com

Made in the USA
Monee, IL
03 January 2025

75856765R00125